CW00336094

# Understanding Sikhism

**Teaching Religions and Worldviews**

*Series Editor: James D. Holt*
This series explores the beliefs and practices of the different religions and worldviews alongside pedagogically supported approaches of how knowledge of each religion or worldview could be taught within the primary and secondary classrooms; this also enhances teaching of those students in the classroom who practice that particular religion or worldview.

Books in the series explore the beliefs and practices of each religion or worldview as a lived experience in the UK. Aspects of each religion or worldview are explored, including the concepts that form the central beliefs, the expression of those beliefs in worship and daily life, and the ethics of believers in the modern day. Each chapter will utilize the authentic voice of those who identify with the religion or worldview today through the use of vignettes and provide reflective tasks for the reader to consider the concepts and how they can be taught in the classroom.

**Forthcoming in the Series:**
*Understanding Buddhism*, James D. Holt

# Understanding Sikhism

# A Guide for Teachers

James D. Holt

BLOOMSBURY ACADEMIC
LONDON • NEW YORK • OXFORD • NEW DELHI • SYDNEY

BLOOMSBURY ACADEMIC
Bloomsbury Publishing Plc
50 Bedford Square, London, WC1B 3DP, UK
1385 Broadway, New York, NY 10018, USA
29 Earlsfort Terrace, Dublin 2, Ireland

BLOOMSBURY, BLOOMSBURY ACADEMIC and the Diana logo are trademarks of
Bloomsbury Publishing Plc

First published in Great Britain 2023

Copyright © James D. Holt, 2023

James D. Holt has asserted his right under the Copyright, Designs and Patents Act,
1988, to be identified as Author of this work.

For legal purposes the Acknowledgements on p. xvi constitute an extension of this copyright page.

Series design by Charlotte James
Cover image © Dinodia Photo / Getty Images

All rights reserved. No part of this publication may be reproduced or transmitted
in any form or by any means, electronic or mechanical, including photocopying,
recording, or any information storage or retrieval system, without prior
permission in writing from the publishers.

Bloomsbury Publishing Plc does not have any control over, or responsibility for,
any third-party websites referred to or in this book. All internet addresses given in
this book were correct at the time of going to press. The author and publisher regret
any inconvenience caused if addresses have changed or sites have ceased to exist, but
can accept no responsibility for any such changes.

A catalogue record for this book is available from the British Library.

A catalog record for this book is available from the Library of Congress.

ISBN: HB: 978-1-3502-6317-8
PB: 978-1-3502-6316-1
ePDF: 978-1-3502-6318-5
eBook: 978-1-3502-6319-2

Series: Teaching Religions and Worldviews

Typeset by Newgen KnowledgeWorks Pvt. Ltd., Chennai, India
Printed and bound in Great Britain

To find out more about our authors and books visit www.bloomsbury.com
and sign up for our newsletters.

They alone are my friends, who travel along with me.

(Guru Granth Sahib 729)

For Sukhbir, Harpreet and Edward

# Contents

## Part 2  Contemporary Issues

# Figures

# Tables

# Series Foreword

*James D. Holt*

The teaching of religion in schools has an interesting history in the UK. It has been through various iterations and paradigm shifts. At the moment, there is a suggestion, and quite a loud one, that we are in the midst of a change of paradigm as it moves from a world religions approach to one that is focused on religions and worldviews. Much is made of this shift, suggesting that it is a seismic, landscape-altering approach within the classroom. Against this background it may seem odd to write a series of books that focuses on subject knowledge for teachers of what can be considered reified religious structures that could be seen to be artificial creations.

Although the nomenclature used in the systematization of religions has changed to include worldviews, I am not convinced that the change is as seismic as has been suggested. The religions and worldviews approach to the teaching of religions and beliefs in schools is, in some ways, a rebranding rather than anything substantive. Effective teaching of religion and belief in schools has, in the recent past, always taken account of worldviews, possibly without recognizing that this is what has been happening. The 'change' to religions and worldviews will still rely on essential aspects of religions/structural worldviews, and it is for this reason that this series of books is being written. What is meant by 'essential' aspects? The essential aspects will differ between religions and worldviews; it is at this point that a discussion of the positive contributions of a religions and worldviews approach will help frame the writing of this and subsequent books.

There are many ways to discuss what is entailed in a religions and worldviews approach to the teaching of religion and belief in schools and other settings. I often speak about the 'messiness' of religions and worldviews, and this messiness has to do with two terms: religions and worldviews.

In exploring the term 'religion', it becomes evident very quickly that the neat structures that we have in our minds, or that are taught in the classroom, are not reflective of the reality that we find in the world today. The various elements that we use in comparative religion enable us to line religions up next to each other and compare various elements, but in some ways in trying to get them to conform to a particular structure of religion we are trying to fit square pegs into round holes. Jonathan Z. Smith (2004, 179–80) noted this:

'Religion' is not a native category. It is not a first person term of self-characterization. It is a category imposed from the outside on some aspect of native culture. It is the other, in these instances colonialists, who are solely responsible for the content of the term.

In having religions fit an artificially constructed paradigm, it is possible to see that both the constituent parts and the whole have been made less, and their vibrancy and meaning have been lost. One such example is in the development of the idea of what Buddhism is in relation to Christianity, or to the religious structure of Christianity, which has meant that the person of the Buddha, Siddhartha Gautama, has developed as the central focus of Buddhism in the West, and certainly the Buddhism that is taught in classrooms. Authors such as Tomoko Masuzawa (2005) highlight that original Buddhism was mined and reified in the nineteenth century with reference to texts in India but with little reference to the lived reality of different Buddhisms in other countries. As a result, Donald Lopez (1995, 7) suggests that Buddhism is a 'hypostatised object ... created by Europe, [which, in turn] could also be controlled by it, and it was against this Buddhism that all the Buddhisms of the modern Orient were to be judged'. Further exploration of this can be found in the volume on Buddhism in this series; but it remains true to say that the Enlightenment understanding of religion was reinforced as colonial powers sought to make sense of the beliefs and practices that they found among the peoples of the empire.

In establishing religion as an observable and static phenomenon, the religions themselves began to reflect the structures and emphases of those who studied and wrote about them. While it is possible to see a continued diversity of expression and understanding, certain principles began to be perceived as normative, and as such an orthodoxy (even if only from the outsider's perspective) began to develop and deviance from the constructed norms began to be seen to be peripheral, where in the past it was part of a vast panoply of loosely related beliefs and practices. This normafication continues even today; in 2021, it was argued by Kalpana Jain that Indian prime minister Modi was attempting to normalize a particular understanding of the Ramayana, and by association the celebration of Diwali. Establishing a Hindu canon or orthodoxy could be seen to be unifying, yet at the same time eroding the diversity and vibrancy of the Hindu community.

It is this approach that, it is argued, developed a post-Enlightenment view of religion and religions. The history of Sikhism, for example, can also be seen to be a reflection of this process where boundaries were established and norms enforced. The typology of religions, in the Western mind, prior to the nineteenth century, tended to reflect a fourfold model: Christian, Jewish, Muslim and Heathen/Pagan. Christianity was the 'norm' while Judaism and Islam were seen to be related (but ultimately wrong), and everything else was put into the equivalent of the 'other' category. During the nineteenth century, religious classifications began to develop further with the first recorded use of terminology such as Buddhism (Boudhism) in 1801, Hinduism (Hindooism) in 1829, Taoism (Taouism) in 1839, Zoroastrianism in 1854 and Confucianism in 1862 (see Josephson, 2012). The nuance of difference within and between religions was not explored in great depth, as is illustrated in the classification of Sikhs as Hindus in the earliest Indian colonial censuses. Up until this point in Sikh history, the self-identification and practice undertaken by Sikhs as followers of the Gurus was seen to be fairly diverse but also not a matter that needed to be delineated. There was evidence of practices associated with Hinduism being followed by Sikhs alongside what could be seen to be more Sikh-like elements. It was the classification of such that provided the impetus for some Sikhs to begin to establish an orthodoxy that separated the *Panth* from Hinduism. The publication of *Ham Hindu Nahin* ('We are not Hindus') in 1899 is evidence of Sikhs feeling the need to establish boundaries where previously they were not perceived to be important (greater exploration of this Sikh 'orthodoxy' is presented in this book).

To some extent the development of a focus on worldviews within the classroom can be seen to be an effort to counter the colonialization of religions and return the understanding of them to a richer and more diverse expression that allows for individual expressions of religion. In exploring worldviews, the Commission on Religious Education (2018, 4) has suggested the following:

> A worldview is a person's way of understanding, experiencing and responding to the world. It can be described as a philosophy of life or an approach to life. This includes how a person understands the nature of reality and their own place in the world. A person's worldview is likely to influence and be influenced by their beliefs, values, behaviours, experiences, identities and commitments.

The Theos Think Tank (2021) video 'No One Stands Nowhere' suggests that a worldview is a complex amalgam of various influences that are constantly shifting and developing. This means that there are personal and institutional worldviews; and that in these institutional worldviews there is a wide variety of experiences and interpretations. This can be seen to build on the work of writers such as Kimberlé Crenshaw (1989) and bell hooks (1994), who have explored aspects of intersectionality. Crenshaw explored what it was to be a Black woman and how race and gender intersect. This develops into a discussion of worldviews and how they are held by individuals; Trevor Cooling Bowie and Panjwani (2020, 29) suggest that people 'inhabit' their worldview.

This is an important development in the study of religion, but, as suggested earlier, it is not new. People like Robert Jackson (1997) have long suggested a listening to the insider or individual voice as a way to understand the complexity of religion. This ethnographic approach recognizes the rich diversity of lived religion. In the wider academic field of religious studies, writers such as McGuire (2008) and Ammerman (2021) have similarly advocated for a focus on the lived experience of religion in the lives of individuals. If this is what is meant by 'worldviews', then it could be argued that teaching about religion in schools has been doing this. The focus on worldviews as a concept is a timely reminder that the religions we explore are not neatly packaged, but they are messy and a result of the confluence of influences and identities in a person's life.

In trying to understand, I imagine a prism, similar to that found on the cover of Pink Floyd's *Dark Side of the Moon* album. The prism is the receptacle where our backgrounds, cultures and experiences coalesce to help make sense of life and the expressions and interpretations of new experiences and the development of values and the like form. These form a different spectrum of colours for each individual. This intersectionality recognizes and emphasizes that no two people are alike. Simply speaking, in the context of this book, a Sikh brother and sister in the UK would have different perceptions of Sikhism despite similar upbringing, because of their gender as well as other experiences that may have coloured their view.

This approach could be seen to problematize the very concept of religions and worldviews to such an extent that religion could be seen to lose all meaning. It reduces religion to an individual expression of an individual belief system.

The argument and purpose of this series of books is to recognize the messiness, intersectionality and worldviews approach to religions, but in a way that does not dismiss everything that is useful about a world religions paradigm. It will recognize the diversity within each tradition but will also use what can be commonly termed the 'essential' aspects of a religion or worldview that enables diversity to be recognized. The essential aspects are needed to frame the discussions that are taking place. Ben Wood (2020, 14) argues:

> Some argue that 'essentialism' narrows and limits understanding and fails to provide a realistic picture of the world and religion and belief. Others, myself included, accept this to a point, arguing that 'essentialism' may be limited, but it is a necessary part of the process of learning about religions in a progressive manner, in that what is learnt in this phase is essential for progress to more sophisticated learning.

The Commission on RE (2018, 6) suggest that

> we need to move beyond an essentialised presentation of six 'major world faiths' and towards a deeper understanding of the complex, diverse and plural nature of worldviews at both institutional and personal levels.

Although it may not be what they intended, I would suggest that a 'moving beyond' essentialism does not mean that we need to dismiss the existence of the central elements of a religion or institutionalized worldview but that we should utilize aspects that are helpful to frame our study. Moving beyond is studying religion in a framework of intersectionality or worldviews that recognizes the problems inherent in the world religions paradigm. This means that adopting a categorization of all religions as having set commonalities is out of date and does not reflect the lived reality of many people in the world. Any study of religion in schools must begin with a recognition of the diversity that is found within the world.

I argue elsewhere (Holt, 2022) that this diversity is appropriate at every level of the school experience. At the very youngest of ages it is possible to use language such as 'many', 'most' and 'some' when speaking of religious belief and practice. As pupils get older it is possible to introduce the nuances and specifics of diversity. It also serves the purpose of exercising a humility of knowledge when we teach; in the intersectional world of religions it is impossible to know everything about the beliefs and practices of all aspects of a religion; using qualifiers ensures that we are not unconsciously establishing boundaries and norms in religions that do not exist.

One of the consequences of exploring religions and worldviews as a paradigm is the inclusion of systems of belief that are not seen to be religious. For many years, groups such as Humanists UK have argued for a recognition and inclusion of non-religious worldviews within the classroom. Many schools, syllabi and specifications now include non-religious worldviews; the worldviews approach can be seen to have expanded what might be explored in the curriculum. In recognizing that the 'big six' have traditionally been prioritized, it is possible that this shift in paradigm will expand what traditions and worldviews should be studied. I have explored the arguments for the inclusion of religions 'beyond the big six', and also the inclusion of expressions of the big six beyond the mainstream, and that we should expand what we understand and teach (Holt, 2019). It is against this background that this series of books works; while recognizing what can be perceived as the 'normative', it will also recognize and explore aspects of diversity within the religious tradition.

It is at point that I feel it is important that I recognize my own positionality with respect to the religions and worldviews that will be covered in this series. For most of the religions, I will be coming from the perspective of an outsider. I recognize both the benefits and hindrances this may bring. I cannot fully understand what it is to live as a Sikh or as a Buddhist. The spirituality of Islam or of Hinduism is not something that I have experienced as a believer. This does not mean, though, that I am unsympathetic. When I present the beliefs and practices of the individual religions, I will do so, as best I can, in a way that would be understood by believers. I understand and appreciate the impact that religions and worldviews can have on the lives of individuals and communities. As an outsider I am also able to recognize debates within the community that may be given short shrift by an insider.

As a teacher, lecturer and professor of religious education over many years, I am also able to understand the nuances of what is needed to teach religions and worldviews in the classroom. I will not be able to cover everything, and the selection of material may leave out things that some people think are important. That is the beauty of intersectionality and worldviews; there are a myriad of ways that religion can be understood and presented. It is my hope that this series of books will provide a basis on which to build in the future. I would encourage the discussion of the contents of this book with fellow professionals, your students but perhaps most importantly with followers of the religions and worldviews explored. The authentic voice is central to understanding the beliefs and impact of religion. This book should provide you with a good foundation on which to develop your teaching and those conversations.

# Acknowledgements

There are many people who contribute to the writing of any book. At many different points throughout my life, there have been people I have met, worked with and become friends with, who have contributed to my understanding of religion and especially, in terms of this book, of Sikhism.

Grateful thanks should first of all be given to Edward Singh and Harpreet Kaur Singh. These two wonderful students introduced me to Sikhism as a lived religion, rather than as something just to be found in textbooks. My journey into learning about Sikhism and experiencing different aspects of this are in no small part due to Edward and Harpreet.

There are many members of the Sikh community who have helped with the answering of questions over the years that have assisted in my understanding that enabled this book to be written. I will not be able to name them all, but Sukhbir Singh, Paramjit Kaur, Jas Singh, Gurmeet Singh, Randeep Singh, Jasveer Singh, Ranvir Singh, Bobby Singh and Hardev Singh have been particularly supportive over the years. I take complete responsibility for anything that might not quite be as understood within the *Panth*.

Within my teaching community so many people challenge and inspire me to be better and understand more. Stephen Darlington, Diane Kolka, Christine Paul and Sally Hunter have been particularly helpful in my understanding of Sikhism.

My own family has been very supportive during the writing of this book. My nieces, Scarlett and Amelia, are just becoming aware of the fact that I write books and are very proud of their author uncle. I'm so proud of each of them and am grateful for their love.

The biggest thanks of all are reserved for my wife, Ruth, and our children, Eleanor, Abi, Ethan, Gideon and Martha, know that sometimes I disappear and hibernate for a while as I write. I am so grateful for their love and support.

As with everything I do, all credit goes to God. I am nothing without the influence of God in my life.

# Note on Texts and Translation

There are different translations available of some of the texts used throughout this book. Although they are in the public domain, I am grateful to searchgurbani.com for their efforts in making these works available for free, and for allowing me to quote freely from them. All references to the following works have page/Ang numbers as given on searchgurbani.com: Guru Granth Sahib, Dasam Granth, Bhai Gurdas Vaaran, Bhai Nand Lai's Ganjnama.

In transliterating from Punjabi or Gurmukhi there are often different spellings in English. The words have been chosen based on their being one of the most frequent ways of spelling. Many Punjabi or Gurmukhi words have been italicized the first time they are used, and for most of these, the meaning will be found alongside usage and in the Glossary.

It should also be noted that in translating the words into English, some of the meaning may be lost. There is a tendency to try and translate one word into another, and this does not always get the meaning across. I have tried, as far as possible, to recognize the incompleteness of these translations.

# Introduction

What is Sikhism? Who is a Sikh? The common translation of 'Sikh' is 'learner' or 'follower'. Guru Granth Sahib uses the term 'Sikh' at different points; for example, Guru Nanak teaches:

> The Guru's Teachings are the gems and jewels; the Sikh who serves Him searches and finds them. (Guru Granth Sahib 1328)

This highlights the relationship between a Sikh and the Gurus. To an extent, this definition seems to provide the basis for definitions in the nineteenth and twentieth centuries. If we consult the *Rahit Maryada* the question seems to be settled. Article I suggests that a Sikh is

any human being who faithfully believes in

- **(i)** One Immortal Being,
- **(ii)** Ten Gurus, from Guru Nanak to Guru Gobind Singh,
- **(iii)** The Guru Granth Sahib,
- **(iv)** The utterances and teachings of the ten Gurus and
- **(iv)** the baptism bequeathed by the tenth Guru, and who does not owe allegiance to any other religion, is a Sikh.

However, if we use the points raised in the series introduction as a background, we realize that this is not as simple a question to answer as is assumed. Although for some the question of 'What is Sikhism?' seems to be settled, there are many answers, and each will reflect the framework within which people are working.

The term 'Sikhism' is loaded with implications and associations that are not always desirable in an exploration of a way of life for millions of people around the world. Arvind-Pal Singh Mandair (2013) has suggested three words that could be used in exploring the religion of Sikhism: Sikhism, Sikhi and *Sikhi*sm. In this understanding 'Sikhism' is the reified religion of the Sikhs that is seen to be neatly packaged in a world religions framework, and that owes its static position to either a colonial imposition or a response to the colonial framework in which it finds itself. While Sikhism is a word that has been used throughout the past century or so, it can be seen to miss the vibrancy and diversity of the Sikh *Panth*. It allows Sikhism to be an observable entity that can be used in comparative religion books and classes. 'Sikhi' is a word that is often seen to be preferred, as it does not have the colonial implications and does not indicate that there is a static position of religion. Rather, it is a vibrant and fluid word that suggests a diversity and lived reality in the Panth. It is a word that helps delineate the lived experience of Sikhs from the reified ideal that we may see expressed in certain textbooks. As indicated in the series introduction it can be noted that Sikhi is 'messy'; there are diverse interpretations and experiences that can form part of our understanding as we teach about the experiences of Sikhs today.

This discussion of 'Sikhism' versus 'Sikhi' can be seen to be reflected in the way that Sikhism is taught within the classroom. The predominant version of Sikhism that is taught seems to utilize an approach that presents it in a way that is analogous to the characteristics that all religions are generally seen to possess. There is a deity, a founder, a holy book, a set of rules, identifiable symbols and so on. None of this is 'false'; rather it adopts a paradigm that suggests that Sikhism is neatly packaged and in some ways has always been so. While it might make Sikhism more understandable in a pupil's eyes, it does not reflect the reality of Sikh identity today, or throughout history.

History is important for all religions, most especially so for Sikhism. Understanding Sikh history helps us understand the various nuances of Sikhism today, and why it is the way it is. The utilization of a historical lens in the exploration of Sikhism enables the teacher to present a more authentic expression of what Sikhism is. In elements that I have seen presented in many schools around the country, and in exam specifications, Sikh history seems to be an exploration of Guru Nanak, and then a fast forward to Guru Gobind Rai/Singh. At that point, Sikh belief, identity and expression can often be presented as being complete and fixed. Although this might be an easy version of Sikh history, it is not justifiable either from a Sikh or from an educational perspective. Throughout this book we will explore 'developments' in Sikh thought, belief and expression. All religious traditions undergo changes and transformations; but most interestingly in this particular situation, Sikhism is a relatively young religion, and the developments are more easily observed and documented.

The chapters in this book will explore central aspects of Sikh beliefs as they are understood by the vast majority of Sikhs today. Chapter 3 focuses on the ten Gurus in human form, and this is a weighty chapter in terms of history and content. It is the argument of this book that understanding the lives and teachings of the Gurus will help lay the basis for understanding Sikhism today. One of the shortcomings of the organization of this book is that there is not sufficient space to explore all the nuances of history and the development of the Sikh Panth between the death of Guru Gobind Singh in 1708 and where we are now over three hundred years later. At this time, there are many events and tensions that lead to the identity of Sikhs. In the classroom, we might leave the impression with pupils that Sikhism taught by Guru Nanak was the same as what we experience today. There are aspects of that which would be accepted, and this is supported by the belief explored in Chapter 3 that the Gurus shared the same light and were contiguous with one another. There are, however, historical developments that affected the focus of the Panth, and how it has been presented to the 'outside' world.

One of the most important movements for the development and articulation of 'modern' Sikhism is one known as Singh Sabha from the nineteenth and twentieth centuries. In the period since the time of Guru Gobind Singh, under the *misl* system, there had been periods of conflict between the Mughal Empire and the Sikh misls. These misls tended to be independent of one another, and only under Maharaj Ranjt Singh (spanning the first part of the nineteenth century) were the misls united and a 'Sikh' Empire established (see Atwal, 2020). Throughout this time, because of the conflicts, a large number of the gurdwaras and the administrative roles fell to *Khatri* Sikhs. Khatri Sikhs, also known as 'Sanatan Sikhs', were those rooted in the ruling elite of India and tended to place themselves above the Khalsa identity. Rather, there was a somewhat fluid relationship between Sikhism and aspects of Hindu belief and practice. Combined with increased Christian missionary activity in India, evidenced, not least, by the conversion of Duleep Singh (the son of Maharaj Ranjit Singh), this diversity of experience and lived reality in the lives of Sikhs led to a push for a distinctive and concrete Sikh identity.

As some point out, it is at this point that the Singh Sabha adopted the structures seen in the British Empire. Just as Christianity had delineators and orthodoxy, many felt that, to enable Sikhism to survive, there needed to be lines drawn and normative ideals established. For members of the Singh Sabha movement this required a reclamation of what it was to be Sikh, and the message of the Gurus. This approach included the implementation of the Tat Khalsa (true Khalsa) as an ideal and the 'correct' way to be Sikh. In this way, Sikhism could be stripped of the Hindu accoutrements that had slipped in; hence the publication of *Ham Hindu Nahin* (*We Are Not Hindus*) in 1899. It is out of this movement that the *Rahit Maryada* developed. Up until the late nineteenth/early twentieth centuries there had been little in terms of distinctive Sikh ritual that had been observed (there were exceptions, including the *Amrit Sanskar*, and aspects of the marriage service, including the recitation of the *lavan* hymns). The establishment of a Sikh calendar that would include *gurpurbs* and distinctive Sikh rituals began during this time period (for a wider discussion of Singh Sabha and their influence, see Oberoi (1994) and Singh Mandair (2009)). An exploration of Sikh history would be interesting to see whether this was a reformation to teachings and practices of earlier times or a codification that restricted the diversity and freedom of expression that had been a distinctive feature of the Panth. Suffice it to say that this is beyond the scope of this book, and the Sikhism that will be explored is that which is lived in the twenty-first century.

In conversations with many Sikhs, there is a predominant view that the Sikh Panth is united and that there is no division within it.

> For me there is only type of Sikhi, it is written in our 11th Guru – Guru Granth Sahib Ji.
> All Sikhs are one. (Holt, interview)

While to the outward observer this may be true, scratch a little and it is possible to see a range of approaches to living as a Sikh. Oftentimes in classrooms there may be a focus on Amritdhari, Sahajdhari and Keshdhari Sikhs, but little beyond these. Amritdhari refers to those who have taken *amrit* and become Khalsa Sikhs; Sahajdhari are sometimes known as 'slow adopters' or people who are living a Sikh life but have not yet taken amrit. This seems a somewhat pejorative term, but it is used within the Panth. Some Sikhs feel as though commitment to the Khalsa, rather than a beginning, is an expression of where they are, and they may not feel they are 'good enough' or 'ready' to make that commitment. Some others, including some Keshdhari, adopt the 'Five Ks' in their daily lives and appear to be Khalsa Sikhs, but will not have gone through the amrit ceremony.

Although this categorization is important, it is not the only diversity that is found within the Sikh Panth. Opinderjit Kaur Takhar (2016) explored the various expressions of Sikhism that could be found, and whether they would be considered as Sikhs by other Sikhs. In her research she explored the place of:

- Guru Nanak Nishkam Sewak Jatha,
- *Namdharis*,
- *Ravidasis*,
- *Valmikis* and
- Sikh Dharma of the Western Hemisphere (3HO).

Interestingly, since 2005 Ravidasis have generally separated themselves from Sikhism. In the 2011 census in the UK they campaigned to be seen as a separate group and were treated as such by the Office of National Statistics. Within the narrower Sikh Panth that may or may not include the above groups, there are others such as the Nihangs who adopt different approaches to a Sikh way of living as well. It is important for the reader to note that there are many different ways to be Sikh. While there may be many who seek to impose an orthodoxy, as teachers we need to ensure that the religions that we teach are 'big tent' religions with space for diversity and self-identification. This is, perhaps, one of the ways that worldviews can impact on our teaching. The way that individual Sikh worldviews will vary based on culture, gender, background and experience; none of these experiences should be negated, rather they should be explored in the context of an essentialized view of Sikhism.

'Sikhi' is a word that is used to highlight the dynamism, fluidity and lived reality of a Sikh's worldview. It is a term that is used in preference to a 'static' understanding of Sikhism. Rather than the noun 'Sikhism', which names something, 'Sikhi' is a verb, a way to describe the active learning from the Guru and the search for the reality of the nature of humanity and existence. 'Sikhi' has begun to be the preferred term that is a better descriptor of the Sikh way of life.

One further note is that even the term 'Sikhi' can be seen to be slightly problematic. For some Sikhs, the preferred term for the 'religion' is *gurmat*. There are some Agreed Syllabuses that are adopting this as a term where previously Sikhism would be used. The reason for the preference of gurmat has been explained in terms of the translation of the terms:

> Guru is what we follow. Gurmat is the way or wisdom of the Guru. In a Sikh setting people will contrast following the Guru's way, gurmat and manmat , the way of the self. Christians follow Christ, they do not follow discipleship. (Holt, interview)

It is important for the teacher to be aware of this. The existing terms may be too embedded to make significant changes at this point, but being able to talk about the challenges of naming a way of life will be significant to enable the voices of Sikhs to be heard.

In the way that Singh Mandair uses *Sikhi*sm throughout his book, he seeks to unite the pre-modern diverse term with the concretized term that we find in the world religions paradigm. In doing so, he can be seen to fuse both understandings in a way that highlights the commonalities of all Sikhs while recognizing its messiness. Throughout this book I will use the term 'Sikhism' in a similar way; I recognize its colonial implications, but its common use within the lexicon suggests that to do otherwise at this stage may complicate matters. Indeed, in my conversation with many Sikhs they seem unaware of the debate over the use of the term. I think 'Sikhi' is perhaps a more evocative and authentic term and recognize that over time this will perhaps become the preferred identifier. For the teacher, I feel it is important to be aware of this discussion and to highlight the use of different terminology. In doing so they will be able to help students understand the importance of language alongside the diversity that they will find within the boundaries of what is termed Sikhism.

In addition to the exploration of various aspects of Sikh belief, practices and history, this book seeks to be a resource for teachers in understanding how Sikhism can be taught within the classroom. It suggests aspects that can be explored and focused on as we strive to understand how Sikhism is lived today. Despite Sikhism being the fifth largest religion in the world, and the fourth largest in the UK (according to the 2011 census) the teaching of Sikhism in UK schools is limited, and, in my experience, the confidence of teachers to teach Sikhism is low. It is often overlooked in the curricula of schools and universities and the writings of religious studies scholars. Juergensmeyer (1979) described Sikhism as the 'Forgotten Tradition', and this would be supported when one considers the writings of people like Stephen Prothero. In his book *God Is Not One* (2010), Prothero explores what are described as the eight major world religions, of which Sikhism is not one. This could be because of the American context within which Prothero writes, but it suggests a wider ignorance of aspects of Sikhism. Much more needs to be done to further the study of Sikhism at all levels. This is also identified as an issue by some in the Sikh community in the UK:

> The UK school system needs to do a lot more to close the gaps between the teaching of Sikhi and other faith groups. For the proportion of Sikhs in the UK, the amount of curriculum time is appalling. (Holt, interview)

It could be the result of a vicious cycle; teachers themselves do not experience Sikhism in their education and so are less prepared to teach about Sikhism as adults. It is for this reason that this book is written, with the main audience being imagined to be teachers. It will be beneficial for all to understand Sikhism better, but it is hoped that with a greater knowledge of Sikhism teachers will be more confident about teaching it in the classroom.

One other note about the use of language in this book should be noted. Even though 'Sikhism' with its colonial connotations is used, the reasons for its use having already been explored, there are other colonial hangovers that will not be perpetuated. Indeed, some of the terminology that I will avoid using has been used by Sikhs themselves, but I think they have been used to help non-Sikhs (especially those with a Christian background) understand Sikhism in a way that is intelligible for them. Thus a *granthi* becomes a priest; Amrit Sanskar becomes Sikh baptism; a Khalsa Sikh becomes a baptized Sikh; *Akal Purakh* or *Waheguru* become God. Each of these terms are 'Christian' or 'Western' and as such come loaded with certain connotations and understandings. Rather than making Sikhism intelligible on Christian terms, an approach that continues the legacy of colonialism, I think it is important for non-Sikhs to understand Sikhism on Sikh terms. I will strive as much as possible to avoid non-Sikh terminology in exploring Sikh beliefs and practices. Where original writers or translators have used such terms I will keep the original language, but it will be in the context of this caveat.

Throughout this book, I utilize the words of Sikhs who have been kind enough to share their views with me. In doing so, it should be noted that for those who use this book as an introduction to Sikhism, it will be valuable to develop relationships with Sikhs and Sikh communities to ensure that the Sikhism you teach is authentic and truly represents the people in your local communities.

# Part 1

## Key Concepts in Sikhism

# Chapter 1

# Waheguru

The opening of Guru Granth Sahib is known as *Mool Mantar*:

> One Universal Creator God, The Name Is Truth Creative Being Personified No Fear No
> Hatred Image Of The Undying, Beyond Birth, Self-Existent. By Guru's Grace. (1)

This passage outlines for Sikhs the nature of *Waheguru* or God. Guru Granth Sahib further
expands on the importance of the *Mool Mantar*: 'The Mul Mantra, the Root Mantra, is the
only cure for the mind; I have installed faith in God in my mind' (675). The translation that
Mool/Mul is the 'root' highlights the truths that it teaches as central to, and the basis for,
an understanding of Sikhism.

The *Mool Mantar* is believed to have been one of the first utterances of Guru Nanak
when he emerged from his river experience. In this experience, which took place at
Sultanpur, Guru Nanak, at the age of thirty, would go to a nearby stream/river for his
daily bath. The *Janamsakhi*s record that on one occasion Guru Nanak disappeared for
three days; many feared that he had drowned. It was during this period of time that he is
believed to have entered into the Divine presence. With a cup of ambrosia he is given a
charge:

> Go, rejoice, in my name and teach others to do so ... I have bestowed upon you the gift
> of my name (nam). Let this be your calling. (Kaur Singh, 2019, 34)

This event is hugely influential but is not necessarily foundational as perhaps may be
taught in schools. It marks the beginning of Guru Nanak's understanding of the nature of
Waheguru, but it is evident from his life up to this point that he embodied Sikh principles
and teachings. This experience has a huge impact on a Sikh, as the understanding of
Waheguru as expressed in the *Mool Mantar* is repeated each day as part of the *Japji*.

At the same time it served to distinguish the message of Guru Nanak, and Sikhism,
as distinct from the traditions with which Guru Nanak was familiar in Punjab. From
a Sikh perspective, while Guru Nanak was aware of and harnessed some of the
teachings of sants and others that he encountered throughout his life, he was doing
far more than developing a syncretism of existing thought. W. H. McLeod (1968, 157)
suggests just this – that he drew on what would be termed 'Hindus' today and aspects
of Sufism, concluding that 'the categories employed by Guru Nanak are the categories
of the Sants, the terminology he uses is their terminology, and the doctrines that he

affirms are their doctrines'. This approach to the thought and teachings of Guru Nanak would be rejected within Sikhism (see Singh, 2009; Grewal, 2010). It reduces the role of Guru Nanak to that of a mere collator; the way that Guru Nanak was able to articulate his religious thought, particularly in relation to the nature of God, shows that he was establishing a new way but one that was able to recognize where his thought lay in relation to the teachings of those that he engaged with. Harbans Singh (1983a, 7–8) articulates this when he suggests that we must view Guru Nanak as independent in the development of his teachings:

> In this perspective, we shall see that Guru Nanak is historically the founder of the Sikh faith. His precept was definitively the starting point. In many significant ways, it signalled a new departure in contemporary religious ethos.

As his life and journeys show, he often interacted with those with complementary or opposing thoughts. He would use these thoughts and beliefs as a basis for discussion. Sometimes he would agree and develop that which was being discussed, while at other times he would reject the teachings being elucidated. It would appear that rather than using these teachings to construct the message which he shared, he was able to express the message in a way that was intelligible to those who he taught. This approach and the uniqueness of Guru Nanak's message are highlighted in a story from the *Janamsakhis* where Guru Nanak is approaching the city of Multan. As he was reaching Multan, he was met by the servants of Shah Rukne Alam with a bowl filled to the brim with milk. The message that was being given to Guru Nanak was that Multan had enough holy men and there was no need for more teachings from one more teacher. Guru Nanak picked a jasmine flower and placed it on top of the milk where it floated. The message was clear: for the teachings of Guru Nanak there was always room.

This is just so with Guru Nanak's teachings about Waheguru. He taught of Waheguru's Oneness; this should not be understood within a Muslim structure; rather Guru Nanak's teachings transcended any that would be found in the world, however close they may appear on the surface. The declaration that Guru Nanak made when emerging from his river experience that 'there is no Hindu or Muslim' suggests that these are only lenses through which the truth is apprehended and that these lenses are clouded; his declaration of the *naam* is unencumbered by such lenses. It is an approach that seeks to find Waheguru through the clarity of vision that is unencumbered by ritual that seeks to distract.

This approach is shown in two events, one with regard to Islam and the other with regard to Hinduism. Firstly, when Guru Nanak is questioned by Daulat Khan and a qazi (both Muslims) about the statement that 'there is no Hindu or Muslim' shortly after the river experience, they are concerned that he is suggesting there is no such thing as a Muslim. On being asked which path Guru Nanak followed, he is reported to have replied:

I am on the path to God and God is neither Hindu or Muslim. (K. Singh, 2004b, 76–7)

Guru Nanak was then invited to pray namaz with the qazi and Daulat Khan. The qazi felt that Guru Nanak had been disrespectful to God during the prayer as he had laughed at the qazi. Guru Nanak had received the impression that the qazi's mind was elsewhere during the prayer, and he explained:

> Your namaz has not been accepted (in the Divine Court) because your mind was somewhere else. (77)

The performance of outward ritual at the expense of inner focus, worship and commitment to Waheguru was rejected by Guru Nanak. His message was much less about ritual and much more about action and the remembrance of the name.

A similar event that shows the emptiness of ritual in trying to understand Waheguru is found in the early life of Guru Nanak. It is narrated that as a child Guru Nanak rejected the sacred thread that was given to boys on their coming of age. Some of his rejection was because his sister was unable to go through the ceremony, but ultimately he rejected it because of the fruitlessness of such a ritual.

> Make compassion the cotton, contentment the thread, modesty the knot and truth the twist. This is the sacred thread of the soul; if you have it, then go ahead and put it on me. It does not break, it cannot be soiled by filth, it cannot be burnt, or lost. Blessed are those mortal beings, O Nanak, who wear such a thread around their necks. You buy the thread for a few shells, and seated in your enclosure, you put it on. Whispering instructions into others' ears, the Brahmin becomes a guru. But he dies, and the sacred thread falls away, and the soul departs without it. He commits thousands of robberies, thousands of acts of adultery, thousands of falsehoods and thousands of abuses. He practices thousands of deceptions and secret deeds, night and day, against his fellow beings. The thread is spun from cotton, and the Brahmin comes and twists it. The goat is killed, cooked and eaten, and everyone then says, 'Put on the sacred thread.' When it wears out, it is thrown away, and another one is put on. O Nanak, the thread would not break, if it had any real strength. Believing in the Name, honour is obtained. The Lord's Praise is the true sacred thread. Such a sacred thread is worn in the Court of the Lord; it shall never break. (Guru Granth Sahib 471)

The centrality of understanding Waheguru independent of ritual and diversions is shown through the Sikh practice of a meditation on/remembrance of the name of Waheguru known as *naam japna* and linked with the practice of *naam simran*. By repeating the name of Waheguru a Sikh is able to meditate on Waheguru's characteristics and seek to develop more in relation to Waheguru (see Chapter 2).

Having explored the basis of the Sikh belief in Waheguru as taught and expressed by Guru Nanak, it is important to explore the various aspects of divinity as taught in the *Mool Mantar*. Each of the different terms used in the *Mool Mantar* will be explored, along with the term 'Waheguru' used by Sikhs in prayer, meditation and devotion.

# Waheguru

Within Sikhism there are many names by which the Divine can be known. It is not incorrect to use the name 'God', but there is always the danger that in so doing it can conjure up in the mind of pupils a deity that shares many characteristics with that which is found within Judaism, Christianity and Islam. One Sikh has suggested:

> WaheGuru is the indescribable and incomprehensible. However, to try … WaheGuru is the connection between all things in creation, destruction and sustenance. Describing WaheGuru as 'God' is sometimes necessary but not really fitting, given connotations of 'God' based on other religions. (Holt, interview)

Throughout Guru Granth Sahib and other writings various names for the Divine are used, including *ChakraPan*, *Govind*, *Gopal*, *GopiNath*, *Hari*, *Jagannath Kamla-pati*, *Krishna*, *Narayan*, *Nath*, *ParaBrahma*, *Paramatma*, *Pyara*, *Ram*, *Saringdhar*, *Sridhar*, *SriRang* and *Vishwambhar*. The two most common names for the Divine used by Sikhs, outside of the words of the *Mool Mantar*, are Waheguru and *Akal Purakh* (eternal one). Throughout his life Guru Nanak recognized the use of different names for the Divine; Guru Gobind Singh did the same in Dasam Granth. The idea within Sikhism is that Guru Nanak felt it inappropriate to question the names of God that people used; but that these names, when used, should be understood in the context of the *Mool Mantar*. At no point were the Gurus suggesting that Krishna or Ram were avatars or manifestations of God, rather that their qualities and the focus of believers would provide a pathway to understand Waheguru. Pashaura Gurmat Singh (2014a) has suggested that 'Akal Purakh' is most often used in discussions of Sikh beliefs and doctrines, whereas 'Waheguru' is most often used in Sikh practice.

Waheguru (Wonderful Sovereign/Eternal Guru) as suggested is often used in devotion; on approaching Guru Granth Sahib in the gurdwara, a Sikh will most often circumambulate the Guru while reciting the name 'Waheguru' as a remembrance and meditation on the Divine. This recitation is often to be found in naam simran (see Chapter 7). The name and concept of Waheguru is emblematic of different elements of Sikh belief.

Throughout Guru Granth Sahib the Divine is often described as the 'True Guru' or 'Supreme Guru' and occasionally as 'Waheguru':

> Vaahiguroo Vaahiguroo Vaahiguroo Vaahi Jeeo
> Waahay Guru, Waahay Guru, Waahay Guru, Waahay Jee-o.
> Kaval Nain Madhhur Bain Kott Sain Sang Sobh Kehath Maa Jasodh Jisehi Dhehee Bhaath Khaahi Jeeo.
> You are lotus-eyed, with sweet speech, exalted and embellished with millions of companions. (Guru Granth Sahib 1402)

Even within this Ang, different phrases of 'True' or 'Supreme' Guru are used in the hymn of praise by Guru Ram Das. The term 'Waheguru' is used sparingly throughout Guru Granth Sahib, and it became more common usage throughout the early history of the Sikhs; it could be suggested that with a Guru in human form other words were used to refer to the Divine to avoid confusion. By the time of Guru Gobind Singh, however, 'Waheguru' was used regularly to refer to God as the greeting of the Khalsa suggests:

Waheguru Ji Ka Khalsa Waheguru Ji Ki Fateh.
The Khalsa belongs to Waheguru; the victory belongs to Waheguru.

Within Sikhism 'Guru' is a word that has significant meaning. It is often translated into the English 'teacher', but this can be seen to be an incomplete and inadequate translation, and it can be said to have other etymological roots, though these interpretations are not accepted by all. 'Gu' is a Punjabi word that means 'darkness', and 'ru' can be seen to mean 'light' or 'shatter' (or even 'heavy', but that does not quite fit here). In essence then a Guru is someone who takes people from darkness to light or shatters darkness. Either of these explanations gives an insight into the role of the Guru in Sikhism. As the 'True', 'Supreme' or 'Eternal' Guru, Waheguru is the source of all light and truth and the 'being' that enables people to find the truth of reality (see the section 'Satnaam' below).

The other aspect of the term 'Waheguru' is 'Sovereign', which has an interesting implication within Sikhism. In using the term 'Sovereign' the image of the Divine as a ruler to which all obeisance is owed is developed in the mind. It does, however, have further implications. Ranveer Singh (2021) has suggested that sovereignty is at the heart of the Sikh message and the teachings and lives of the Gurus. According to him, Sikh sovereignty is 'a means of expressing the self-regulating and autonomous nature of the Sikh Panth' (i). Understanding Waheguru as sovereign enables Sikhs to recognize their, and the Panth's, place as a sovereign empire and as such live according to the gurmat. Understanding the Divine as Waheguru helps Sikhs understand both their relationship to the Divine and their place in the world. Waheguru places them in a relationship with the Divine and the world that is at once dependent and of a sovereign heritage. This can have implications for the message of the Panth in a spiritual sense but also in a temporal and secular sense (this will be explored in greater detail when discussing the concept of miri-piri in Chapter 3).

Akal Purakh means 'eternal one' or 'being not subject to death'. The two words will be explored in detail in relation to the Mool Mantar below, but it is important to note that in Guru Granth Sahib and the Dasam Granth the phrase is used to refer to the Divine. One chapter of the Dasam Granth is entitled Akal Ustat, and one of its first lines is:

The non-temporal Purusha (All-Pervading Lord) is my Protector. (Dasam Granth 35)

This discussion, and the exploration of the characteristics of Waheguru outlined in the discussion of the Mool Mantar below, presents those teaching Sikhism with a unique challenge. Each of these names represents something different about the Divine, and each can be rightly used within a discussion of Sikhism. The teacher should explore each of these concepts as appropriate, but in the general discussion of Sikhism it is possibly necessary to choose one of the names of the Divine to use as the default, and then this to be used throughout the school. Although 'God' is not wrong, it might be more representative to use the term 'Waheguru'.

## Ik

The first word of the *Mool Mantar* is '*Ik*', meaning 'One', and it is represented in the numeral, '1', rather than in the word. This suggests the indivisible and concrete unity of the Divine. Most translations of the *Mool Mantar* into English append the word 'God' to the translation. This is perhaps what is meant, as Guru Nanak is describing the ultimate reality, Waheguru, but the word God is nowhere to be found in the *Mool Mantar*. However, it is intimated throughout in suggesting that Waheguru is unique and has no partner. The focus on the 'One' is throughout the teachings of the Gurus:

> My Lord and Master is One; He is the One and Only; O Siblings of Destiny, He is the One alone. (Guru Granth Sahib 350)

The 'One' is above understanding and is incomprehensible to the human mind because it is shrouded by the ego; it is unable to look beyond the illusory nature of reality that has been created by the ego. Only by an orientation to the One can illusion be overcome and the true nature of the One and of existence be understood (this will be explored in greater detail in Chapter 2).

## Onkaar

In some ways *Onkaar* is inextricably linked with Ik and in many writings is presented as *Ikonkaar*. The translation of Onkaar is difficult to render, and there are different translations. The most common is that of 'God' suggesting that there is one God that is indivisible. Pashaura Singh (2014a, 227) suggests 'The Divine is One' as the translation of Ikonkaar; in so doing he links this first phrase with the first sound that is the force within creation. Onkaar, in this understanding, is described in Guru Granth Sahib:

> From Ongkaar, the One Universal Creator God, Brahma was created. He kept Ongkaar in his consciousness. From Ongkaar, the mountains and the ages were created. Ongkaar created the Vedas. Ongkaar saves the world through the Shabad. Ongkaar saves the Gurmukhs. Listen to the Message of the Universal, Imperishable Creator Lord. (Guru Granth Sahib 929–30)

In Pashaura Singh's translation of this passage he replaces 'One Universal Creator God' with 'Primal Sound' conjuring up images of the word/syllable AUM/OM within Hinduism. This similarity is explored by Wazir Singh (1969, 20):

> The 'a', 'u', and 'm' of aum have also been explained as signifying the three principles of creation, sustenance and annihilation ... aumkār in relation to existence implies

plurality … but its substitute Ekonkar definitely implies singularity in spite of the seeming multiplicity of existence.

As a teaching of Guru Nanak, this articulation of Onkaar as a creative power is challenging in that it suggests the reality of Brahma. To understand this we have to return to the way that Guru Nanak taught; he taught the people that were in front of him, and in so doing he would use aspects of their understanding to develop the teaching that he was imparting. This does not suggest that Brahma is real, though Guru Nanak recognized that the Divine was known by many names. It highlights further that all are subject to Ikonkaar.

Kapur Singh (1993, 85) suggests that the translation of Onkaar should be 'Being-Becoming', which could also be considered as reference to the transcendent and immanent qualities of the One. Waheguru is both above and beyond as indicated later in the *Mool Mantar* but is also intimately involved in creation. Waheguru is both visible and invisible. In terms of prevailing Hindu understandings where the Divine was either *nirguna* (beyond all attributes) or *sagun* (possessing all attributes), Guru Nanak taught an understanding that was both. Both attributes are shown in Guru Granth Sahib, firstly, nirguna and the uniqueness of the One:

> For endless eons, there was only utter darkness. There was no earth or sky; there was only the infinite Command of His Hukam. There was no day or night, no moon or sun; God sat in primal, profound Samaadhi. There were no sources of creation or powers of speech, no air or water. There was no creation or destruction, no coming or going. There were no continents, nether regions, seven seas, rivers or flowing water. There were no heavenly realms, earth or nether regions of the underworld … No one was seen, except the One Lord. (Guru Granth Sahib 1035)

Secondly, sagun, where the Divine is in the multiplicity of the world:

> He is near to all, and yet far from all; O Nanak, He Himself remains distinct, while yet pervading all … Many millions are born, live and die. Many millions are reincarnated, over and over again … Wherever He wills, there He keeps us. O Nanak, everything is in the Hands of God … Many millions are searching for God. Within their souls, they find the Supreme Lord God. (Guru Granth Sahib 276)

This is key in understanding Waheguru; the Divine is within everything but because of ego could be seen to be inaccessible.

In discussing Sikh monotheism it is important for those with a background in studying the Abrahamic faiths to note that there is a distinct difference between the two monotheisms. Eleanor Nesbitt (2016, 21) suggests that 'English renderings tend misleadingly to reinforce a Semitic understanding of monotheism, rather than the Gurus' mystical awareness of the one that is expressed through the many'.

Ikonkaar is also an important symbol within Sikhism that is used in many gurdwaras and in the home (Figure 1.1).

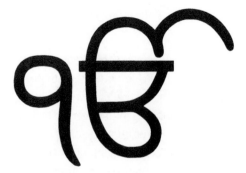

**Figure 1.1** *Ikonkaar*. https://commons.wikimedia.org/wiki/File:Ek_onkar.svg. Original: SukhVec
tor: Mrmw, CC0, via Wikimedia Commons.

## Satnaam

*Satnaam* is variously translated as 'the true name' or 'the name is truth'. The two aspects
of this word are crucial in realizing its importance in understanding Waheguru within a
Sikh way of life.

Describing Waheguru as *sat* enables a Sikh to understand the true nature of reality and
how they should be living their lives. Further lines from the *Japji* suggest the importance
of truth in describing Waheguru:

> True In The Primal Beginning. True Throughout The Ages. True Here And Now. O Nanak,
> Forever And Ever True. (Guru Granth Sahib 1)

Sat or 'truth' as Waheguru's name indicates a quality of the Divine but also the end of a
person's search for truth. There is no falsity in Waheguru, and by living life in communion
with the Divine a Sikh is able to find the truth of reality through the Guru's grace (*nadar*).
Without the truth a person is left to wander in *maya* (materialism or the illusion of reality that
leads people away from the Truth):

> Lost in egotism, Maya and attachment, the mortal earns pain, and eats pain. The
> great disease, the rabid disease of greed, is deep within him; he wanders around
> indiscriminately. (Guru Granth Sahib 1123)

Truth is thus found in Waheguru and in the realization of the naam within oneself. The
truth then enables maya to be stripped away from the mind; and this is accomplished by
listening to or obeying the *hukam* (command) of Waheguru:

> So how can you become truthful? And how can the veil of illusion be torn away? O
> Nanak, it is written that you shall obey the Hukam of His Command, and walk in the Way
> of His Will. (Guru Granth Sahib 1)

How this is expressed and found in the life of a Sikh will be explored in Chapter 2.

Naam literally means 'name' and appears over 2,500 times in Guru Granth Sahib. One such example is:

> The One God is my Intimate, Best Friend and Companion. The Naam, the Name of my Lord and Master, is Nanak's only Support. (Guru Granth Sahib 197)

This passage suggests the 'naam' as underpinning all of Guru Nanak's teachings and philosophy. Within Sikhism naam can be seen to have three different, but related meanings:

1. It refers to Waheguru – the all-pervading spirit/power that is throughout the universe. It lies latent in every person and is actualized or realized by engagement with the Guru. The One Lord is permeating and pervading amongst all; without the Guru, this understanding is not obtained (Guru Granth Sahib 1132).

2. It can refer to *Gurbani* – the words of the Gurus.

3. It refers to the praise and glorification of Waheguru – by giving utterance to the divine naam, a person is able to fine peace (see Dogra and Gobind Singh, 1995, 328).

Naam, within everything, is representative of the Divine spark. The aspect of the Divine that is within all living things. Once a person becomes aware of the naam, they have the responsibility to bring their mind and actions into union with Waheguru. For this reason, naam simran, or remembrance of the name of the Divine, is key to the life of a Sikh (the concept of union with the Divine will be explored in Chapter 2 and the practice of naam simran in Chapter 7).

## *Karta Purakh*

*Karta* means 'Doer' or 'Creator', and *Purakh* refers to an individual being. Therefore, Waheguru is the being who is the creator. As the Eternal One, and as described earlier, Ang 1035 of Guru Granth Sahib outlines that for aeons before creation there was only Waheguru. The role of Waheguru as Creator refers to the initial creation, but Waheguru continues to be the ontological cause, creator or sustainer of the world and of the many universes.

> Having created the creation, He watches over it. By His Glance of Grace, He bestows happiness. There are planets, solar systems and galaxies. If one speaks of them, there is no limit, no end. There are worlds upon worlds of His Creation. As He commands, so they exist. He watches over all, and contemplating the creation, He rejoices. (Guru Granth Sahib 8)

For a Sikh, as important as the initial creation is, the ongoing role of *Karta Purakh* today is equally important. The Creator is not separate from creation. The example is often used that if a human, as a carpenter, creates a statue, the two are separate, whereas Waheguru is indivisible from creation. This, again, returns to the teaching that Waheguru is both nirguna and sagun; immanent and transcendent; beyond and within creation. This immanence and transcendence are key to understanding the relationship of humanity to Waheguru and the command to become *gurmukh* (which will be explored in Chapter 2).

For the teacher in the classroom who is sometimes persuaded that a comparison of creation 'stories' is important, the place of Sikhism is difficult to navigate. The essential events suggest that there was nothing except Waheguru, and from that point Guru Nanak suggests that it is difficult to describe what happened. Guru Granth Sahib teaches that from a primal void,

> By His Command, the world was formed. By His Command, the heavens, this world and the nether regions were created; by His Command, His Power supports them. The Hukam of His Command is the mythical bull which supports the burden of the earth on its head. By His Hukam, air, water and fire came into being. (Guru Granth Sahib 1035)

The word 'Command' is often translated as 'Word'. Essentially Waheguru commanded it, and the universes and the elements were created. While the 'story' may not have established phases or the narrative structure of other creation stories, when exploring creation within Sikhism it is important to study the relationship of Waheguru with creation. It is this that is most important rather than the intricacies of order.

## Nirbhau

*Nir* means without or no and *bhau* means fear. In this description Waheguru is literally without fear or fearless.

> O Nanak, the Fearless Lord, the Formless Lord, the True Lord, is One. (Ang 464)

As the being who is above and beyond all things, why should Waheguru have fear? The description could be used for different reasons. Firstly, as a quality of Waheguru, in a much lesser way it is important for Sikhs to be without fear. The knowledge they have of the naam within them and their place within creation and in relation to Waheguru means that there is no need for a person to fear anything.

A further reason might be the positive aspect of this 'negative' statement where Waheguru could be described as 'All-Bliss', meaning that all is wonderful (see Guru Granth Sahib 464) and that those who seek and find union with Waheguru do not just find an absence of fear, but also bliss.

## Nirvair

'Nir' again means without, and *vair* means hatred or enmity. Therefore, Waheguru is without hatred or enmity. Waheguru is free from rancour towards anything or anyone. Linked with the concept of Ikonkaar, that Waheguru is unique and supreme, and there can be no being at the level at which they can become an enemy. The lack of an enemy reinforces the supremacy and uniqueness of Waheguru.

Again, this could suggest a quality that those seeking union with Waheguru should emulate. The corollary to 'no hatred' is 'all love', which helps a Sikh understand the generosity and forgiving nature of Waheguru.

## Akal Moorat

*Akal* means 'eternal', 'not subject to death', 'timeless' or 'beyond time', and *moorat* can mean 'being', 'image' or 'shape'. This would suggest that Waheguru is a timeless being or being outside of time. The Dasam Granth describes this timeless quality:

> He is the Primal Purusha, Unique and Changeless … He is deathless and a non-temporal Entity … He doth not come within the trap of death. (35–6)

We have already seen that before creation, Waheguru existed alone for aeons. Time only began with creation, and this reinforces the fact that Waheguru is unique and One.

The concept of time means that things change; being Timeless or outside of time means that Waheguru does not change but is eternal. This enables Sikhs to be firm in their belief in the knowledge that Waheguru is constant and changeless.

## Ajooni

'A' means beyond or without, while *jooni* means birth or incarnation. Waheguru, in contrast to other beliefs about deities, is not born or incarnated into humans or any other form. Waheguru is within creation, and the naam is found within all living things, but that does not mean that Waheguru takes human form:

> He does not fall into misfortune, and He does not take birth; His Name is the Immaculate Lord. Kabeer's Lord is such a Lord and Master, who has no mother or father. (Guru Granth Sahib 339)

Waheguru can be known through the word/Gurbani/*shabad* and the Gurus. Each of these have the attributes of Waheguru but are not Waheguru. The Gurus in human form are manifestations of the qualities and characteristics of Waheguru:

> Accepting Guru and God as one, the gurmukh has erased the sense of duality. Knocking down the wall of ego, the gurmukh has united the pond (self) with the river (Brahm). Undoubtedly the river remains contained within its two banks neither one knowing the other. (Bhai Gurdas Vaaran, Vaar 29, Pauri 14)

Waheguru is *satguru* (the True Guru) and people can become gurmukh (united with satguru) and manifest the associated qualities, but none of these are born or incarnated as Waheguru.

# Saibhang

*Saibhang* is translated as 'self-existent'. This is an attribute of Waheguru that has been explored as we have discussed Ikonkaar, *Satnaam* and Karta Purakh. Before creation there was only Waheguru:

> He created Himself – at that time, there was no other. He consulted Himself for advice, and what He did came to pass. At that time, there were no Akaashic Ethers, no nether regions, nor the three worlds. At that time, only the Formless Lord Himself existed - there was no creation. As it pleased Him, so did He act; without Him, there was no other. (Guru Granth Sahib 509)

Waheguru is, in philosophical terms, a necessary being – dependent or contingent on none else.

# Gurprasaad

*Gurprasaad* is often translated as 'by Guru's grace' with the suggestion that Waheguru can only be known through the Guru's grace. This can be interpreted in two ways, which essentially are the same thing. Firstly, that through the grace of satguru a person is able to realize the truth of satguru. Secondly, it is through the teachings of the eleven Gurus that the truth of Waheguru/Satguru is known. It is only through Waheguru's grace (*prasaad*) that people are able to understand the truth of the Divine.

In translating Guru Granth Sahib into English, Gopal Singh (1960, 1) suggests an alternate translation of 'Enlightener':

> [Here] Guru Nanak is giving, in monosyllables, the attributes of God. The Guru here, therefore, is Guru-in-God whose Grace is invoked. As such, 'Guru' can only be rendered as 'Enlightener' which is also its literal meaning in Sanskrit.

Either of these interpretations helps a Sikh understand more about Waheguru and the way to become gurmukh.

A further exploration of the term 'prasaad' is the idea that the *Mool Mantar* is a list of Waheguru's characteristics, and as such the Divine is full of grace. This links with the idea of attaining *mukti* which will be discussed in the next chapter. The grace of Waheguru enables a person to attain union with Waheguru.

# Summary

In exploring the nature of Waheguru within Sikhism it is impossible to summarize Waheguru in any other way than through the *Mool Mantar*. The first part of Guru Granth Sahib enables a person to begin to apprehend the qualities of Waheguru. The most important aspect of the Divine enables Sikhs to know their place in relation to Waheguru. Learning about Waheguru enables them to learn about themselves and how they can best live their lives. It is for this reason that meditation on/remembrance of the naam takes on such importance within Sikhism. With the background established as to the nature of Waheguru, it is now possible to move on to the nature of humanity and the importance of seeking union with Waheguru.

# Chapter 2

# The Nature of Humanity/Becoming *Gurmukh*

In exploring the nature of Waheguru in Chapter 1 we were able to observe the importance of *naam*. One of the meanings of naam as an expression of Waheguru is that it is the all-pervading spirit/power that is throughout the universe. It lies latent in every person and is actualized or realized by engagement with the Guru. This one teaching outlines the nature of all living things and, in particular, humanity. The world has been created to enable humanity to realize their true nature and for individuals to achieve unity with Waheguru. To help us understand the nature of the reality of existence and humanity, we will explore a number of concepts within this chapter, including *maya*, *haumai*, *manmukh* and *gurmukh*.

## *Maya*

'Maya' can be translated as 'delusion' and refers to the idea that the only true focus in the world is Waheguru; everything else is transitory and an illusion. It is only Waheguru that is timeless, not subject to change and worthy of attention. Existence is not an illusion, but a person's focus is illusory as it draws them away from an awareness of the truth of existence. Maya is also created by Waheguru.

A complementary understanding within Sikhism is that maya is synonymous with ignorance. It is a wall or a fog that hides the truth of reality from people. Ignorance can be overcome by refocusing on priorities and a recognition of the truth of naam and Waheguru. It is metaphorically described in Guru Granth Sahib in a way that illustrates the danger of mistaking/misinterpreting reality with illusion or false perception:

> In the darkness of maya, I mistook the rope for the snake, but that is over, and now I dwell in the eternal home of the Lord. (Guru Granth Sahib 332)

> Like the story of the rope mistaken for a snake, the mystery has now been explained to me. Like the many bracelets, which I mistakenly thought were gold; now, I do not say what I said then. (Guru Granth Sahib 658)

The perception of the rope causes a person to act in a particular way; a perception of the reality of existence can cause a person to live in a particular way that does not reflect the truth of the naam within. It is only in the way of living that a person is able to eradicate the influence of maya from their life. That reality can be grasped through the teachings of the Gurus:

> Raajas, the quality of energy and activity; Taamas, the quality of darkness and inertia; and Satvas, the quality of purity and light, are all called the creations of Maya, Your illusion. That man who realises the fourth state – he alone obtains the supreme state. (Guru Granth Sahib 1123)

Maya is, in Sikh belief, any distraction that moves a person away from Waheguru. Sikhism is not, however, world rejecting; rather, it is world affirming. It is in the world that a Sikh can achieve unity with the Divine.

> Impurity does not come from the earth; impurity does not come from the water ... O Nanak, the one who has no Guru, has no redeeming virtues at all. Impurity comes from turning one's face away from God. (Guru Granth Sahib 1240)

It is within the world that a Sikh lives the principles of the Gurus. While a lack of understanding of the true nature of the world can lead a person away from union with the Divine, a true understanding of the world enables a Sikh to utilize what is in the world to seek that same union:

> Nanak, meeting the True Guru, one comes to know the Perfect Way. While laughing, playing, dressing and eating, he is liberated. (Guru Granth Sahib 522)

Union with Waheguru is to be found within the living of life. In this way, Guru Nanak and his successors taught against the duality of the world and the need to be world renouncing to realize the reality of the world. Guru Nanak rejected the sannyasi or renunciate ashrama common in Hinduism. Life could be lived and union achieved while living as a householder, and, in fact, it was designed to be so. For Guru Nanak, and for Sikhs, there is no spiritual life and temporal life; rather the two are inseparable. In a similar way to the nature of Waheguru being *nirguna* and *sagun*, immanent and transcendent, the religious life of a Sikh is indivisible and incorporates every aspect of living. With Waheguru being present throughout creation and throughout the world, it is possible for a person to find union there, without an artificial separation.

In exploring the Sikh concept of maya within the classroom, it may be important to explain it in the context of maya in Hinduism or Buddhism. This is not necessary, as it is a concept that stands alone and does not need to be compared. However, if students are already aware of the concept of maya in other religious traditions, then it is important to highlight the different way in which maya is understood in Sikhism, or they may be under the impression that it means the same thing. The work of Wittgenstein (1968, 109) helps us understand the need to explore the usage, rather than just its appearance: 'One cannot guess how a word functions. One has to look at its use and learn from that', summarized as 'don't ask for meaning ask for use'. Maya, in Hinduism, would similarly be translated as 'illusion', but rather than disguising the reality, it is a creative force that provides the perception of reality in existence. There are certainly commonalities between the two concepts, but Sikhism would see it as merely an empty force misleading the world.

Maya is also a term within Sikhism that can denote wealth; and in this understanding, it is similarly used to distract people from naam and the reality of existence:

> The household which is filled with abundance – that household suffers anxiety. One whose household has little, wanders around searching for more. He alone is happy and at peace, who is liberated from both conditions. (Guru Granth Sahib 1019)

## *Haumai*/self-centredness and ego

One of the main aspects of maya is the focus on the ego or the self. By focusing on the haumai a person deludes themselves that life is all about them and the seeking of worldly pleasures to satisfy the ego. As part of maya, haumai provides the illusion that there is a duality in the world and that Waheguru and creation are separate. The focus on the self and the separateness from Waheguru is highlighted in Guru Granth Sahib:

> In ego they come, and in ego they go.
> In ego they are born, and in ego they die.
> In ego they give, and in ego they take.
> In ego they earn, and in ego they lose.
> In ego they become truthful or false.
> In ego they reflect on virtue and sin ...
> In ego they are ignorant, and in ego they are wise.
> They do not know the value of salvation and liberation.
> In ego they love Maya, and in ego they are kept in darkness by it. (Guru Granth
>     Sahib 466)

Interestingly, Cole and Sambhi (2006, 79) render a different translation of this where 'In ego they' is translated as 'In ego one', which highlights the self-centredness of the ego; it is not about 'they' but about 'one', meaning an individual.

In seeking attachment, and being attached, to the material world a person is seeking to satisfy themselves. In so doing, they are succumbing to the illusion of existence. Haumai provides, as part of maya, a screen or a cloud that masks true understanding and union with Waheguru. The goal of a Sikh is to escape the influence of maya and haumai, achieving liberation and ultimately union with Waheguru.

It is maya and haumai that keep the cycle of reincarnation going. A person is reborn because they have failed to grasp the reality of the naam within creation and within themselves. As such, people are subject to the Five Thieves that draw them away from the truth and make them subject to maya. The Five Thieves are inextricably linked to haumai and the focus on the self:

> Within this body dwell the five thieves: sexual desire, anger, greed, emotional attachment
> and egotism. (Guru Granth Sahib 600)

They are *kam* (lust), *krodh* (rage or uncontrolled anger), *lobh* (greed), *moh* (attachment or emotional attachment) and *ahankar* (ego/pride). Kam or lust is a perversion of the quality of love. Using the example of the rope and the snake in explaining the concept of maya, we can see how lust is used as an ego-centred perception of love. Rather than focused on expressions of true love towards others, kam is an expression of self-gratification that is only focused on the self. Lust is a negative emotion that adversely impacts an individual. Love is properly expressed in service of others; this is in any kind of relationship, whether within the community or within married life. It is evident from the teachings of the Gurus that relationships are important, and that the seeking of union with Waheguru should be carried out as a householder. The renunciate could be just as susceptible to lust: 'The Yogis, wandering ascetics and renunciates – this net is cast over them all' (Guru Granth Sahib 1186). Lust cannot be overcome by its denial but by a true understanding of the naam. Like all of the other 'thieves', lust provides a skewed perception of reality that needs to be overcome.

Krodh or wrath/anger is a feeling or state of mind that is focused on an individual, event, thing or even one's own actions. In common with all aspects of maya and the Five Thieves it is possible to see that it skews a perception of reality. Anger is often focused on the self and how the actions of others or circumstances have impacted on the individual. This channels an unwanted focus on the needs of the self. Again, in a similar way to kam, krodh can be seen to be a manipulation or perversion of a positive feeling and response. It is right to be angry at certain things such as inequality among human beings, but when that anger focuses on the self and becomes uncontrolled, a 'mist' descends that increases the influence of maya in a person's life.

Lobh or greed is an outworking of a natural impulse. It is necessary for a person to want to have enough to live their life and provide for their family. When this becomes the main focus of a person's life, it can be all-consuming. It is not wrong to be wealthy within Sikhism, but it is wrong to seek wealth for selfish reasons. It may begin for positive reasons but can quickly become all-consuming as people focus on the material aspects of life and the desire to accumulate and have more. This is a distraction from the naam, the true focus of life. It is an expression of haumai, where a person's wealth is shown to glorify the self. Where wealth is used to benefit others this would be seen to be a positive thing.

As with all of the Five Thieves, lobh is used in a way to cloud the mind and change a person's focus. The solution to maya and all of the Five Thieves is meditation on the naam. This could be likened to applying a lens to reality that enables everything to come into focus. Lobh is a lens that is self-prescribed and that creates a distortion to the nature of reality. Following the Guru and realizing the truth of naam enables these lenses to be replaced with the only prescription that will work.

Within the context of moh or attachment, it can be seen that attachment to the material is indicated, but perhaps, in distinction to lobh, it can also include emotional attachment. Guru Granth Sahib describes such attachment as being like drowning in a muddy swamp:

> In the swamp of emotional attachment, their feet cannot move. I have seen them drowning there. (Ang 12)

This is, perhaps, one of the most difficult of the Five Thieves to avoid. It is not overcome by non-attachment, but rather through a proper understanding of a person's relationships to all things and people. There is an emotional attachment to many things and people in life; for example, a person's family. This is right and proper, but how can this emotional attachment be a distraction to union with Waheguru?

A person who is subject to moh is perhaps focused solely on those people and things within their sphere of existence. As such there may be an unhealthy obsession/attachment which means that anything outside of the realm of the self is ignored. It may appear to be positive as the needs of others are considered, but this is often only in relation to the individual. It is an unhealthy relationship with aspects of a person's experience that are subject to change and even end. At the extreme, a person can develop obsessions with keeping people, things and relationships the way that they are. At the same time they are uninterested in anything else.

In contrast to a Buddhist worldview, the solution, again, to this attachment, for a Sikh, is not non-attachment but to live a life in relationship with others. A Sikh is to place the attachments that they have into the proper perspective. Giving up all attachment is not the way of a Sikh, but using the reality of the naam to understand their nature and place is that which will enable moh to be overcome.

Ahankar or ego/pride is similar to and different from the concept of haumai. The two terms are used separately within the teachings of the Gurus, and so it will be useful to explore the difference between the two, if, indeed, there are any. The term 'ahankar' is translated as ego or pride. The term haumai is translated as ego/self-centredness, but it is also a cognate of the words 'I' and 'me' – perhaps reflecting it as part of the worldview of maya. It is inextricably linked in the sense that pride can be seen to lead to haumai. Haumai is to do with the nature of a person's existence and their place within that, while ahankar is to explore a person's view of their own importance. In some ways this can be seen to be splitting hairs. In this context a person's focus on their own place in the world is both selfish and self-congratulatory.

Pride is the antithesis of equality (see Chapter 5). It seeks to laud oneself and to relegate others. It makes a person feel responsible for all that they have and all that they are; in so doing it means that the person forgets Waheguru and makes themselves the most important being in their lives. Pride can be seen to be the worst of the Five Thieves, perhaps because it is the source of each of the others. They are all rooted in how the individual is affected or satisfied in life.

The Five Thieves and haumai are evidenced in a person's life as they are described as manmukh, whereas they can be overcome by a person becoming gurmukh. It is to these two concepts that we now turn, to understand both the reality and maya of existence.

## Manmukh

Under the influence of haumai and the Five Thieves a person can be seen to become manmukh (self-willed or self-focused). This is the opposite of the desired way of life within Sikhism – that of becoming gurmukh (see below). A person who is manmukh is focused on the ego or the self and is shrouded in the cloud of maya. Instead of a lens that brings everything into focus, a manmukh person has the nature of reality obscured. Indeed, they have by their own choice been left to themselves in navigating existence:

> O my mother, Maya is so misleading and deceptive. Without meditating on the Lord of the Universe, it is like straw on fire, or the shadow of a cloud, or the running of the flood-waters. (Guru Granth Sahib 717)

Those who are manmukh have followed their own will and their own guidance and live subject to the Five Thieves, attached to many or all aspects of the material world. Guru Granth Sahib has many passages that describe the 'lost' nature of those who are manmukh:

> The Gurmukh knows the Divine Light, while the foolish self-willed manmukh gropes around in the darkness. (Guru Granth Sahib 20)

> The self-willed manmukhs are totally without virtue. Without the Name, they die in frustration. (Guru Granth Sahib 27)

This last passage that describes the death in frustration of those who are manmukh refers to the continued reincarnation of such. Within Sikhism continued reincarnation of a human's soul is the result of them not being gurmukh, and therefore having characteristics of someone who is manmukh:

> Some are very knowledgeable, but if they do not know the Guru, then what is the use of their lives? The blind have forgotten the Naam, the Name of the Lord. The self-willed manmukhs are in utter darkness. Their comings and goings in reincarnation do not end; through death and rebirth, they are wasting away. (Guru Granth Sahib 19)

The purpose of existence within Sikhism is to purify the soul by becoming united with Waheguru. Someone who is manmukh is unable to understand the naam and be blessed by the Guru's grace. Within aspects of Sikhism there is the belief that the soul, or aspect of naam, must pass through 8.4 million life forms or reincarnations before achieving mukti (liberation/union with Waheguru). One Sikh has suggested:

> If I fail to achieve mukti in this life, then I will have to start my progress with the 8.4 million life forms again. Only by going through each of these reincarnations will I be able to have the opportunity of living as a human again. (Holt, interview)

This may be an individual's view; for many Sikhs, depending on the life that people live, they will be reborn as a lower life form, but not necessarily as all of them. This cycle of reincarnation is driven by the ego, mired in maya:

> This soul has lived in many wombs. Enticed by sweet attachment, it has been trapped in reincarnation ... Maya has infused attachment to itself in each and every heart. (Guru Granth Sahib 251)

Implicit in the continued reincarnation of beings is the concept of *karam*/karma. Within Sikhism karam has three main interpretations: the law of cause and effect, the grace of the Guru, and actions. At this point we will only explore karam as the law of cause and effect. This is the most oft-understood meaning of karam, perhaps because of its relationship to the concept of karma/*kamma* found within Hinduism and Buddhism. This is certainly an aspect of karam that is found within Guru Granth Sahib. Karam is a law which means that every action has a consequence whether in this life or in lives to come:

> The body is the field of karma in this age; whatever you plant, you shall harvest. Says Nanak, the devotees look beautiful in the Court of the Lord; the self-willed manmukhs wander forever in reincarnation. (Guru Granth Sahib 78)

In a Sikh understanding the law of cause and effect is subject to the *hukam* or command of Waheguru. There are two types of karam within this understanding as part of hukam: *dukrit karam* is thinking against hukam (it is thinking because a person can only think against hukam rather than act against hukam or the command of Waheguru), and *sukrit karam* is following hukam. This distinction is in terms of how a person lives their life, and how they think they will gain good and positive karam.

As karam is subject to hukam, it is not an immutable force or law. Performing good acts or gaining good karam does not wipe away bad karam. Rather, the law of karam, in reference to reincarnation, can be broken only by the grace of the Guru. Karam is subject to the Divine command, and this will be discussed in further understandings of karam in the section below exploring the way to be gurmukh.

Those who are living a manmukh life are subject to the effects of karam. Indeed, as Dogra and Mansukhani (1995, 173) suggest, 'however noble and benevolent a devotee may be, he cannot get salvation or liberation from transmigration'. Even with positive or sukrit karam it is impossible to break out of the cycle of reincarnation. The idea is that after death the soul is brought into the Court of Waheguru and the cycle of rebirth continues based on the karma that has been accumulated.

## Gurmukh

To attain union with Waheguru and escape the cycle of reincarnation it is necessary for a person to become gurmukh or to live a gurmukh life. In contrast to manmukh, which is self-willed or self-focused, a person who is gurmukh is united with the Divine and is Guru (meaning Waheguru) focused. The gurmukh person has recognized the truth of reality and is aware of the naam within everything. They have seen through the clouds of maya and understood the truth of their relationship with the Divine. In an irony that is not lost on Sikhs, the truly gurmukh has turned and looked inside themselves and found Waheguru; they have realized the true nature of the self by discovering the naam. Those who have always sought to serve the ego and self will be ever searching through maya, but those who allow themselves to be guided by the Guru will realize the true self.

Throughout the writings of the Gurus it is clear that the realization of the naam and the ability to become gurmukh are possible only with the assistance of the True Guru:

> The key is in the hands of the True Guru; no one else can open this door. By perfect destiny, He is met. (Guru Granth Sahib 124)

This links with the second understanding of the term karam when it is translated from the Arabic as 'grace'. As mentioned earlier, the law of karam condemns everyone, no matter how noble, to continue in reincarnation. The law of karam is thus balanced by the Guru's grace: 'It is the inner transformation brought about through awakening of the power of the Holy Name which helps in the nearness of the devotee to the Lord. Then He takes over and man feels one with Him' (Dogra and Mansukhani, 1995, 173).

The discovery of the naam, and the beginning of the uniting with Waheguru, transforms an individual. While this sounds straightforward, Guru Nanak, in the *Japji*, has described the process or spiritual realms that a person will go through in seeking union with Waheguru:

> Along this path to our Husband Lord, we climb the steps of the ladder, and come to merge with Him. (Guru Granth Sahib 7)

These stages are named *Dharam khand*, *Gian khand*, *Saram khand*, *Karam khand* and *Sach khand*. These form an understanding of the different stages of the spiritual evolution of the minds of people. Each stage outlines where the mind is focused, and how the person acts. It is important to note that these stages are not developed in isolation from the other stages and also from the rest of the community. Individuals will have characteristics of each and do not necessarily leave behind the previous stages as ascent is made. Again, the five *khand*s are not world rejecting but are developed in relation to the living of a life in a community or a family, and to the *Panth*.

Figure 2.1 illustrates that while there is progression, the latter realms incorporate the actions and qualities exhibited in the earlier realms, meaning that it is a progression within the physical realm, rather than a transcendence and renunciation of such. An exploration

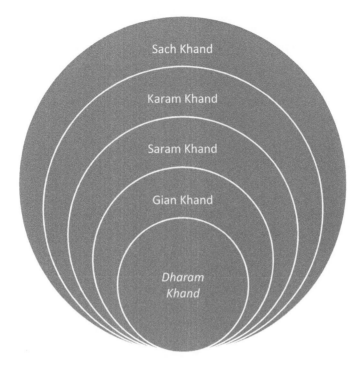

**Figure 2.1** The realms of spiritual consciousness.

of each of these stages or realms (Punjabi: khand) is important to understand the search for union with Waheguru or the path of a gurmukh.

## Dharam Khand

*Dharam* can also be transliterated as 'dharma' and has as the meaning 'duty'. This is the earth, which has been created so that people can fulfil their duty and live a good life:

> In the midst of these, He established the earth as a home for Dharma. Upon it, He placed the various species of beings. Their names are uncounted and endless. By their deeds and their actions, they shall be judged. (Guru Granth Sahib 7)

In this realm of consciousness a person acts and reaps the consequences of their actions. The world has been established as the home of dharam. By recognizing the impact of karam in their lives and in others, people are able to begin their spiritual journey. A person, in this stage, is beginning to recognize the truth of reality and to meditate on the naam and, because of this, is motivated to live an ethical life, recognizing that there are consequences to all actions. Beginning to recognize this truth and live accordingly, people 'receive the Mark of Grace from the Merciful Lord' (Guru Granth Sahib 7). The actions that a person performs form the ethical basis of Sikhism and will be explored in greater detail in Chapters 5, 7 and 8.

## Gian Khand

Through their recognition of dharam and karam a person is able to develop spiritually into Gian khand or 'the realm of spiritual wisdom' (Guru Granth Sahib 7). While the realm of duty has motivated a person in terms of action, in Gian khand a person is engaged more in a development of wisdom or mental satisfaction. In this realm, Waheguru is made known, and there is a fountain of wisdom that begins to be understood:

> In the realm of wisdom, spiritual wisdom reigns supreme. The Sound-current of the Naad vibrates there, amidst the sounds and the sights of bliss. (Guru Granth Sahib 7)

Recognizing their true place within creation, alongside the multiplicity of the other aspects of the universe, a person develops humility. The truth of creation is widened for the individual, and the person at this stage is able to recognize the falsity of haumai and the truth of the naam. A person moves closer to Waheguru by rejecting haumai and developing all forms of wisdom. As indicated by the Sikh worldview, this wisdom and knowledge is not just that which might be considered 'religious', rather all knowledge can be part of wisdom when viewed through the lens of the naam. Understanding the truth, everything in and outside of the world is made possible by Waheguru.

## Saram Khand

Saram khand is variously translated, but it can mean the 'realm of effort' but also modesty and humility. In this realm it is suggested that the person becomes more humble as their knowledge of the Divine increases. Guru Nanak describes it thus:

> In the realm of humility, the Word is Beauty. Forms of incomparable beauty are fashioned there. These things cannot be described ... The intuitive consciousness, intellect and understanding of the mind are shaped there. The consciousness of the spiritual warriors and the Siddhas, the beings of spiritual perfection, are shaped there. (Guru Granth Sahib 7)

This passage from the *Japji* suggests that it is in this realm that mental, intellectual and spiritual capacities are developed and honed. The humility and qualities that are part of Gian khand are formed, and a person is able to be described as a spiritual warrior – someone who is, at the same time, at one with both eternity and the temporal world. A person is intuitively one with eternity and the naam as they live their lives. It is in this realm that the apex of reason and knowledge is reached. Pashaura Singh (2014, 233) has noted that the Divine word/teachings of the Guru (*bani*) transform 'the "perception" (*surati*) into higher intellect (*mat*)' and 'emotive reflection (*man*), and discerning intelligence (*budhi*)' into '"self-luminous consciousness" (*sudhi*)' where the gurmukh 'experiences mystic identity with *Akal Purakh*'. This experience may be fleeting; to make it lasting, a person must develop mental and spiritual discipline to hone those faculties that have been affected.

The realm or stage of Saram khand is seen to be, very much, a preparation for the further stages in the development of a person's spiritual consciousness and union with Waheguru.

## Karam Khand

As outlined earlier karam (or karma) has different meanings within Sikhism. The realm of karam is not the same as that of dharam where the law of cause and effect holds sway. Rather, the further meaning of karam as 'grace' is the meaning of this realm. In this stage of spiritual progression the grace of Waheguru breaks through and enables people to experience bliss as this grace is experienced. At this point, as we return to the *Mool Mantar*, it becomes clear that the grace of Waheguru is central to the characteristics of Waheguru, but it is also the way that Waheguru is known in the fullest sense by a person who is seeking union.

> In the realm of karma, the Word is Power. No one else dwells there, Except the warriors of great power, the spiritual heroes. They are totally fulfilled, imbued with the Lord's Essence. Neither death nor deception comes to those, Within whose minds the Lord abides. The devotees of many worlds dwell there. They celebrate; their minds are imbued with the True Lord. (Guru Granth Sahib 7)

This description of Karam khand highlights the union with the Divine; the ego has been overcome and people experience the bliss of the naam because they are 'imbued with the Lord's essence'. Their relationship with the naam is realized and is expressed in the qualities they possess. The evils have been overcome, and the person is exemplary in their living of the Five Virtues: *sat* (truth), *santokh* (contentment, including an overcoming of attachment), *daya* (compassion), *nimrata* (humility) and *pyare* (love). Each of these is lived with courage and a remembrance of the naam (these virtues will be explored in greater detail in Chapter 8). Guru Arjan spoke about the concept of *braham-giani* (God-conscious being) which may sit well in a description of a person in this realm. The qualities, actions and influence of a braham-giani are described in Angs 273–4 of Guru Granth Sahib; a selection of these qualities is given here. A braham-giani

- lives a lifestyle which is pure;
- focuses on the development of spiritual wisdom;
- is absorbed in meditation of the naam;
- is solely reliant on Waheguru;
- is humble;
- does good to others cheerfully;
- has no worldly entanglements;
- loves only Waheguru;

- dwells with Waheguru;
- is aware of the truth of reality and existence;
- is free of ego;
- is such because of the grace of Waheguru;
- helps those who cannot help themselves;
- knows the immanence of Waheguru;
- is honoured in the court of Waheguru; and
- is shown the mercy of Waheguru.

These descriptions begin to help a Sikh understand the qualities of someone who is seeking to be gurmukh. The realization of such is made possible only through the expression of Waheguru's grace. A person is fully awake to the reality of existence and, viewing everything in its proper perspective, is able to act accordingly. Achieving spiritual liberation or the status of gurmukh in this life, a person in the realm of karam khand is able to enter the final stage/realm.

## Sach Khand

*Sach* means 'truth', and as such the final realm is the 'realm of truth'; it is the dwelling place of *Nirankar* (the formless one):

> In the realm of Truth, the Formless Lord abides ... O Nanak, to describe this is as hard as steel! ... Such is the karma of those upon whom He has cast His Glance of Grace. O Nanak, the Merciful Lord, by His Grace, uplifts and exalts them ... Those who have meditated on the Naam, the Name of the Lord, and departed after having worked by the sweat of their brows. O Nanak, their faces are radiant in the Court of the Lord, and many are saved along with them! (Guru Granth Sahib 8)

It is here that complete unity with the Divine is experienced. The description of Sach khand suggests that the universe and all of existence are contained therein. As such, it might be suggested that it is the realm where only Waheguru is, but as Waheguru is within everything it is a 'place' where, united with Waheguru, people are able to attain the highest level of consciousness. This realm of consciousness is possible to attain in this life; one who does so will achieve mukti or liberation from the cycle of reincarnation:

> One who, in his soul, loves the Will of God, Is said to be Jivan Mukta – liberated while yet alive. As is joy, so is sorrow to him. He is in eternal bliss, and is not separated from God. (Guru Granth Sahib 275)

In this realm no more karam/karma is attached to a person, and the karmic process has ended because of the intervention and grace of Waheguru. This union of bliss with the Divine is described by Guru Gobind Singh:

Just as millions of sparks are created from the fire although they are different entities, they merge in the same fire. Just as from of waves are created on the surface of the big rivers and all the waves are called water. Just as from of waves are created on the surface of the big rivers and all the waves are called water. Similarly the animate and inanimate objects come out of the Supreme Lord having been created from the same Lord, they merge in the same Lord. (Dasam Granth 49)

While the concept of life after death is spoken about, and the interrelated concepts of reincarnation and mukti are important, the focus of a Sikh's life is to seek to become united with Waheguru during this lifetime. It is this life that they can currently control; by seeking to live a gurmukh life they can hope for mukti, but the focus is on now.

## Summary

One Sikh has suggested that the purpose of life is

to remember the Lord every second and to do good deeds so as to become one with the Lord. (Holt, interview)

It will become evident as we move through the coming chapters that understanding the purpose of life and the nature of existence underpins all of the Guru's teachings and the way that Sikhs live their lives. It is clear from a discussion of the five realms of spiritual consciousness that the way a Sikh lives and the qualities they develop enable a person to begin to live a gurmukh life. Just as Waheguru is within and outside of the world, in the spiritual and temporal worlds, so a gurmukh must straddle the physical and spiritual. Actions are imperative in living a gurmukh life in that they prepare a person to realize the truth of existence; but once realized they are evidence of a person's remembrance of the naam and the grace (karam) of Waheguru that they are receiving in their lives. These actions are evidence of living in the light and path of the Guru.

# Chapter 3

# The Ten Gurus

As explored in Chapters 1 and 2, the concept and role of a Guru is central to Sikhism and the life of a Sikh. The nomenclature of modern society has reduced the concept of a 'guru' to a teacher. There are relationship gurus, self-help gurus and many more. As a teacher of Sikhism it is important to note that these are the understandings of the term that our pupils may come to our classroom with. It is important in introducing the concept of 'Guru' within Sikhism to recognize their pre-eminent place in understanding the nature of Waheguru and the nature of existence. The Gurus within Sikhism (including Guru Granth Sahib) are more than teachers. This chapter will be devoted to an exploration of the lives and teachings of the ten Gurus in human form. The following chapter will explore the nature, place and importance of Guru Granth Sahib.

## What is a Guru?

The previous two chapters have made clear that a Guru is someone, possibly best described as a teacher, who brings a person from darkness to light. The darkness of *maya* is shattered by the teachings of the Gurus as a person comes to know the truth of the *naam* within themselves. Similarly, the Guru's grace makes it possible to break the bindings of *karam* and thus enables a person to develop through the realms of consciousness and achieve *Sach khand* – freedom from the cycle of reincarnation and union with Waheguru. That there is a link between Waheguru and the Gurus in human form is a truth that cannot be overemphasized within Sikhism. One Sikh has suggested that the terminology 'human Gurus' is best replaced by 'Gurus in human form' to emphasize the Guruship of each before their mortality:

> 'Human form Gurus' may be better to reflect the understanding the Gurus were a reflection of Akal Purakh. The Gurus are vital. They are a way for us humans to understand 'God' (WaheGuru) and we should have a personal relationship with our Gurus. (Holt, interview)

One aspect of the above quotation suggests an understanding of who the Gurus in human form really are. They are described as a 'reflection of *Akal Purakh*'; what does this mean for Sikhs? W. Owen Cole and Piara Singh Sambhi (2006, 89) have suggested that when a soul unites with Waheguru, it is eternal, with one exception:

It may be that God wishes a perfected being to return to earth in order to undertake some particular task. Such a person will already be brahm-gyani at birth. Entry into the world will be ... because of God's commandment.

Such a birth provides an opportunity for *sewa* (see Chapter 6) in bringing people to the knowledge of the naam through their teaching and example. The *Janamsakhis* (see below) make it clear that Guru Nanak's birth was of such a type, and Guru Gobind Singh in Dasam Granth (Book of the Tenth) suggests the same of himself. As *braham-giani*, the Gurus are those beings described in the previous chapter based on the teachings in Guru Granth Sahib:

> O Nanak, the God-conscious being is Himself the Supreme Lord God. The God-conscious being cannot be appraised. The God-conscious being has all within his mind. Who can know the mystery of the God-conscious being? Forever bow to the God-conscious being. The God-conscious being cannot be described in words. (Ang 275)

The Guru is always united with Waheguru, living in a state of bliss. Their words are *amrit vachan*s, meaning they are saturated with the grace/energy of Waheguru. The Gurus are expressions of Waheguru in the sense they are united. Guru Nanak's description of himself makes clear the role and importance of a Guru:

> I was a minstrel, out of work, when the Lord took me into His service.
> To sing His Praises day and night, He gave me His Order, right from the start.
> My Lord and Master has summoned me, His minstrel, to the True Mansion of His Presence.
> He has dressed me in the robes of His True Praise and Glory.
> The Ambrosial Nectar of the True Name has become my food.
> Those who follow the Guru's Teachings, who eat this food and are satisfied, find peace.
> His minstrel spreads His Glory, singing and vibrating the Word of His Shabad.
> O Nanak, praising the True Lord, I have obtained His Perfection. (Guru Granth Sahib 150)

With this description it becomes evident that the Gurus are far more than inspired teachers, while neither being born of Waheguru, nor avatars. One Sikh has suggested:

> They are the form of Divinity. Perfect in every way. (Holt, interview)

They are braham-giani, beings who are united with Waheguru and manifestations of the qualities and teachings of the naam, who bring others to the same state of existence:

> The Palace of the Lord God is so beautiful. Within it, there are gems, rubies, pearls and flawless diamonds. A fortress of gold surrounds this Source of Nectar. How can I climb up to the Fortress without a ladder? By meditating on the Lord, through the Guru, I am blessed and exalted. The Guru is the Ladder, the Guru is the Boat, and the Guru is the Raft to take me to the Lord's Name. The Guru is the Boat to carry me across the world-ocean; the Guru is the Sacred Shrine of Pilgrimage, the Guru is the Holy River. If

it pleases Him, I bathe in the Pool of Truth, and become radiant and pure. (Guru Granth Sahib 17)

As such, the respect shown to the Gurus in human form within Sikhism and within the classroom is of paramount importance. Although there are many pictures of each Guru, there are some Sikhs who would rather not have them pictured as it is impossible to capture the essence of who they are in a picture. The focus should be on discovering the True Guru within:

Meditate on the image of the Guru within your mind; Let your mind accept the Word of the Guru's Shabad, and His Mantra. Enshrine the Guru's feet within your heart. (Guru Granth Sahib 864)

While this is a minority view and pictures are used within the Sikh community, and we might want to use images within the classroom, it is important to note the dignity with which they are held and that they are, also, not objects of devotion.

There is also a prohibition against portraying any of the Gurus in human form in film, drama or anything akin to it. This was extended in 2019 when the Shiromani Gurdwara Parbandhak Committee (SGPC) opposed the release of the animated film *Dastan-E-Miri Piri*. This depicted Guru Hargobind, and film-makers were asked to remove all animations and vocals portraying him. In 2018, Harinder Singh Sikka was excommunicated by the Akal Takht for directing a film, *Nanak Shah Fakir*, which depicted Guru Nanak. In our classrooms it is important to respect the approach taken throughout most, if not all, of the Sikh *Panth* and not represent any of the Gurus in drama; and also to not create activities that would ask pupils to write/imagine how a Guru would have felt in a particular situation. Newspaper stories would be fine, but journal entries and the like, less so. One example of a documentary that is created in a way that is respectful of the role and depiction of the Gurus is the series available on thegurunanak.com. In this twenty-four-part documentary series, the director and presenter Amardeep Singh follows in the footsteps of Guru Nanak and explores the events of his life without depicting them except with illustrations from early *Janamsakhi*s.

One further example of honour paid to the Gurus by some Sikhs is in the use of the pronoun 'they'. Ranveer Singh (2021) does this throughout his book *Patshahi Mehima: Revisiting Sikh Sovereignty* as a sign of respect. This book has not adopted that approach, no disrespect is meant, but it is purely for functional reasons of language that male pronouns are used.

## The relationship between the Gurus in human form

One further point that I made in the introduction is that in the classroom, and sometimes in our historical reading, we explore the life and teachings of Guru Nanak and then fast forward to Guru Gobind Singh. This is a disservice to Sikh history and to the Gurus themselves. We may do this because of the time available on the curriculum, or the primacy-recency effect, where only the first and last are remembered; or we may be perpetuating the teaching that we have received. None of these are sufficient reason to explore only two. It is important for teachers to understand that each of the Gurus in human form is important and that they should be explored in turn.

There is sometimes the discussion about the complementarity of the teachings and religion of Guru Nanak and Guru Gobind Singh. Some are at pains to point out the exact relationship between all of their teachings, while some would suggest that the peaceful religion of Guru Nanak was militarized by some of his successors, especially Guru Gobind Singh, and that there is a disconnect. It is important to recognize that such a discussion misses the importance of the continuity of each of the Gurus in human form. One Sikh has suggested:

> They are the guiding light and each guru highlighted one aspect of life more than other aspect e.g. concept of langar, concept of miri-piri, concept of sacrificing one's life for the right of freedom of religion of other religions, strict equality, and creation of the khalsa brotherhood, etc. (Holt, interview)

There are central themes that run through all the teachings of the Gurus, but to suggest that Sikhism was 'completed' at the death of Guru Nanak is to fail to recognize the continuity of the Gurus. As the teachings of the Gurus spread, new challenges were met and each Guru had a role to play in sharing the teachings and way of life that would enable people to break through maya and experience the naam.

The continuity of the Gurus in human form is shown in the passing of the Guruship from one to the other. This is described in Guru Granth Sahib when Guru Angad was installed as Guru:

> Nanak established the kingdom; He built the true fortress on the strongest foundations. He installed the royal canopy over Lehna's head; chanting the Lord's Praises, He drank in the Ambrosial Nectar. The Guru implanted the almighty sword of the Teachings to illuminate his soul. The Guru bowed down to His disciple, while Nanak was still alive. The King, while still alive, applied the ceremonial mark to his forehead. Nanak proclaimed Lehna's succession – he earned it. They shared the One Light and the same way; the King just changed His body. The immaculate canopy waves over Him, and He sits on the throne in the Guru's shop. He does as the Guru commands; He tasted the tasteless stone of Yoga. (Ang 966)

Symbolically or literally, Guru Angad was given a sword to represent the spiritual teachings of the Guru. One aspect of the passage above that stands out is the teaching that they (Guru Nanak and Guru Angad (Lehna)) 'shared the One Light and the same way'. What does this mean? Bhai Gurdas suggests:

> During his life time he waved the canopy of Guru seat on the head of Lahina (Guru Angad) and merged his own light into him. Guru Nanak now transformed himself. This

**Table 3.1** A list of the ten Gurus in human form and their dates

| Name of the Guru in human form | Dates of Guruship |
| --- | --- |
| Guru Nanak (Nanak 1) | 1469 (birth)–1539 |
| Guru Angad (Nanak 2) | 1539–52 |
| Guru Amar Das (Nanak 3) | 1552–74 |
| Guru Ram Das (Nanak 4) | 1574–81 |
| Guru Arjan (Nanak 5) | 1581–1606 |
| Guru Hargobind (Nanak 6) | 1606–44 |
| Guru Har Rai (Nanak 7) | 1644–61 |
| Guru Har Krishan (Nanak 8) | 1661–4 |
| Guru Tegh Bahadur (Nanak 9) | 1664–75 |
| Guru Gobind Singh (Nanak 10) | 1675–1708 |

mystery is incomprehensible for anybody that awe-inspiring (Nanak) accomplished a wonderful task. He converted (his body) into a new form. With the same mark (on the forehead), the same canopy he radiated on the Throne. The power Guru Nanak had is now with Guru Angad was publicly proclaimed all around. Guru Angad left Kartarpur and scattered his light while sitting at Khadur. (Bhai Gurdas, Var I: 45–6)

The light of the naam that infused every aspect of Guru Nanak is transformed into Guru Angad; the relationship with Waheguru is the same. Nikky-Guninder Kaur Singh (2011, 19) describes the impact of these passages from Guru Granth Sahib and Bhai Gurdas as 'the First Guru is physically, intellectually and spiritually absorbed into the Second'. What this completely means is perhaps beyond the scope of human understanding, but the continuance of the Panth and teachings established by Guru Nanak would continue through the ten Gurus in human form, and from thence in Guru Granth Sahib. This unity of light between the Gurus is further exemplified in the assignation of the titles Nanak 2, Nanak 3 and so on to each of his successors (Table 3.1).

Throughout the remainder of this chapter we will explore the lives and contributions of each of the Gurus in human form. This exploration will, I hope, form the basis of what can be taught within the classroom.

# Guru Nanak (1469–1539)

## Janamsakhis

Before exploring aspects of the life of Guru Nanak, it is important to note the sources that are used to narrate the story of his life. The main source of contemporary narrations of the life comes from Guru Granth Sahib. One such example was explored in the introduction where, as a child, he rejected the wearing of the sacred thread as it was ultimately going to break and become dirty. The saying is related in Guru Granth Sahib, but this will have formed some of the source material for the narration of the story in the *Janamsakhi*s.

The *Janamsakhi*s are narratives of the events of the life of Guru Nanak. Initially, some of these were pictures that illustrated events from Guru Nanak's life. They quickly became written narratives:

> In the language of myth and allegory, the Janamsakhis depict the divine dispensation of the First Sikh, his concern for kindness, social cohesiveness, and his stress on the divine unity and the consequent unity of humanity. (Kaur Singh, 2019, 69)

For some, the *Janamsakhi*s have been seen as unreliable sources of accurate information about the life of Guru Nanak. The suggestion is that because they were written after his death, they tell us more about the world and beliefs of the people who recited the narrative than they do about Guru Nanak. Kirpal Singh (2004a) wrote *Janamsakhi Tradition: An Anaytical Study* to reassert the importance of the *Janamsakhi* tradition. He suggests that the writers of the earliest *Janamsakhi*s relied on two main sources:

- The *bani* (teachings) of Guru Nanak which were found in the Adi Granth (later Guru Granth Sahib).

- The first Var of Bhai Gurdas, who was a close companion of Baba Buddha, an important figure in Sikh history, who had observed the events of the creation of the Panth. Bhai Gurdas was also a companion of the next four Gurus.

Further, Singh argues that the *Janamsakhi*s are not intended as either biographies or hagiographies but as anecdotes put together to help people understand the life and teachings of Guru Nanak. To try to read them as history would perhaps be problematic, but to dismiss them as such would be similarly problematic. However, their mythical and allegorical dimension does not reduce their importance for Sikh history (Kaur Singh, 2019, 69). The main *Janamsakhi*s that have been used at different points throughout history include:

- *Bhai Bala Janamsakhi*: In the nineteenth century, it was seen to be the authoritative, and certainly the most popular, *Janamsakhi*. It is claimed to have been written by Bhai Bala in 1592 at the instruction of Guru Angad. Bhai Bala identifies himself as a close companion of Guru Nanak and accompanied him on his many travels. There are many indications that the provenance asserted in the *Janamsakhi* is not true. There is no evidence of the existence of Bhai Bala, who seems not to have been known to Guru Angad, and he is also not mentioned by Bhai Gurdas. With regard to the dating, there is evidence of anachronism in terms of the language used, which was not seen until the late seventeenth century. *Khalsa* phrases such as 'Waheguru Ji Ki Fateh' are also used throughout. While its provenance may be suspect and it may be an eighteenth-century production, it does utilize stories that are associated with Guru Nanak, and if read carefully is able to provide some understanding of the life of Guru Nanak and how it is viewed.

The following two *Janamsakhi* collections are part of the *Puratan Janamsakhi*s, 'puratan' meaning ancient or early. These two *Janamsakhi*s were rediscovered in the late nineteenth century. Although up until that point the *Bhai Mala Janamsakhi* held sway in terms of popular use, these next two were seen to be more rational explanations of Guru Nanak's life. They are to be found in a composite volume often called the *Puratan Janamsakhi*.

- *Vilayat Vali Janamsakhi*: This *Janamsakhi* had been donated to the India Office Library in the nineteenth century by a man named Colebrook. It formed the basis of Trumpp's work and is said to have been written by Sewa Das in 1588.

- *Hafizabad Vali Janamsakhi*: This *Janamsakhi* was found by Gurmukh Singh of the Oriental College, Lahore, at Hafizabad. It agrees with various aspects of Guru Nanak's life outlined in the *Vilayat Vali Janamsakhi*.

- *Bhai Mani Singh's Janamsakhi:* This is, perhaps, the latest of the four *Janamsakhi*s outlined so far. It was written by a Bhai Mani Singh, a Sikh in the court of Guru Gobind Singh. Initially, he was against writing a *Janamsakhi* suggesting that the Var of Bhai Gurdas was sufficient. On being convinced to write, he outlined his purpose in writing:

  > Just as swimmers fix reeds in the river so that those who do not know the way may also cross, so I shall take Bhai Gurdas's var as my basis and in accordance with it, and with the accounts that I have heard at the court of the tenth Master, I shall relate to you whatever commentary issues from my humble mind. (McLeod, 1980, 37)

  There is also the suggestion that Guru Gobind Singh signed the *Janamsakhi* on its completion, indicating he accepted it as a source for Sikh belief and teaching.

- *Miharban Janamsakhi*: The *Miharban Janamsakhi* holds a controversial place within Sikhism. It was written within the Mina tradition, which grew up around the person of Prithi Chand, the eldest son of Guru Ram Das. Within the lineage of the Sikh Gurus, the youngest son of Guru Ram Das, Guru Arjan, succeeded him, but Prithi Chand felt that as the eldest child he should be the next Guru. They flourished for much of the seventeenth century and controlled Amritsar and Harmandir Sahib. Guru Gobind Singh named them as one of the Panj Mel, or five reprobate groups, in 1699. In the eighteenth and nineteenth centuries their numbers dwindled, and now they no longer exist. The author is said to be Prithi Chand's son and successor, Sodhi Miharban. The *Janamsakhi* was largely unknown and thought lost until the mid-twentieth century.

  Many see Bhai Gurdas's Var to have been written in response to this *Janamsakhi*, which was written to narrate the life of Guru Nanak, but also in praise of Prithi Chand. Its association with the Mina sect means that it is little used in comparison to the others, though it is in this text that the name of Bhai Mala is mentioned.

## Thoughts for the classroom

Within an exploration of the sources for the narratives surrounding the events of the life of Guru Nanak, there are a range of possibilities that arise for their use in the classroom. The stories of Guru Nanak are normally narrated in the classroom with little discussion, but in a similar way to the Christian Gospels, the narrations of the life of the Buddha, along with texts from many religions, there are opportunities for critical reading of such. At no point does this mean that the teacher or pupils seek to criticize the person or role of Guru Nanak. We could follow the approach suggested by Khushwant Singh (1999, 291):

> Although none of these janamsakhis are contemporary, they are certainly based on some biography which was written earlier but is now untraceable. A historian can neither discard nor accept the janamsakhis in their entirety. Everything they state must be tested.

It is possible in analysing the writing of the texts to explore them in terms of understanding both the life of Guru Nanak and the communities which produced them.

Within the classroom there has been a development in the use of hermeneutics in terms of reading sacred texts. As historical texts that are used within the Sikh community, it is possible to see that the *Janamsakhi* can be used in the same way. As we understand a hermeneutic approach to be about 'the art or science of interpretation, concerned with meaning and significance' (Bowie, Panjwani and Clemmey, 2020, 3), it is possible to move beyond sacred text to read the *Janamsakhi*s to see how the narratives are imbued with meaning and significance.

This type of approach should include the reading of the text (most likely in English) to explore the things we learn about Guru Nanak from the narrative; what we learn about the community that produced it; what links there are to Guru Granth Sahib; the possible historicity claims that can be made; and how the text links with, and is used by, Sikhs today. Pupils in schools are used to having narrative curated or mediated for them, and engagement with the source material helps pupils engage with the narrative in a much more effective and authentic way.

There are many stories told of the childhood of Guru Nanak. There have been volumes filled with stories from throughout his life; and there is only the opportunity to draw on brief examples. It should also be noted that throughout this book there have been, and will be, examples from Guru Nanak's life that are used to underpin or illustrate his life and teachings as given expression in Sikhism. For example, in Chapter 1, we explored his rejection of the sacred thread to illustrate the futility of empty ritual in trying to understand Waheguru. Similarly, in Chapter 6, we explore the story of the twenty rupees and the establishment of the first *langar*. The narrative undertaken below will, necessarily, only touch on brief aspects of his life.

## The early life of Guru Nanak

Guru Nanak was born on 15 April 1469 at Rai Bhoe Talwaṇḍi (renamed as Nankana Sahib, in Punjab, modern-day Pakistan) to Kalyan Chand Das Bedi (Mehta Kalu) and Mata Tripta. He was named after his sister Nanaki. His father was a Hindu, and a *patwari* or accountant in modern terms.

At this point it is important to note the disparity between the birthdate listed above and the celebration (*gurpurb*) of the birth of Guru Nanak, which takes place on the full moon night in November. This November date was established based on the *Bhai Bala Janamsakhi*, whose provenance is questioned and contradicted by what are seen to be the more reliable *Janamsakhi*s. It could also be considered a later interpolation; Hari Ram Gupta (1994) suggests that the gurpurb was celebrated during the time of Ranjit Singh (as late as 1815) in April. Tradition since the mid to late nineteenth century is such that it continues to be celebrated in November, though most people recognize his birth took place on 15 April.

His birth, in contrast to that of other religious figures, was fairly normal – a normal delivery as reported by the midwife Daultan. The earliest *Janamsakhi* pictures show Tripta holding her son in her arms. The only indication of it being a momentous event is that the hut in which he was born was flooded with light at that moment. This is a birth that reflects both the spiritual and the physical aspects of reality. Just as Waheguru is *nirguna* and *sagun*, so is Guru Nanak of the physical world, as shown through his natural birth, but it is of spiritual significance as the hut was filled with light. It is possible that I am reading too much into the symbolism, but it seems significant that the birth of Guru Nanak fully places him in the world, which is where all are to live their lives.

In exploring Guru Nanak's schooling, there are many stories that show his ability and knowledge, especially his spiritual knowledge. By the end of his first day, when he was taught the alphabet, it is recorded that he had learned the letters and composed an acrostic celebrating and worshipping Waheguru. This acrostic is found in Ang 432 of Guru Granth Sahib, the first part of which is:

Raag Aasaa, First Mehl, Patee Likhee ~ The Poem Of The Alphabet:
One Universal Creator God. By The Grace Of The True Guru:
Sassa: He who created the world, is the One Lord and Master of all.
Those whose consciousness remains committed to His Service – blessed is their
    birth and their coming into the world.
O mind, why forget Him? You foolish mind!
When your account is adjusted, O brother, only then shall you be judged wise.
Eevree: The Primal Lord is the Giver; He alone is True.
No accounting is due from the Gurmukh who understands the Lord through these
    letters.

Ooraa: Sing the Praises of the One whose limit cannot be found.

Those who perform service and practice truth, obtain the fruits of their rewards.

Nganga: One who understands spiritual wisdom becomes a Pandit, a religious scholar.

One who recognizes the One Lord among all beings does not talk of ego.

As an aside, the opportunity for students to develop an acrostic to show their understanding of the nature of existence and of Waheguru in Sikhism would be an appropriate stimulus activity in the classroom.

Other events in his childhood show his mature spiritual knowledge; it was this knowledge that he sought, at the same time frustrating and inspiring others. He responded to one of his teachers asking whether he was of sufficient knowledge to teach him, and that he desired to develop his knowledge of spiritual matters. This disinterestedness in the affairs of the world continued at different points – once when asked to look after cattle, Guru Nanak was so caught up in contemplation that he did not notice the cattle eat up a farmer's crop in the field. Tradition holds that the field was replaced with the crop that had been destroyed. Although this highlights a miraculous event, the spiritual bent of the Guru is what is most important.

## Guru Nanak's marriage

It is suggested that one way Mehta Kalu tried to ground his son and involve him in the 'real' world was by arranging his wedding. Guru Nanak was married to Mata Sulakhani in 1487. The *Janamsakhi*s tell that he eschewed many traditions in the build up to the wedding; one example is his refusal of consult horoscopes to establish an auspicious time, suggesting that any time would be auspicious. The couple are also reported to have walked around the fire four times, instead of the seven required as per Hindu ritual. Guru Nanak and Mata Sulakhani had two sons, Sri Chand and Lakhmi Das.

Guru Nanak continued to be distracted from the real world, and so a job was arranged for him at Sultanpur Lodhi, where he moved with his family and his childhood friend, Bhai Mardana, a Muslim. At Sultanpur Lodhi, he worked hard in the Governor's office and was responsible for stores and accounting. It was while he was here that he would meditate by the river, and he experienced the Court of Waheguru in the river (see Chapters 1 and 2).

## Guru Nanak's *udasis*

Having received his errand in the Court of Waheguru, Guru Nanak embarked on a series of spiritual journeys (*udasis*) with Bhai Mardana. Travelling for a total of approximately twenty-four years, and a distance of over twenty-five thousand kilometres, Guru Nanak is believed to have embarked on five udasis:

1. 1500–6: This journey lasted approximately seven years and included visits to Sultanpur, Tulamba, Panipat, Delhi, Varanasi, Nanakmata, Tanda Vanjara, Kamrup, Asa Desh, Saidpur, Pasrur and Sialkot.

2. 1506–13: This journey lasted approximately seven years and included visits to Dhanasri Valley and Sangladip.

3. 1514–18: This journey lasted approximately five years and included visits to Kashmir, Sumer Parbat, Nepal, Tashkand, Sikkim and Tibet.

4. 1519–21: This journey lasted approximately three years and included visits to Makkah and the surrounding countries.

5. 1523–4: This journey lasted approximately two years and included visits around Punjab.

This list is not exhaustive, and other cities such as Rome are mentioned in some traditions of Guru Nanak. His journeys enabled him to spread the message of Waheguru but also to experience the lives and teachings of others. These experiences on his udasis led to the composition of some of his *shabad*s (hymns) that would later form the basis of the Adi Granth and then Guru Granth Sahib. One example of a shabad that was given in response to an experience on one of these udasis followed the visit to Gorakhmata. In this village were a group of yogis who adopted certain practices that they invited Guru Nanak to join them in. He composed the following shabad rejecting all of their practices:

> Yoga is not the patched coat, Yoga is not the walking stick. Yoga is not smearing the body with ashes. Yoga is not the ear-rings, and not the shaven head. Yoga is not the blowing of the horn. Remaining unblemished in the midst of the filth of the world – this is the way to attain Yoga. By mere words, Yoga is not attained. One who looks upon all with a single eye, and knows them to be one and the same – he alone is known as a Yogi. Yoga is not wandering to the tombs of the dead; Yoga is not sitting in trances. Yoga is not wandering through foreign lands; Yoga is not bathing at sacred shrines of pilgrimage. Remaining unblemished in the midst of the filth of the world – this is the way to attain Yoga. (Guru Granth Sahib 730)

The yogis immediately accepted the teachings of Guru Nanak and renounced their ways.

Another example from the udasis shows further the message of Guru Nanak in worshipping the ever-present *Akal Purakh* and the futility of empty ritual. In Makkah, Guru Nanak was accosted by a Muslim leader who angrily told him to move his feet from the direction of the Kab'ah when he was resting. Guru Nanak responded patiently that the man should not speak so rudely. He then moved his feet, but wherever the Guru moved his feet the doors of the Kab'ah followed. It is said that the Guru recited a verse from the Qur'an:

> And to Allah belongs the east and the west. So wherever you [might] turn, there is the Face of Allah. Indeed, Allah is all-Encompassing and Knowing. (Surah 2:115)

On recognizing the greatness of Guru Nanak and the truthfulness of his words, the Muslim leader begged forgiveness and kissed the Guru for his true teaching.

The *Janamsakhi*s are full of such stories that illustrate the events and teachings of Guru Nanak and as such are a rich source for exploration in the classroom. The importance of this storytelling will be explored at the end of this chapter.

One final example from his travels involves Guru Nanak being imprisoned. In about 1520 the Mughal emperor Babur (Zahir-ud-Dīn Muhammad) invaded Saidpur (Eminabad) and imprisoned all of the surviving inhabitants. Guru Nanak and Mardana were in the city and were taken prisoner too. The Guru was ordered to carry a pack, while Mardana was given a horse to lead. Here the narratives differ; either Guru Nanak performed his task while singing shabads or the pack was carried without any support and the horse was led without reins. Reports of these happenings reached Babur, who demanded to meet the Guru. So impressed was the emperor on meeting Guru Nanak that he offered Guru Nanak a gift. The Guru requested the freedom of all from Saidpur, and that they should have their goods returned to them. Tradition holds that over eleven thousand prisoners were released that day. This highlights the importance, for Guru Nanak, of protecting the rights of all people and serving all regardless of status or religion.

## Kartarpur

After the last of his long journeys, Guru Nanak settled in Kartarpur in 1552. One tradition holds that Guru Nanak asked a wealthy follower to donate a piece of land. The other tradition holds that having arrived at a place close to the river Ravi, he stopped near Batala, which was surrounded by farmland. One day at lunchtime, he and Mardana were singing *Gurbani*. Meeto, a local farmer's wife, heard the singing while she was preparing her husband's lunch. Entranced by the Gurbani, she carried the lunch to Guru Nanak and Mardana.

On finishing his singing, Guru Nanak noticed Meeto standing nearby and began to converse with her. Meeto offered the meal she had prepared to the Guru, who accepted it and served it to both Meeto and Mardana, after which all three ate together.

Having excused herself, Meeto went to meet her husband, Karoria, to excitedly tell him of the Guru. When she arrived, her husband was cross and too hungry to pay attention to her exuberance. Realizing that he would not listen, Meeto served him and the workers some food. After eating, Karoria agreed to meet Guru Nanak.

On meeting Guru Nanak, Karoria explained that all the fields in that area, as far as the eye could see, belonged to him. The Guru asked him who they belonged to before him. Karoria responded that they were his father's. 'And before him?', the Guru asked. Eventually, Karoria realized that the land did not really belong to him but all belonged to Akal Purakh. He then asked the Guru to stay with him for a while.

Soon people came to know of Guru Nanak and his divine message. They were delighted to hear his soul-inspiring songs and discourses. They accepted him as their spiritual guide and became his disciples. The Guru's fame soon spread far and wide.

Hindus and Muslims, people of all classes and castes, and sadhus and faquirs flocked to him. Inspired by his songs and discourses, they gave up their mutual hatred and jealousy and began to live together like brothers.

While staying on Karoria's land, the Guru received many visitors which began to make the place busy. Karoria then decided to ask the Guru to leave so that all could return to normal. However, each time he set out to meet the Guru he was prevented from reaching his destination either because his horse stumbled or because it refused to move, and on one occasion he temporarily lost his eyesight.

He realized that he was unable to reach the Guru because of his pride and anger and, therefore, decided to walk to the Guru and ask for forgiveness. On seeing the Guru and feeling the love and joy of the music and presence of the Guru, Karoria offered the land to Guru Nanak and suggested they call it Nanakpur.

Guru Nanak demurred and suggested that as it was the land of the Creator (*Kartur*) it should be called Kartarpur, or the seat of the Creator.

People came from far and wide to pay homage to, and visit with, the Guru. Many houses and a dharmsala were built. Hymns were sung, and the Guru taught the community. Perhaps the most noticeable aspect of life in Kartarpur was the langar, where all sat and ate together regardless of caste, religion or gender, with no distinction.

Guru Nanak lived a householder's life; he grew food and spent time in devotion to Waheguru. Through the way he lived in Kartarpur, Guru Nanak showed how one could live a householder's life in devotion to the Divine. The way to become *gurmukh* was not a life of retreat and denial, but it was available only through living an involved life.

## The Guru's death

Prior to Guru Nanak's death, he installed Lehna as his successor, Guru Angad. As his death drew near, there arose a difference of opinion between his followers. Those from a Muslim background wanted to bury him, while those from a Hindu background wanted to cremate his body. With his followers gathered around him, he explained that it was only his body that would be dying, and his light would be passing to Guru Angad (through the principle of *joti jot*). He asked Muslims to place flowers on his left-hand side and Sikhs and Hindus to place them on his right. Whichever flowers survived would determine what should happen to his body. He died on the evening of 22 September 1539, and the following morning, both sets of flowers remained while the body had disappeared. His followers had forgotten his teaching that there was no Hindu or Muslim but only the path of Waheguru. Muslims buried his flowers, while Hindus and Sikhs cremated them. A gurdwara now stands at the place of his death.

## Thoughts for the classroom

In some ways as we explore the narrative of Guru Nanak's life, it is impossible to separate the events from the teachings they illustrate. The previous two chapters highlight the teachings of Guru Nanak, and they find expression in the events and his shabad. When we use the stories of Guru Nanak it is essential that we use them as a springboard to understand the teachings of Sikhism. Although I suggest that current classroom practice focuses solely on Guru Nanak and Guru Gobind Singh, this is not to suggest that they should not be focused on, but rather that the others should also find a place. The life of Guru Nanak is rich with experiences that can be utilized in the classroom. There many events that link with Sikh living today, and it is imperative that these links be made.

## Guru Angad/Nanak 2 (1504–52)

Guru Angad (meaning 'limb', suggesting that he was like a limb of Guru Nanak in their closeness) was appointed Guru by Guru Nanak in the manner described above. He was the leader of the Sikh Panth from 1539 to 1552.

Guru Angad had been born Bhai Lehna in 1504, in Harike, Punjab, but lived most of his life in Khadur. Before meeting Guru Nanak, Guru Angad had been a Hindu teacher, but in his devotion to Waheguru he had shown his faithfulness. Indeed, it is reported that twice Guru Nanak encouraged him to go home to his family in Khadur, but on both occasions he returned to the Guru.

It is thought that some time in his twenties, during the Kartarpur period of Guru Nanak's life, Guru Angad became a Sikh, or a disciple of the Guru. His devotion to the Guru, his spirituality and humility are seen to be some of the many reasons why he was chosen as Guru by Guru Nanak. Many at the time would, perhaps, have expected one of Guru Nanak's two sons, Sri Chand and Lakshmi Das, to succeed him as Guru, but a couple of stories are told as to why Guru Nanak chose Lehna to be the second Guru, Guru Angad.

The first story tells of a jug that had fallen into a muddy ditch. On being asked to retrieve it, Sri Chand felt that the jug was too dirty and that the dirt would possibly pollute him. Lakhmi Das refused, the suggestion being that it was too menial a task for a son of the Guru. On the other hand, Lehna retrieved it, cleaned it and brought it to Guru Nanak filled with clean water.

The second story tells of Guru Nanak leading a group of Sikhs into a forest; he made gold coins and gems appear on the path. Most of those who were with him scrabbled to pick up the gold and the gems. Only Lehna and Baba Buddha ignored the jewels and gold. In the second part of the story, on finding Lehna and Baba Buddha to be the only ones with him, Guru Nanak invited them to eat off a corpse on a funeral pyre. Baba Buddha refused and left, whereas Lehna went ahead and on lifting the shroud found Guru Nanak.

Both of these stories, and others, show the humility of Guru Angad and help Sikhs understand why he was chosen over the sons of Guru Nanak.

As the first successor to Guru Nanak, it is felt by many that Guru Angad's main role was the consolidation of the Sikh or, as it was then known, the Nanak Panth. It might have been assumed that Guru Nanak was just one of many charismatic teachers in Indian society; indeed, many sants had lived and taught within the area in which Guru Nanak had established the Panth. In appointing a successor it could be seen that he wanted the community which he had founded to continue. There are perhaps many examples of the disciples of charismatic teachers being dispersed on their death, but with Guru Angad having been installed, Guru Nanak had indicated his wish for it to continue. Guru Angad consolidated the Sikh community during the thirteen years from the death of Guru Nanak to his own in 1552.

It would seem that before Guru Nanak's death, he suggested that Guru Angad relocate the bulk of the Sikh community to Khadur. It is seen to have been a way for Guru Angad to establish himself as Guru and to avoid any possible machinations and divisions caused by Sri Chand and Lakhmi Das. Cole and Sambhi (2006) suggest that this may not have been the reason, but that it might just have been an indicator of the comfort he felt in his hometown of Khadur; it did, however, set the precedent that it was not a requirement for Gurus to situate themselves in the village or 'seat of power' of their predecessor.

His leadership of the Nanak/Sikh Panth is remembered for a number of developments and consolidations.

## The development of Gurmukhi script

Gurmukhi literally means 'from the mouth of the Guru' and was established to preserve the words of Guru Nanak. Guru Angad drew on existing languages to develop a unique composite language. Although suggesting that Guru Angad developed the Gurmukhi script, it is more than likely that he worked with Guru Nanak in its development. Believed to be the words of Guru Nanak, there is an acrostic poem (*Paintis Akhari*) that utilizes all thirty-five letters of the Gurmukhi alphabet at the beginning of each line to describe the qualities of *Ikonkaar*. Guru Angad is seen to be the author of sixty-two or sixty-three of the hymns in Guru Granth Sahib (approximately 1 per cent). In terms of teaching and writing in the Gurmukhi script, his major role seems to have been the articulation of the bani of Guru Nanak. It was Guru Angad who, when writing a hymn, appended the name 'Nanak' and began the tradition of the naming of the Gurus as 'Nanak 2' and so on.

Establishing a script different from those found in the surrounding areas can be seen as an act of creating a separate identity.

[The Gurmukhi script showed] they were something distinct from the common mass of Hindus. It also dealt a powerful blow to the domination of the priestly class, whose importance rested on their knowledge of Sanskrit which had so far been the language of religion. (Singh and Singh, 1950, 19)

There is a suggestion that many people at the time saw Sikhism as one of several traditions within what came to be known as Hinduism. As such, the teachings of Guru Nanak sat easily within the *sanatan* tradition, and some might suggest that Guru Nanak was not trying to establish a new 'religion'. His actions in choosing a successor and also the actions of Guru Angad in establishing a distinctive alphabet suggest that the separation from existing traditions was an important part of Sikhism from the earliest days.

It is important to note a debate about the origin, dating and development of the Gurmukhi script. It may have been developed by Guru Nanak, but, at the very least, it was harnessed by Guru Angad in a distinctive way to preserve the bani of Guru Nanak.

## Expansion of the langar

During the time of Guru Angad, there was an expansion of the langar and how it was practised within the Sikh Panth. The community had grown significantly, and as such the administration of langar was simplified to enable *sewadars* to meet all the needs of the increasing number of guests. The food was standardized, and sewadars were instructed to be polite and attentive. In tandem with this development, Ranveer Singh (2021) suggests that Guru Angad developed the concepts of 'court' (*darbar*) and 'sovereignty' begun by Guru Nanak. He established a community close to a river where he sat on a throne, and there were orders of etiquette and behaviour established. There seems to have been a transcending of worldly and spiritual sovereignty during this time.

One story highlights both the humility and groundedness of Guru Angad but also his position in relation to 'worldly powers'. The sovereignty of Guru Angad was contemporaneous with the Mughal emperor Humayun. Tradition holds that following Humayun's defeat at the hands of Sher Shah Suri (1550), he visited Guru Angad. On entering the court of Guru Angad, Humayun was kept waiting for over three-quarters of an hour, either because Guru Angad was playing with children (Singh, 1926, 53) or because he was performing kirtan (Fenech, 2014, 42). Humayun was deeply offended, but when he started to draw his sword and smite the Guru, his sword would not move. The Guru reproved him:

> At this Angad looked up smiling, and said, 'Beaten by Sher Shah, you can do no better than strike a faqir with your sword. Better go back to your motherland before you seek to regain your throne.' (Singh, 1926, 53)

The treatment of the emperor suggested that there is a separation between the court of the Guru and that of the emperor. This becomes a much more explicit issue as we explore the lives of the subsequent Gurus.

## Physical exercise

As part of the development of the court of the Guru, following morning services, members of the community were encouraged to engage in exercise drills and wrestling matches. In this way, the physical health and strength of the members were encouraged. Each dharmsala (community gathering place of the Sikhs) was encouraged to have a gym attached. This, again, provided a foundation on which future Gurus would build.

## Consolidation of the *sangat*

The consolidation of the Sikh/Nanak Panth was perhaps the greatest contribution of Guru Angad. At the time of his Guruship, he was able to hold together in the community those who might have wanted to follow the deeply contemplative practices of Sri Chand, as he was seen by many to be Guru Nanak's successor. A schism did not develop, and he was able to hold the community together.

As the community grew, Guru Angad appointed leaders at the various dharmsalas of Sikhism that developed. These leaders would be responsible for the collection of offerings to help meet the expenses of langar, and other aspects of the community.

Guru Angad had two sons, Dasu and Dattu, to whom he did not pass on the Guruship; neither was Sri Chand, the surviving son of Guru Nanak, nominated. Instead, before his death in 1552, he nominated Amar Das as his successor in front of a congregation of Sikhs. He did this by placing a coconut and five paise in his lap before prostrating before him as his Guru.

## Thoughts for the classroom

As already mentioned, the significance of Guru Angad is often overlooked within the teaching of Sikhism. Perhaps his naming as Angad, or 'limb', is mentioned, but the great work that Guru Angad performed in consolidating and holding the Sikh community together is not explored as it should be. When Guru Nanak died, he left a community that had been focused on his teachings and his role as Guru; it would have been easy for the community to diminish. However, the actions of Guru Angad established aspects of a Sikh community that were true to the life and work of Guru Nanak but also served as a bridge to future Gurus. The establishment of the darbar at Khandur, as well as the development/completion of the Gurmukhi script enabled Sikhism to flourish in a way that delineated it from the beliefs and practices found in the area at that time. Guru Angad's life and work would serve as an interesting exploration of the development of religions and religious communities.

The stories of his life enable all to see the qualities and priorities of a Guru and also a gurmukh. He applied the teachings of Guru Nanak in establishing a community, a *sangat*, that transcended the physical and the spiritual.

# Guru Amar Das/Nanak 3 (1479–1574)

Guru Amar Das was installed as Guru at the age of seventy-two and was Guru for twenty-two years until his death in 1574. He was born in May 1479 in Basarke village in Punjab. He married Mansa Devi, and they had four children: Mohri, Mohan, Dani and Bhani. He was a Vaishnava Hindu for most of his life and is reported to have completed approximately twenty different pilgrimages to places such as Haridwar on the River Ganges. At about the age of sixty, while on one of these pilgrimages, a Hindu sadhu suggested that he find a teacher. It was to this task that he then set his mind. On returning home, he heard the *Japji* being sung by a daughter of Guru Angad, Bibi Amro, who happened to be married to Amar Das's nephew. She was living in Basarke at the home of her husband's family; when leaving home she had been asked by her father to continue singing the hymns of the Guru and to share Sikh beliefs.

Bibi Amro taught Amar Das about Guru Angad and the teachings of Guru Nanak. She arranged for him to meet Guru Angad, at which point he accepted the teachings of the Sikh/Nanak Panth and accepted Guru Angad as his Guru. On becoming Sikh, Amar Das rejected Vaishnavism and began to live a life of selfless service (sewa). This was evidenced in his drawing the Guru's bath, cooking and cleaning for the Guru and members of the community. He was often engaged in meditation and prayers, eventually becoming gurmukh under the Guru's teaching and through his grace.

As cities began to be developed under Guru Angad's influence, one at Goindwal was built for the Guru, and his disciples wished for him to live there. Guru Angad could not do so because of his ill health, and so he asked Amar Das, his devoted disciple, to make Goindwal his residence.

These events led to two aspects that arose when Guru Amar Das became Guru. In a similar way to Guru Angad, to avoid confrontation with and a schism between him and the two sons of Guru Angad, he moved the base of his court to Goindwal. It was this selfless service that led to one of the sons of Guru Angad to oppose the Guruship of Amar Das (both were initially opposed, but Dasu was quickly reconciled):

> Datu, the son of Angad, was for a while, at enmity with Amardas. Once he proclaimed himself a Master at Khadur, but he was not accepted. At this, Datu, full of rage, went out to Goindwal, and kicked Amardas; having always regarded him as a poor servant of the family. 'What! a servant of ours, made into a master?' cried Datu. But Amardas only knelt down and began rubbing Datu's feet in deep reverence, 'Sire', he said, 'my flesh is old and hard; it must have hurt your foot.' (Singh, 1926, 57)

At this, Datu flew into a rage and called Guru Amar Das a usurper. It was not until the time of the fifth Guru, Guru Arjan, that Datu was reconciled with the wider Sikh Panth.

During his time as Guru, the Sikh community continued to grow and spread over a large area. This underpinned much of his leadership of the Nanak/Sikh Panth, which is remembered for a number of reasons.

## Manjis

With the increasing numbers of Sikhs and the attendant larger geographic area, it became necessary to develop the manner in which the community was served and kept together. Guru Amar Das established a network of twenty-two *manjis*. These were geographic centres that roughly equated to the same twenty-two areas covered and governed by the Mughal Empire. Each was headed by an individual who was authorized to exercise authority in the name of the Guru's darbar. In addition to the twenty-two manjis, Guru Amar Das created fifty-two *puris*, which were smaller centres of governance. The number fifty-two mirrored the number of bodyguards held by the emperor.

In exploring this as an innovation within the Sikh Panth, it is possible to view it in a pragmatic sense. It was necessary for the communities that were spread out to receive guidance and leadership on behalf of the Guru. Utilizing the twenty-two geographic areas already served by the Mughal Empire could have been a purely sensible approach that used existing boundaries and seats of governance. However, authors such as Ranveer Singh (2021) and Louis Fenech (2000) suggest that there could have been a reason for the continued establishment of the Sikh Panth as sovereign. Ranveer Singh (2021, 41) suggests that the establishment of the manjis and the puris 'laid down the gauntlet of rebellion'. Whether this symbolism was appreciated or noticed by those at the time is questionable. Indeed, when the emperor visited Goindwal, based on the complaints of Hindu rulers, he was so impressed that he gave the revenues of a number of surrounding villages to the Guru's daughter, Bibi Bhani. This hardly seems the actions of an emperor whose authority was being challenged; however, it could have been a political move to assuage any feelings of rivalry.

What is certain, however, is that the foundation for future developments, and possible conflicts, was laid. Indeed, Guru Amar Das continued with the exercises and competitions established by Guru Angad.

## Equality

As has been explored in relation to Guru Nanak, and as will be developed in Chapter 5, the concept of equality lies at the heart of the Sikh message. Every person has the naam within, and as such all have the capability of union with Waheguru. The treatment of women had always been something that set Sikhs apart from Hindus and Muslims in the surrounding areas. Guru Amar Das established some practices that highlighted this equality and reinforced the importance of women in the Sikh Panth. In the manjis and puris, mentioned above, there were women who were appointed as administrators, including Bibi Amro, his niece who had introduced him to Guru Angad. Women were also appointed, as part of this system, for preaching the teachings of the Gurus. Other developments that separated Sikhs even further from their Muslim and Hindu neighbours included women being forbidden from wearing the veil (purdah) and the practice of sati (burning a widow on the funeral pyre of her husband):

> Do not call them 'satee', who burn themselves along with their husbands' corpses. O Nanak, they alone are known as 'satee', who die from the shock of separation. (Guru Granth Sahib 787)

Guru Amar Das also allowed remarriage and forbade the practice of female infanticide. In terms of modern society, these may seem to be sensible and much needed reforms, but at the time of Guru Amar Das these changes overturned generations of religious and/or cultural practices. The place of women established by the Gurus was radical for the time.

## Demarcation of Sikh belief and practice

As has been noted, the developments and strictures in place with regard to the treatment of women was a marker of Sikh identity in contrast to surrounding Hindu and Muslim practices. This is true of two other developments within the Sikh Panth initiated during the time of Guru Amar Das.

Langar had always been a practice since the time of Guru Nanak, but under the Guruship of Guru Amar Das the practice and the recognition of the egalitarianism that it embodied seemed to have been taken note of by people outside of the Sikh Panth more. The eating together as equals, with no distinction being made, was in direct opposition to the established order of society manifested in caste. Guru Amar Das is reported to have adhered to the policy of 'Pehle pangat piche sangat', meaning 'First eat together, then meet together'. It was concern over these egalitarian practices that led to the visit of Emperor Akbar to Goindwal. When the emperor arrived, instead of being ushered into a meeting with the Guru, he was invited to sit on the floor and share the communal meal. In this way, and by the expansion of the langar, Guru Amar Das was able to reinforce and highlight the equality of all as a central tenet of Sikhism, in contrast to the practices prevalent in wider society.

The second development, which is seen by some to be more controversial, is the establishment of certain rituals within the Sikh Panth. As has been explored in relation to the teachings of Guru Nanak, outward ritual expressions were often rejected as empty, and it was the internal search for Waheguru that was most effective. Empty rituals, such as the sacred thread ceremony, offerings being made or pilgrimage, had constantly been rejected and eschewed by Guru Nanak. The developments in this area by Guru Amar Das are seen by many Sikhs to be necessary in the establishment of a distinctive Sikh identity, and a separation from the rituals that were associated with life events and the yearly calendar for most of their Hindu neighbours.

Three such developments were a *baoli* (well) at Goindwal; the gathering of the community at Baisakhi and Diwali; and the adoption of certain rituals at a wedding.

Guru Amar Das oversaw the construction of a baoli at Goindwal that would serve as a pilgrimage site (*tirath*) for Sikhs. Rather than visiting other places of pilgrimage popularized by Hindus, Sikhs were able to visit the well at Goindwal. The well had 84 steps, symbolic of the 84 cycles of existence within Hinduism, or the 8.4 million species within creation. The initial impetus for the building such a well was the refusal to allow Sikhs to draw water from a local well. It has served as a blueprint for other wells in different gurdwaras. It can also be seen to reflect the Sikh emphasis on cleanliness and the need to bathe. In serving many purposes, one of the impacts that it had was that if a Sikh felt the need to make a pilgrimage, then there was a distinctively Sikh site.

As the Sikh community grew, the need for people to feel a connection with the Guru increased. The first generations of Sikhs had been able to know the Gurus and seek personal audiences. This became increasingly difficult as time went by. One 'solution' to this was an innovation of Guru Amar Das when he established Diwali and Baisakhi as two existing festivals where Sikhs were invited to gather together at Goindwal to celebrate with the Guru. This served the purpose of bringing the community together, but also separated the Sikh Panth from the surrounding Hindus. If Sikhs were celebrating these festivals in the local communities where they lived, it was likely they would join in the Hindu celebrations. In bringing them together at Goindwal people were able to feel a distinctive Sikh identity in the celebrations:

> Although the historical events which Sikhs associate with these occasions still lay in the future, they now became times when the Guru's followers were required to decide which faith they belonged to. Sikhs could not enjoy the celebrations that took place in their Hindu villages and be disciples (Sikhs) of the Guru. (Cole and Sambhi, 2006, 22)

The third aspect of 'ritual' developed by Guru Amar Das surrounded life-cycle events. He suggested the recitation of Gurbani at times of birth and death, but the most noted development was during wedding ceremonies. He composed a forty-verse hymn titled '*Anand*', which was to be sung at Sikh wedding celebrations or at other events of significance. This is still sung by many Sikhs at different times of religious importance. It would be developed further in subsequent years, but it established Sikh events as distinct from others.

It has been suggested by Fenech (2014) and McLeod (1976) that the needs of the ever-expanding community necessitated the development of these rituals. In trying to unify the community, which may have been more removed from the direct influence of the Guru, Guru Amar Das needed to institute these developments to help people feel connected to the Guru and to their Sikh identity. There was a possibility that people would fall back into rituals from Hinduism, and the lines between the two worldviews would be blurred. In a manner similar to the establishment of the manjis, these were developments that enabled people to feel a connection with the Guru.

## Social action and charitable giving

As has been noted with regard to the langar, the role of women and the rejection of caste, Guru Amar Das continued social teaching and action to try and enact equality to enable all to recognize the naam within and develop a gurmukh life. As outlined earlier, one of the distractions of maya involves wealth – either an abundance of it or the lack of it. People can begin to focus so much on wealth that they are drawn away from a contemplation of the naam and a continued separation from Waheguru. The concept of langar, as outlined, continued to be important, and its concept was emphasized. As a part of this, and also because of the growing numbers within the community, there needed to be a formalization of the contribution of Sikhs to the community. Guru Amar Das introduced a system of giving, whereby a Sikh is asked to give of their wealth for social and charitable purposes. This was an offering to the Guru and used for many purposes. In enabling the community to be self-sustaining, this practice enabled, and continues to enable, Sikhs to not be subject to maya, which suggests that material wealth is the goal of existence. Rather, charitable giving enables people to put wealth into its proper perspective.

The following two contributions of Guru Amar Das laid the basis for future developments of Sikhism which can, perhaps, be considered two of the most important aspects of Sikhism today.

## Guru Da Chakk

Although only involved during the planning stages, Guru Amar Das selected the site of Amritsar, which he named Guru Da Chakk. This was later to be developed by Guru Ram Das and Guru Arjan into the Harmandir Sahib (house of God).

## *Goindval Pothis*

Guru Amar Das began the compilation of the words of the previous two Gurus, elements of his own words and the writings of certain Hindu *bhagats* and Sufis, whose hymns and teachings aligned with that of Sikhism. These are known either as the *Goindval Pothis* or the *Mohan Pothis*. They were the precursor to the compilation of the Adi Granth by Guru Arjan, which in turn became known as Guru Granth Sahib. A total of 907 of Guru Amar Das's hymns are to be found in Guru Granth Sahib.

His continuity with Guru Nanak and Guru Angad is described in Guru Granth Sahib:

> The same mark on the forehead, the same throne, and the same Royal Court. Just like the father and grandfather, the son is approved. He took the thousand-headed serpent as his churning string, and with the force of devotional love, he churned the ocean of the world with his churning stick, the Sumayr mountain. He extracted the fourteen jewels, and brought forth the Divine Light. (Guru Granth Sahib 968)

Prior to his death, he nominated his son-in-law, Bhai Jetha, as the next Guru and renamed him Ram Das (servant of God):

> Amar Das sent for his two sons Mohan and Mohri, and for Bhai Budha and other Sikhs. In this shining assembly of disciples, Amar Das, having obtained five pieces and a coconut, got down from his seat, placed Jetha thereon, and set the offerings before him, saying, 'Thou art myself. The light of our Master Nanak is in thee.' Jetha was acclaimed by the whole assembly as Ram Das, the Master. (Singh, 1926, 64)

## Thoughts for the classroom

All of these 'developments' enabled Sikhism to flourish as an expanding community. Guru Amar Das continued the work of Guru Nanak and Guru Angad. He lived in a different time, and the community had different needs. It is important to note that for the developing religion to be consistent between Gurus is central to a Sikh self-understanding. This does not mean that everything has to be the same; Guru Nanak established the Panth, but being of the same light it was incumbent on succeeding Gurus to articulate and develop how the teachings of the Guru could be applied in different circumstances. Guru Amar Das developed aspects of Sikhism that enabled it to begin to have a place independent of religious traditions.

In exploring the life of Guru Amar Das in the classroom, there are interesting elements that serve as a bridge between the past and the future. Guru Amar Das did not know Guru Nanak but was devoted to his teachings. Perhaps the various developments he initiated could serve as the basis for teaching about Sikhism. His focus on equality, social action and the langar are particularly important in developing these as distinguishing features of Sikh identity. In examining the development of a religious tradition, the question of how a community develops from one which is built on a personal connection to one which utilizes intermediaries and why that was felt needed will be particularly interesting.

# Guru Ram Das/Nanak 4 (1534–81)

Guru Ram Das, originally named Jetha, was born to Hari Das and Mata Anup Devi, in Lahore, on 24 September 1534. He was orphaned at the age of seven and was brought up by his maternal grandmother. Living in Basarke, there is evidence that he knew Guru Amar Das (before he was Guru). At the age of twelve, they moved to Goindwal, where he accepted Guru Amar Das as his Guru. There, he served the community with humility and Waheguru and Guru Amar Das with great devotion. Guru Amar Das noted this and allowed Jetha to marry his daughter Bibi Bhani in 1554. After their marriage Jetha and Bibi Bhani remained in Goindwal and continued selfless service to the community and were also involved in the digging of the well with eighty-four steps.

During his time at Goindwal, Guru Amar Das often relied on him. One such instance took place prior to the visit of the emperor to the Guru at Goindwal, when Guru Amar Das was summoned to the Mughal emperor's court. Perhaps suggesting that he was not subject to the political authorities of the time, the Guru sent Jetha in his place. The concerns which precipitated this visit surrounded the egalitarian emphasis of the Sikh community, which was evidenced in the langar and the number of people, particularly those belonging to the lower castes, who were joining the Sikh Panth. These issues had been raised by Hindu teachers and brahmins. In defence of what was happening within the Sikh Panth, he gave a robust defence that both articulated the teachings of Sikhism and rejected the practices of Hindus and Muslims. He reiterated the oneness of humanity that rejected all divisions between people. He further suggested that sin or wrongdoing could only be overcome through compassion and surrender to Waheguru, rather than through ritual ablutions or the life of an ascetic. Even before his nomination as Guru he was reinforcing the central elements of the Sikh Panth.

As Guru, he continued the teachings of the previous three Gurus and also gave insight on what it was to be a Sikh during that time. In what is now found in Guru Granth Sahib, he records:

> One who calls himself a Sikh of the Guru the True Guru shall rise in the early morning hours and meditate on the Lord's Name. Upon arising early in the morning, he is to bathe, and cleanse himself in the pool of nectar. Following the Instructions of the Guru, he is to chant the Name of the Lord, Har, Har. All sins, misdeeds and negativity shall be erased. Then, at the rising of the sun, he is to sing Gurbani; whether sitting down or standing up, he is to meditate on the Lord's Name. One who meditates on my Lord, Har, Har, with every breath and every morsel of food – that GurSikh becomes pleasing to the Guru's Mind. (Ang 305)

Guru Ram Das was Guru for seven years, from 1574 to 1581. During this time, he both continued and developed the teachings and practices of the Gurus that came before him. There are 688 hymns of Guru Ram Das in Guru Granth Sahib. In a similar way to Guru Amar Das he also laid the foundation for further consolidation of the Panth. This underpinned much of his leadership, which is remembered for a number of reasons.

## Reconciliation and humility

One seemingly small event showed his ability to bring about a reconciliation with Sri Chand, the only surviving son of Guru Nanak. Sri Chand had formed an ascetic way of life that still honoured the teachings of Guru Nanak, which developed into a group called the Udasi. While not becoming one with the wider Sikh Panth, because of the focus on the householder life within Sikhism and on asceticism and celibacy within the Udasi, the reconciliation of Sri Chand was an important moment for unity and development. This reconciliation was a result of the humility of Guru Ram Das. On meeting Guru Ram Das, Sri Chand commented on the length of the Guru's beard, and asked why he had such a long beard. Guru Ram Das replied that it was used to wash the feet of sants such as Sri Chand; then, he bent down to Sri Chand's feet. Sri Chand immediately jumped up in protest, embraced the Guru and said:

> It's enough. This is the kind of character by which you have deprived me of my ancestral heritage. Now, what more is left with me that I could offer you for your piety and goodness of heart? (Pruth, 2004, 67)

The humility of Guru Ram Das reconciled Sri Chand and washed away any hard feelings between Sri Chand and his father's successors.

## Ramdaspur

Mohan and Mohri, the sons of Guru Amar Das, were hostile to the succession of Guru Ram Das. As a result of this, Guru Ram Das moved his headquarters/darbar to Guru Da Chakk, the area chosen by Guru Amar Das as the site of a new town. There is a tradition that the land for Guru Da Chakk was given by the emperor; however, as the Guru was unable to accept the gift, the emperor bestowed it to the Guru's wife, Bibi Bhani. The alternative version is that Sikhs bought the city for seven hundred rupees from the owners of the village of Tung.

The plan had been to construct a town with a pool at its centre. In 1577, the digging of the tank under the direction of Guru Ram Das began. This site was fortuitous in that it enabled the Sikh Panth to flourish and grow. Its location near the Delhi–Kabul trade route enabled it to prosper; the Guru invited merchants and tradesmen of all kinds to establish their businesses in Guru Da Chakk, which was renamed Ramdaspur, and later Amritsar.

Guru Da Chakk also developed into the centre of Sikh identity. The celebrations of Baisakhi and Diwali now took place at Ramdaspur, continuing the tradition that had begun with Guru Amar Das at Goindwal.

There are suggestions that the sovereignty and independence of the darbar of the Guru continued under the Guruship of Guru Ram Das at Ramdaspur. The combination of spiritual and temporal sovereignty may be suggested in Guru Granth Sahib:

> The Great and True Guru, Guru Amar Daas, has preserved honour in this Dark Age of Kali Yuga. Seeing His Lotus Feet, sin and evil are destroyed. When His mind was totally satisfied in every way, when He was totally pleased, He bestowed upon Guru Raam Daas the Throne of Raja Yoga. (Ang 1399)

Raja yoga is sometimes translated as political and spiritual rule or sovereignty (R. Singh, 2021, 51). This was evidenced in the Guru's darbar and also in his development of the manji system.

## The manji system

The manji system set up by Guru Amar Das seemed to have been a success both in unifying the community, thereby keeping people in touch with the Guru, and in collecting donations. One of the changes brought about by Guru Ram Das was the appointment of *masand*s, or territorial deputies. These masands were selected on the basis of their knowledge of the teachings of the Gurus and also their integrity. 'Masand' was the 'official' name given to the administrators that had been established under Guru Amar Das.

## Music

The previous Gurus had been known for their composition of hymns, and Bhai Mardana had been the *rababi* for Guru Nanak's bani. Fenech (2014) and Hans (1988) have argued that Guru Ram Das's contribution in the area of music is important in the development of Sikhism, though it is often overlooked. Although there are comparatively fewer compositions (sixty-eight) by him in Guru Granth Sahib, he began to introduce different musical modes/measures (rags) using over thirty different rags in his compositions. This enabled a more robust sharing of Gurbani, besides making them perhaps more musically diverse and appealing.

## *Lavan* hymns

Perhaps the most evident aspect of Guru Ram Das's influence in the Sikh community today, outside of the city of Amritsar, is his composition of the *lavan*. These four hymns written by Guru Ram Das were, and still are, to be repeated at Sikh wedding ceremonies. The verses can be found in Angs 773–4 of Guru Granth Sahib. In these hymns, the Guru outlines the journey of each soul towards Waheguru and then the duties of those who are married. The purpose of marriage, and its desirability for all people, is suggested later in Guru Granth Sahib by Guru Ram Das:

> They are not said to be husband and wife, who merely sit together. They alone are called husband and wife, who have one light in two bodies. (Ang 788)

Reading this, it is impossible not to note the similarity that the purpose of life is to unite with Waheguru. As such, marriage can be seen to be a state that enables a person to develop those qualities that are needed to attain union, perhaps first with a spouse and then with Waheguru.

It is evident in the creation and use of the lavan hymns that Guru Ram Das was at pains to separate Sikh practice from Hindu rituals. Although he founded the city of Ramdaspur, and assisted in the building of the well at Goindwal, he spoke about the emptiness of pilgrimage:

> The Ganges, the Jamunaa, the Godaavari and the Saraswati – these rivers strive for the dust of the feet of the Holy. Overflowing with their filthy sins, the mortals take cleansing baths in them; the rivers' pollution is washed away by the dust of the feet of the Holy. Instead of bathing at the sixty-eight sacred shrines of pilgrimage, take your cleansing bath in the Name. When the dust of the feet of the Sat Sangat rises up into the eyes, all filthy evil-mindedness is removed. (Guru Granth Sahib 1263)

In this passage, Guru Ram Das reiterates the teaching of Guru Nanak that it is recitation of the naam that purifies. Indeed, it is not the places of pilgrimage that make a person holy but those who visit that can make the places holy. This is not, and cannot be seen to be, inconsistent with the teachings of Guru Amar Das. The condemnation is perhaps of empty ritual; when descending the eighty-four steps at Goindwal a Sikh would be repeating the *Japji*, and thus meditating on the naam.

Prior to his death, Guru Ram Das nominated his youngest son, Arjan, to succeed him as Guru. He had the ageing Baba Buddha perform the rite, who expressed his hope that

> as one lamp is lighted from another, so the Guru's spirit will pass into him and will dispel the darkness in the world. (K. Singh, 1999, 53)

## Thoughts for the classroom

Guru Ram Das is remembered mainly for the founding of, what would become, Amritsar and his consolidation of the system of masands. In seven years he accomplished much, and his example of devotion and humility is inspiring to Sikhs today. The exploration of his life is perhaps best served in the classroom by studying the large number of stories that are associated with him, and also the development and influence of the lavan, particularly as it is still used as part of the Sikh wedding ceremony. Following a study of the remaining six Gurus in human form, this chapter will explore the importance of storytelling within the teaching of Sikhism.

# Guru Arjan/Nanak 5 (1563–1606)

Guru Arjan was born on 15 April 1563 at Goindwal as the youngest child of Guru Ram Das and Meta Bhani, the daughter of Guru Amar Das. For the first eleven years of his life he lived at Goindwal in the home of his grandfather, with his mother and father. His grandfather, Guru Amar Das, is reported to have noted his specialness at a young age and predicted that he would one day be a wellspring of poetry and bani. The suggestion is that even at this early age he was destined for Guruship. At the age of eleven, he moved to Ramdaspur with his father when Guru Ram Das became Guru.

A well-known story is told of his attendance at a wedding in Lahore when he was seventeen. His father had been invited and wanted one of his sons to attend. His eldest son, Prithi Chand, had already refused. A couple of reasons have been suggested for his refusal, the first being that he held an important position in the treasury and was worried about being replaced. The other reason was similarly self-serving, if true: it has been suggested that he was apprehensive that if he was away, it might present the opportunity for someone else to be appointed to succeed as Guru. The second brother, Mahadev, similarly refused to go because of his lack of interest in the matter. Guru Arjan, however, happily fulfilled his father's request. This is, perhaps, one motivating factor in the decision of Guru Ram Das to appoint his youngest son, rather than either of his two older sons.

At the end of the wedding, Arjan was asked to stay on in Lahore and oversee the sangat there. This was a time of suffering for Arjan, in that he suffered the pain of separation from his Guru. During his time away he wrote three letters to Guru Ram Das, but only the third, marked with a '3', reached its destination. On inquiring why the letter had a '3' marked on it, it was discovered that Prithi Chand had intercepted the first two and hidden them from their father. In the letter Arjan had lamented:

> I cannot endure the night, and sleep does not come, without the Sight of the Beloved Guru's Court.

On his return home, Guru Ram Das asked him to complete the poem:

> I am a sacrifice, my soul is a sacrifice, to that True Court of the Beloved Guru. By good
> fortune, I have met the Saint Guru. I have found the Immortal Lord within the home of
> my own self.

Again, these events are seen by many to be contributing factors to the appointment of
Guru Arjan, rather than Prithi Chand. Moreover, because of Prithi Chand's duplicitousness,
it is perhaps no surprise that he was openly hostile to the appointment of Guru Arjan and
was a constant source of opposition throughout his time as Guru and into the Guruship
of Guru Hargobind. His actions, which will be touched upon throughout this section, led
to his designation as *mina*, meaning 'charlatan' or 'dissembler'. This appellation was also
attached to his son and successors in the group that followed him.

Guru Arjan came to the Guru's throne at a time where things seemed to be going
well for Sikhs. The Panth had grown under the previous four gurus; they enjoyed the
tolerance and good graces of the Mughal emperor, and it appeared as though there was
opportunity for the community to flourish. There were many developments during the time
of Guru Arjan that led to the physical, spiritual and doctrinal foundation to be solidified.
The end of his time as Guru similarly marked a turning point in Sikh relationships with
the surrounding powers, and perhaps an understanding of the place of Sikhism in the
world. The 'accomplishments' or developments during the time of Guru Arjan included
the following.

## Harmandir Sahib

Harmandir Sahib refers to the modern-day Golden Temple, literally meaning home/abode
of God. Guru Arjan's father had begun the founding of the town of Ramdaspur and the
digging of the pool that was to sit at the heart of the city. One of Guru Arjan's first works
was to finish building the Harmandir that was to sit next to the great pool. There is a
suggestion that Guru Arjan invited the Muslim Mian Mir to lay the foundation stone of the
new temple. However, most modern Sikh writers suggest that this is not so but that Mian
Mir would have been in attendance.

The design of Harmandir Sahib reflected important aspects of Sikh teaching. In contrast
to Hindu mandirs which were built on plinths, Harmandir Sahib is built slightly below
ground level, so that worshippers would have to descend to enter it. This is symbolic of
the Sikh teaching that in order to find Waheguru, a person must 'descend' in humility and
service. This is a physical reminder that would help Sikhs understand the way to find the
naam within and overcome maya. The second design feature is that of four doors. There
are a couple of symbolisms for the doors: they are open to the four directions and show
the universality of the Sikh message and the opportunity to discover Waheguru. Also, the
four doors stand in contrast to Hindu mandirs that have only one entrance; these doors
symbolically show that the Guru is available to all of the four castes:

The four castes – the Kh'shaatriyas, Brahmins, Soodras and Vaishyas – are equal in respect to the teachings. (Guru Granth Sahib 747)

Once inside, there was only one causeway to the inner sanctum, suggesting that there is only one way to Waheguru for all. Once the foundation stone had been laid, the pool was filled with water and the city renamed Amritsar (the pool of nectar).

The importance of the construction of Harmandir Sahib cannot be overstated for Sikhs at the time of Guru Arjan, and also for Sikhs today. It provided a place of pilgrimage, but more than that, it provided a centre of Sikh identity, spirituality and community. In the novel *The English Patient*, the author Michael Ondaatje (1992, 271) describes Harmandir Sahib thus:

Singing is at the centre of worship. You hear the song, you smell the fruit from the temple gardens – pomegranates, oranges. The temple is a haven of the flux of life, accessible to all. It is the ship that crossed the ocean of ignorance.

There would be times in the future when the Guru did not make his home at Amritsar, but this was not to negate its importance.

Its importance today is similarly shown in descriptions of its impact on visitors and worshippers. Nikky-Guninder Kaur Singh (2011, 39) explains her experience therein beautifully:

Through its finite structures, the Harmandar creates an energetic movement toward the Infinite Transcendent … In this revelatory process, constricting barriers are broken down, and we are ushered into our innermost recesses.

Its importance is also evidenced in the Sikh reaction to Operation Bluestar in 1984. This was an operation by the Indian government that was seen to desecrate the Harmandir Sahib. As a background to Operation Bluestar, Jarnail Singh Bhindranwale, leader of Dharam Yudh Morcha, was living in the complex around Harmandir Sahib. With Bhindranwale was General Shabeg Singh, who was seen to be a great military strategist. With little reason or justification, in June 1984, then Indian prime minister Indira Gandhi ordered her army to enter the complex. Severe damage was caused to buildings in the complex, including the Akal Takht; the official figures show deaths of 492 civilians and 83 members of the Indian army. This caused the mutiny of up to 2,000 Sikh soldiers from the Indian army, and ultimately led to Indira Gandhi's assassination by her Sikh bodyguards. The rights and wrongs of Bhindranwale are secondary to the desecration of the Harmandir Sahib, made worse by it being enacted on the anniversary of the martyrdom of Guru Arjan.

## Dasvandh

The other long-lasting impact on Sikhism of the construction of Harmandir Sahib was the introduction of *dasvandh* by Guru Arjan. This was an extension of the charitable giving encouraged by Guru Amar Das, and continued by Guru Ram Das, which required the Sikh to donate 10 per cent of their earnings to the Guru and, by extension, to the Sikh community. It was dasvandh, collected by the masands, that enabled the construction of Harmandir Sahib, but also the continued assistance to people through the langar, and other sewa within the community.

## Expansion of the Sikh community and authority

With a centre of the community in place, and other cities throughout Punjab being part of the Sikh Panth, the opportunity was there for the expansion of the community. It was not for that purpose that Guru Arjan set out on a tour of the Majha and Doaba regions of Punjab for a period of five years, but it was a happy consequence.

The Sikh community was expanded with the building of the cities of Taran Taran, Kartarpur and Hargobindpur as well as completion of sacred pools at Santokhsar and Ramsar. This provided construction projects and work for people. As Guru Arjan travelled across Punjab, he was able to assist in the digging of wells and other projects that benefitted villages. His travels around Punjab also brought many more people into the sangat, and particularly noteworthy were the large number of Jats that became Sikh. Jats have contributed much to Sikhism throughout history, and even today, they form a large part of the Sikhs in Punjab and the heritage of Sikhs in the diaspora. Jats were a caste of peasant farmers from among whom some Sikhs had already been drawn, but the time of Guru Arjan marked a much larger influx. They have been described in many ways. Khushwant Singh (1999, 15) has described them as people possessing a 'spirit of freedom of equality', who refused to submit to religious or political authorities: 'the Jat was born the worker and the warrior'. This enabled the Sikh sangat to flourish during the time of Guru Arjan, but also in the future.

Guru Arjan's impact in growing the community should not be underestimated; his humility, travels and pragmatism in the development of construction works and encouraging trade enabled an appeal to people in the surrounding areas.

The second aspect of the expansion under Guru Arjan surrounded the understanding of the place of Sikhs and their Gurus within the world. As has already been noted, in the times of the earlier Gurus there had been suggestions about the sovereignty of the Gurus in terms of temporal and spiritual matters. Under Guru Arjan, a further appellation of Sacha Padshah began to be used of the Guru, meaning 'true emperor', language that found echo in Guru Granth Sahib:

> Guru Arjun sits on the throne; the royal canopy waves over the True Guru. From east to west, He illuminates the four directions. (968)

Others have noted the development of the Sikh 'commonwealth' during the time of Guru Arjan. He himself reinforced this idea of a theocracy, a 'state within a state' if you like, when he wrote a poem to welcome the birth of his son, the future Guru Hargobind. For

Guru Arjan this solidified a dynasty that would continue the Sikh Panth, in temporal and spiritual terms:

> The True Guru has truly given a child. The long-lived one has been born to this destiny. He came to acquire a home in the womb, And his mother's heart is so very glad. A son is born – a devotee of the Lord of the Universe. This pre-ordained destiny has been revealed to all. In the tenth month, by the Lord's Order, the baby has been born. Sorrow is dispelled, and great joy has ensued. The companions blissfully sing the songs of the Guru's Bani. (Guru Granth Sahib 396)

The phrase 'a devotee of the Lord of the Universe' has also been translated as 'the saint of the World-ruler Lord (Gobind)', suggesting a great destiny and continuation of the 'commonwealth' in the person of Hargobind. This confirmation of the importance of the Guru in all matters would be continued from the moment of Guru Hargobind's installation as Guru (see below).

## Adi Granth

On returning from his travels Guru Arjan discovered that his brother Prithi Chand had continued in his opposition to his Guruship. Prithi Chand has been raising concerns with the Mughal emperor (see below), but the most pressing issue, with perhaps the most long-term effects, involved the attempts of Prithi Chand to produce a book of hymns, including compositions of his own that he was penning under the name of 'Nanak' in the same way that the previous Gurus had, thus trying to make his collection seem to be authoritative for Sikhs. Whether this was the precipitating force, or merely an added impetus, with the help of Bhai Gurdas in 1603 Guru Arjan began the compilation of what would become the Adi Granth (the first volume).

In addition to combatting any 'pretended' writings of others, the compilation of the Adi Granth would ensure that the ever-expanding community would have access to the Guru's bani, and continue to feel a connection to the Guru however geographically distant they may be. The process was arduous and large in scale, and the compilation process had certain stages, though, of course, they overlapped and intermingled. The outline below is purely to help understand the various steps undertaken by Guru Arjan, with the assistance of Bhai Gurdas.

- A message was sent out to Sikhs requesting the hymns of the preceding four Gurus. Baba Mohan, Guru Amar Das's son, was in possession of the two pothis that his father had collected. Initially, Baba Mohan refused to relinquish possession of the pothis; it was only when Guru Arjan travelled to Goindwal and requested him himself that Baba Mohan agreed to give them to him. So important were these pothis as the bani of the Gurus that they were accorded the respect given to royalty as the collections were transported. They were carried in a palanquin on the shoulders of four Sikh attendants. Guru Arjan walked beside them, rather than ride his horse and place himself in a higher position than the Gurbani.

- As a workplace he chose a quiet spot on the outskirts of Amritsar. To keep this spot cool, he dug a pool which he named Ramsar after his father. Today, there is a gurdwara that marks the spot of compilation. It is also at this spot that Guru Arjan composed the prayer *Sukhmani* (psalm/jewel of peace), which can be found in Angs 262–96 of Guru Granth Sahib.

- The writings of the previous Gurus were placed alongside Guru Arjan's poetry. As part of this process Bhai Gurdas was asked to scrutinize each and indicate whether it was authentic Gurbani. The final decision was not with Bhai Gurdas, rather Guru Arjan was the one to approve the inclusion of each of the bani in the Adi Granth.

     The writings of the Gurus were not the only ones to be included; Guru Arjan used verses from Hindu and Sufi saints, whose writings were in line with the words of the Gurus. Against a background of religious division, particularly between Hindus and Muslims, the work of Guru Arjan in creating a synthesized body of work that reflected common spiritual ideas and the search for meaning was both unique and inspired. Like Guru Nanak before him, Guru Arjan did not adopt a syncretistic approach to religious belief; rather he harmonized the path of the True Guru and the search for the naam by utilizing those writings which spoke of such. Showing the truth of Guru Nanak's reported saying that 'there is no Hindu or Muslim' and that there is only the way of the True Guru, Guru Arjan was willing to chart the course of the Gurus recognizing liberation was available only through the Truth, not through partisan teachings of either Hindus or Muslims.

- Once all of the bani to be included had been collected together, Guru Arjan organized them into an order that reflected their musical pattern. The first section of the Adi Granth is liturgical and includes three daily prayers. The *Japji* (Meditation) by Guru Nanak consists of thirty-eight stanzas and two couplets. The *Rehras* (Supplication) contains nine hymns: four composed by Guru Nanak, three by the fourth Sikh guru, Guru Ramdas (born 1534, guru 1574–81), and two by the fifth Sikh guru, Guru Arjan. The *Sohila* (Praise) consists of five hymns: three by Guru Nanak, and one each by Guru Ramdas and Guru Arjan (Singh Mann, 2001, 5).

     There are exceptions, but generally the main section of the Adi Granth was organized into thirty-one sections, with each containing poems set to one rag. The final section contains a variety of hymns from a variety of the sources already mentioned, not set to any specific rag.

     The order of the sections was, first, the words of the Gurus arranged in the order of their succession. Guru Arjan wrote *mahalla* (body) at the beginning and appended the number of the Guru to avoid any confusion. The choice of the word 'mahalla' was deliberate, reinforcing that each of the Gurus were of the same body and the same light – a point that was first introduced in the installing of Guru Angad as the second

Guru (Nanak 2) (see above). This was followed by the writings of the Sufi and Hindu saints. The final section was a collection of various couplets and writings not set to any particular rag.

The choice of rag for each section of bani was deliberate to ensure they had particular resonance for seasons and emotional moods.

Ang 1429 is seen to be a seal placed on the Adi Granth by Guru Arjan and describes its importance to the Sikh community:

> Upon this Plate, three things have been placed: Truth, Contentment and Contemplation. The Ambrosial Nectar of the Naam, the Name of our Lord and Master, has been placed upon it as well; it is the Support of all. One who eats it and enjoys it shall be saved. This thing can never be forsaken; keep this always and forever in your mind. The dark world-ocean is crossed over, by grasping the Feet of the Lord; O Nanak, it is all the extension of God.

The Adi Granth, containing Gurbani, enables a Sikh to realize the truth of reality and cross 'the dark world ocean'. Maya can be overcome and union with Waheguru attained.

The different aspects of the bani and how it is used will be explored in the next chapter. This section lays the basis for a discussion of how its use evolved over the years until today.

- Once it was complete, the Sikh community celebrated with much festivity; indeed, the celebrations were likened to those of a wedding. Sikhs came from far and wide to see the new volume, and vast quantities of *karaprasad* were made and served.
- The Guru sent Bhai Banno to Lahore to have the volume bound. On his journey, Bhai Banno made a copy of the Adi Granth and returned to Ramsar with two copes, one for the Guru, and one for the sangat. Guru Arjan was surprised to see him return with two volumes, and subsequently placed his seal of approval only on the original written in the hand of Bhai Gurdas. There is a tradition that Bhai Banno added some bani that had been rejected; a copy of the rejected Granth is in possession of the descendants of Bhai Banno today.
- On 16 August 1604, the Adi Granth was carried on the head of Baba Buddha, with Guru Arjan walking behind holding a whisk over it. This was an event of great pomp as it was to be installed in the Harmandir Sahib. Baba Buddha was appointed the first *granthi*; he opened the Adi Granth and read:

> The Lord Himself has stood up to resolve the affairs of the Saints; He has come to complete their tasks. The land is beautiful, and the pool is beautiful; within it is contained the Ambrosial Water. The Ambrosial Water is filling it, and my job is perfectly complete; all my desires are fulfilled. Congratulations are pouring in from all over the world; all my sorrows are eliminated. The Vedas and the Puraanas sing the Praises of the Perfect, Unchanging, Imperishable Primal Lord. (Guru Granth Sahib 783)

This passage is most appropriate as it fuses the past and the present; the Adi Granth perhaps completes Guru Arjan's 'job', and at the same time takes the wisdom of the past and with the Guru's grace marks the way of the Guru.

As dusk settled at the end of the day, the Adi Granth was wrapped in silks and placed in a specially built chamber, where Guru Arjan slept by its side. In the morning, the Adi Granth was then taken back and placed in front of the sangat. These practices continue even today, and will be explored in the next chapter.

The compilation and publishing of the Adi Granth was perhaps the greatest achievement during the time of Guru Arjan. It met the needs of the growing community, both then and in the future. It provided a focus for the sangat and established an authentic collection of bani which Sikhs could use in their search for a more gurmukh life and unity with Waheguru.

## Martyrdom

As already alluded to, the opposition to Guru Arjan from his brother, Prithi Chand, continued unabated. Indeed, during the compilation of the Adi Granth, Prithi Chand sent word to Emperor Akbar that there were passages within the Adi Granth that were offensive and derogatory to Muslims. When Akbar visited the Guru, Baba Buddha and Bhai Gurdas brought out the manuscript as it then stood and read out passages to him. The emperor was impressed and felt the message of the Adi Granth reflected the beliefs he held and valued. As a result, he donated fifty-one gold mohurs for the Adi Granth and gave robes of honour to Baba Buddha, Bhai Gurdas and Guru Arjan.

It would seem that Emperor Akbar was focused on a respect for, and tolerance of, different communities and religious perspectives. Under his rule of the Mughal Empire, the Sikh Panth was able to flourish. However, upon his death, all was to change for Sikhs in Punjab.

Upon the death of Akbar, his son Jahangir became emperor, above the claims of Jahangir's own son Khusrau who was seen to be more temperate and favoured by his grandfather. Under Jahangir the claims of anti-Muslim writings in the Adi Granth were resurrected. Jahangir was also under the influence of a close advisor, Ahmad Shah, who was important in the promotion of Sunni Islam in the Mughal Empire. Annemarie Schimmel (2004, 132) suggests that 'Akbar's tolerance and his syncretism were completely at odds with Ahmad's narrow conception of true Islam'. It was against this background and jealousy of the increasing popularity of the Sikh Panth that Jahangir vowed 'to put a stop to this vain affair or to bring him [Guru Arjan] into the assembly of the people of Islam' (Rogers and Beveridge, 1909, 72).

An occasion/pretext presented itself when Khusrau travelled past Taran Taran and experienced Guru Arjan's hospitality. He was invited to the langar and provided a place to stay overnight. This was characterized by enemies of Guru Arjan as providing assistance and support to Khusrau. Following the suppression of the rebellion of Khusrau, the emperor was unrelenting in his punishment of those who he felt had aided his son. As such, Guru Arjan was charged with treason and levied with a heavy fine. When he refused to pay the fine, he was arrested, taken to Lahore and sentenced to death.

It is at this point that two traditions have arisen as to Guru Arjan's actions with regard to the succession of his son, Hargobind, to the Guruship. It is certain that he chose him as his successor, but it was either before he left for Lahore that he nominated him or he sent word from his prison in Lahore. Apart from the continued machinations of Prithi Chand, there is generally seen to be no opposition to this succession. The installation of Guru Hargobind following his father's death will be explored below.

Tradition suggests that Guru Arjan was tortured by Diwan Chandu Shah, an enemy of the Guru, since he had refused to agree to the marriage of his son, Hargobind, to Chandu Shah's daughter. Chandu Shah was deeply offended by this, though some reports suggest that Guru Arjan refused because of the way Chandu Shah had spoken about the Guru and his family's position. There are also suggestions that it was Chandu Shah's dissimilitude that led to Jahangir sanctioning the arrest and sentencing of Guru Arjan.

Jahangir had ordered Guru Arjan to convert to Islam or be tortured to death. As is evident from the life of Guru Arjan, and his continuation of the teachings of the preceding Gurus, he would not countenance giving up the way of the True Guru. Waheguru was neither Hindu nor Muslim; he had shown his belief in this concept through the main actions of his life, especially in the compilation of the Adi Granth. A bani that he had written emphasized this fact:

> I do not keep fasts, nor do I observe the month of Ramadaan. I serve only the One, who will protect me in the end. The One Lord, the Lord of the World, is my God Allah. He administers justice to both Hindus and Muslims. I do not make pilgrimages to Mecca, nor do I worship at Hindu sacred shrines. I serve the One Lord, and not any other. I do not perform Hindu worship services, nor do I offer the Muslim prayers. I have taken the One Formless Lord into my heart; I humbly worship Him there. I am not a Hindu, nor am I a Muslim. (Guru Granth Sahib 1136)

For Sikhs, this focus on the One is evident through the days of torture that Guru Arjan endured. Throughout each day he remained immersed in *naam simran*. Guru Arjan suffered the following tortures at the hand of Chandu Shah:

- He was deprived of food, water and sleep.
- He was placed in a large copper cauldron and water was added and a fire lit underneath. The Guru's body was burned, but he sat in a meditative state focusing on the naam. At the end of this stage of torture, the Guru's skin was blistered.
- He was boiled in water, while burning hot sand was poured on him from above. It was during this torture that one tradition holds that Mian Mir (a Sufi sant) offered to save him; the Guru refused saying that it was the will of Waheguru and that his

suffering would set an example to others (another tradition holds that Mian Mir arrived too late to help the Guru).

- He was seated on a red hot iron plate while hot sand was poured on him.
- On 30 May 1606, while Chandu Shah was thinking up new ways of torture to cause the most amount of pain, Guru Arjan asked to bathe in the Ravi river. Chandu agreed, assuming that the shock of the cold water on the Guru's blistered body would be a source of great pain. Guru Arjan, as he walked to the river, forbade his followers to intervene. As he entered the river in meditation on the naam he was swept away, died and his body was never recovered.

For Sikhs, this martyrdom is of great significance. He is known as the first martyr (shahid) or proto-martyr.

> It was this event, according to tradition, that changed forever the course of Sikh history, for it was the martyrdom of Guru Arjan which led to the transformation of the Sikh Panth. From mere farmers and shopkeepers to brave warriors, this new Panth had a mala or garland in one hand and a sword in the other. (Fenech, 2000, 80)

Fenech suggests that it may be that the martyrdom as an exemplar, or Sikh ideal, is not focused on in the immediate aftermath of Guru Arjan, and that it is a later interpolation in the succeeding years. It would appear to be evident, however, in the actions of Guru Arjan's son and successor, that the implications of this first martyrdom, if not fully articulated at the time, were certainly understood. There are many elements in the life of Guru Hargobind that would suggest a turning point for the development of Sikh relations with the empire, which had previously not been antagonistic, but now the sovereignty of the Sikh Panth as an independent 'power' began to be noticed and expressed. The question of it being a departure from the message of Guru Nanak and his successors would be rejected as each Guru is of the same light, and the martyrdom and its effects were in perfect consonance with the message of Guru Nanak. Sunita Puri (1993, 191) suggests that this event was 'the fulfilment of Guru Nanak's spirituo-ethical vision and injunctions'. Similarly, Jitenda Uberoi (1996, 91–2) suggests, 'The life, work and death of Guru Arjan perfectly represented all that Guru Nanak had founded and anticipated.' The suggestion of later interpolations does not seem to be settled, but the martyrdom and the responses to it do seem, in the Sikh mind, to be entirely congruent with what came before.

## Thoughts for the classroom

It would appear that the time of Guru Arjan marked a significant point in the history of Sikhism. It has been noted that the actions of Guru Arjan solidified the doctrinal and community basis of the Sikh Panth. It marked a change in the place of Sikhism and the Panth within the wider world. As such, the time of Guru Arjan has an important place in the study of Sikh identity and history in the classroom. There were no beliefs that were changed or introduced, but the codification of Gurbani in the Adi Granth provided the basis for a greater Sikh identity, as well as method for the ever-growing Panth to have links with the Gurus through their bani. The events of the compilation of the Adi Granth are rich to explore the creation of a volume of scripture, along with the way it has been revered since the time of Guru Arjan. It is important to note in the classroom that these are not modern innovations but have their roots in the time of Guru Arjan and its first installation in Harmandir Sahib in 1604. Although laying the basis for what would become Guru Granth Sahib, it is important to note that there were developments in what it contained before it attained the status of Guru (see the section on Guru Gobind Singh below and the next chapter).

Care should be taken when exploring the place and history of Harmandir Sahib. Throughout history, this sacred place has been subject to attack and damage. The image we see of the 'Golden Temple' is not the same edifice that would have been recognized by those at the time of Guru Arjan. For, perhaps, the first time Sikhs had a 'permanent' place that would generally remain the centre of Sikh belief and identity throughout the ensuing years. The way that it was viewed then, and now, is comparable, and the symbolism that it evokes in a person's relationship with Waheguru should be explored in great depth.

The influence of the increasing number of Jat Sikhs in the development of Sikhism, and also for Sikhism today, will be explored in greater depth. In the classroom, the efforts of Guru Arjan to spread the message of Sikhism is important and marked a significant change in the place of Sikhs. With increasing numbers this became a factor in the way that Jahangir viewed them; they appeared to no longer be benign, rather their numbers caused the empire to pause.

Similarly, martyrdom is an important element within Sikh identity. This will be explored in greater detail below when discussing the 'reclaiming' of Sikh identity during the time of the British Empire. Although some would argue that this is a creation of the nineteenth century, the martyrdom of Guru Arjan is not in doubt, and its immediate impact is evident in the life of his son, Guru Hargobind. It will be interesting for the teacher to explore how religions can develop in relation to their social and political situations, without in any way negating the fact that it is divinely inspired.

# Guru Hargobind/Nanak 6 (1595–1644)

Guru Hargobind was only eleven when his father was martyred and he was installed as Guru by Baba Buddha. The last words of his father, relayed to him, were to praise Waheguru but also to 'let him sit fully armed on his throne and maintain an army to the best of his ability' (Macauliffe, 1985, 99). These two instructions can be seen to lie at the heart of some of the most important developments during the time of Guru Hargobind. This effort to harmonize the temporal and the spiritual is shown during the events of his installation as Guru. Macauliffe records that on his installation, Guru Hargobind was dressed with two swords by Baba Buddha. When questioned about its appropriateness by Baba Buddha:

> The Guru replied, It is through thine intercession I obtained birth; and it is in fulfilment of thy blessing I wear two swords as emblems of spiritual and temporal authority. In the Gurus house religion and worldly enjoyment shall be combined the caldron to supply the poor and needy and the scimitar to smite oppressors. (Macauliffe, 1909b, 4)

The dressing of him with two swords was different to the previous Gurus, who had traditionally been robed with one sword – the *salli* symbolic of spiritual power. This use of one sword was congruent with the teaching of Sikhism and the previous Gurus, of *Degh* and *Tegh*. Degh has reference to the cauldron/kitchen mentioned by Guru Hargobind above, while Tegh has reference to the sword. Guru Hargobind's use of two swords reflected the belief that has come to be known as *miri-piri* – the two swords of spiritual and temporal authority. This teaching was a significant development of the ideas of Tegh and Degh; each member of the community would be protected from want through the Degh, but would also be protected from persecution and violence through the two complimentary swords of miri and piri.

## Miri-piri

The use of temporal and spiritual authority as a central focus within the time of Guru Hargobind is made intelligible by the circumstances at the time when he became Guru. He, and the Sikh Panth, faced threats and challenges from a variety of sources:

- Emperor Jahangir was worried that the Guru and the Sikhs, more widely, would seek revenge for the death of Guru Arjan.
- Ahmad Shah (one of Jahangir's closest Muslim advisors mentioned above) and Chandu Shah (who had tortured Guru Arjan) transferred their ill-feeling and opposition to Guru Hargobind, retaining their hatred of the Sikhs.
- Prithi Chand, the new Guru's uncle, retained his feelings that his position as the rightful Guru had been usurped. Indeed, even when Guru Hargobind was a baby, Prithi Chand had tried to poison him. At Guru Arjan's death, Prithi Chand had declared himself the new Sikh Guru, but Baba Buddha and Bhai Gurdas's support of Guru Hargobind as the legitimate successor was important in settling the dispute. In Mina sources, however, Prithi Chand is still known as Sahib Guru (eminent Guru) or Mahala Chhevan (the sixth master).
- There is also the suggestion that the masands (manjis) had become somewhat corrupt and could be opposed to the new Guru, not least because of his youth and the worry that their sources of income would be affected (see Macauliffe, 1909b).

These threats posed a challenge to the continued existence of the Sikh Panth. It was, therefore, necessary for Guru Hargobind to act in a way that was in harmony with the previous Gurus but safeguarded Sikhs:

> Arjan (Dev) transformed himself into Harigobind and sat majestically ... This Guru, the vanquisher of armies, is very brave and benevolent. (Bhai Gurdas, Var 1, Pauri 28)

It is important to recognize that that same light continued to pass from one Guru to the next. Guru Hargobind continued to speak out and act for the protection of, and justice for, all people, just as all the Gurus before him had done.

However, it is evident from passages in the Var of Bhai Gurdas that there was a shift in emphasis during the time of Guru Hargobind. Many Sikhs would see this as a natural development reflecting the martyrdom of Guru Arjan and the need to maintain the Sikhs' place in society. These passages highlight the 'complaints' made against Guru Hargobind:

> The earlier Gurus considered that to give instructions and to preach to the people, one has to sit at one place known as dharamshala, but this Guru (Hargobind) does riot stick to one place. Earlier emperors would visit the house of the Guru, but this Guru has been interned by the king in a fort. The sarigat coming to have his glimpse cannot find him in the palace (because generally he is not available). Neither he is scared of anybody nor does he scare any one yet he is always on the move. Earlier Gurus sitting on the seat instructed people to be content but this Guru rears dogs and goes out for hunting. The Gurus used to listen to Gurbani but this Guru neither recites nor (regularly) listens to hymn-singing. He does not keep his follower servants with him and rather maintains nearness with the wicked and the envious ones (Guru had kept Painde Khan nearby) (Bhai Gurdas Var 26).

The emphasis of Guru Hargobind needed to be on the safety of the Panth. Some critics might suggest that this was a result of the large number of Jats and their independent spirit that was affecting the direction of the Guru and the wider Panth. It is evident, however, that elements of the 'martial' spirit and the focus on temporal and spiritual authority had been seen in the work of the previous Gurus. Up until this point, however, it had generally been the case that temporal authority, and the protection of the Panth, had not had to be exercised. However, his continuity with previous Gurus and the appropriateness of his actions are seen with the response to the complaints made above:

> But the truth is never concealed and that is why on the lotus feet of the Guru, the mind of Sikhs hover like a greedy black-bee. Guru Hargobind has borne the unbearable and he has not made himself manifest. (Var 26)

The last line is sometimes translated as 'he has not complained of it'. This shows, at least, the understanding of Bhai Gurdas that Guru Hargobind faced circumstances unlike any of the previous Gurus: he 'has borne the unbearable'. Yet through all of this, the Sikh Panth can be seen to have thrived.

There is, sometimes, the distinction drawn between the 'temporal' authority exercised by the Guru and the 'political' authority that some assume he sought. It can be argued that the Guru sought only the protection of all of those within his care; he saw that he operated in a different sphere and realm than the emperor. However, this distinction may well have been lost on observers, and may have even been a later interpretation to suggest that Sikhs do not need their own political authority. At this stage, however, the goal of the Guru was to use the intertwined concept of miri-piri to ensure the protection of all. To illustrate this, there are a number of developments that integrate the saintliness/spirituality with the martial spirit of the Sikh, what has become known, in English, as saint-soldier.

Although the first few years of the time of Guru Hargobind as Guru were relatively peaceful in terms of Sikh relationships with the Mughal Empire (perhaps the Mughals could have believed that the death of Guru Arjan would have pacified or even demoralized the Sikhs to the point of dissipation), Guru Hargobind enacted measures that would ensure the continuation and protection of the Panth:

- He welcomed offerings of arms and horses. Mobad (2001, 61) records that later in his time as Guru:

  > He [the Guru] had seven hundred horses in his stable. Three hundred battle-tested horsemen and sixty musketeers were always in his service. Among them a set of persons occupied themselves in trade, service and work [on his behalf]. Whoever left his own place, took refuge with him.

- He raised a small army, and spent time training these soldiers, developing (re-emphasizing) martial exercises.

- He built Lohgarh (the castle of steel) as a fortress in Amritsar (there are other forts named Lohgarh that are different and associated with Guru Gobind Singh).

- In addition to the chanting of Gurbani, congregations of Sikhs would often be sung/ told the ballads of heroic figures.

All of these would develop the martial spirit of Sikhism, and at certain points it is reported that the Guru fought in defensive wars against the Mughals. It could be suggested, however, that the addition of miri overtook the importance of piri. As noted, tegh and degh were important aspects of the previous Gurus, and for all of the martial activities of Guru Hargobind, he remained the 'Guru'; he was a manifestation of the attributes of the almighty, who sought to help others realize the naam within. He continued to seek to grow the Sikh Panth; he sent people to places such as Bengal and Bihar to teach Gurmat and the Gurbani.

The Udasis were a group that was considered part of the Sikh Panth, who followed the teachings of Sri Chand (the son of Guru Nanak) and his successors. While the two groups had remained separate, there had been a rapprochement during the time of Guru Ram Das, and this continued under Guru Hargobind. He allowed, or possibly even encouraged, their preaching of the message of Guru Nanak and the Sikh Panth, and through their preaching, Sikhism was able to expand. Reports suggest that in 1629, Sri Chand requested of Guru Hargobind that one of his sons join him as he preached. Guru Hargobind's son Baba Gurditta was allowed to join the Udasis, and before he died, Sri Chand appointed him his successor.

## Akal Takht

Another of Guru Hargobind's achievements as Guru was the building of the Akal Takht (Throne of the Timeless/Eternal One) at Darbar Sahib, opposite the Harmandir Sahib. This was built as a seat of authority where Sikhs could come to have temporal and spiritual matters addressed. It was a symbol of the greater recognition of the sovereign status of the Sikh Panth; although it was part of the Mughal Empire, it was increasingly seen, especially by Sikhs, as a state within a state. Ranveer Singh (2021, 84) has explained the symbolism of the proximity of the Akal Takht to Harmandir Sahib:

> The Akäl Takht stands in close proximity to Harmandir Sähib to represent the Sikh centrality of Akal within Kal; Divine existence within the temporal structures of worldly governance. There is no hierarchy between the two, but instead, a fluid dynamism woven into the tapestry of the entire Sri Darbar Sähib, reflecting how the Divine is at the nucleus of temporal Sikh thought and action. The greatness of the two structures in Sikhi is that they complement each other. It is not a mere unity of two separate institutions but a representation of Sikh agency, and it epitomises the concept of oneness that is a core aspect of the Sikh world view.

The building itself, when built, was known as Akal Bunga (abode/home of the Timeless/Eternal One); the Takht is the seat of authority within. However, it is more common today to refer to Akal Bunga and Akal Takht as synonymous and use the term 'Akal Takht' to refer to both. The Akal Takht was built slightly lower than the Harmandir Sahib, suggesting the order of importance between the spiritual and the temporal.

The foundation stone of the Akal Takht was laid by Guru Hargobind and then completed by Baba Buddha and Bhai Gurdas. It was originally a platform twelve feet in height, on which Guru Hargobind would sit and administer issues of justice for Sikhs. The height of the Takht was significant, in that the emperor had issued an edict saying that no one but the emperor could sit on a raised platform of more than three feet. Again, this highlighted the independent nature of the Sikh Panth and the authority of the Guru.

The Akal Takht was a central feature of Guru Hargobind's life at Amritsar. He would usually begin the day by worshipping at Harmandir Sahib, hunt later in the morning and spend the afternoon in the Akal Takht fulfilling his responsibilities there. This would be followed by further worship at Harmandir Sahib, ending the day at Akal Takht with stories of heroic individuals.

On 13 December 1612, when Guru Hargobind was taken prisoner at Gwalior, he installed Bhai Gurdas at the first *jathedar* of Akal Takht. The jathedar is the official who has the authority from the Guru to issue justice from the Akal Takht.

One further note is that, during the time of Guru Hargobind, the Akal Takht was most likely to have been restricted to the platform and its decoration. Today's Akal Takht is a building that houses a platform and to which Guru Granth Sahib is taken in the evening and awoken in the morning.

## Selflessness

There are many elements of Guru Hargobind's life, work and teaching that go beyond the focus on the physical strengthening of the Sikh Panth. He was, in every sense of the word for Sikhs, the successor to the previous Gurus and their message. At one point, Guru Hargobind was held prisoner by the Mughal emperor Jahangir Khan. There are various stories that suggest how he came to be interred at Gwalior Fort. There are two events that are recorded as a part of his imprisonment that show his humility, selflessness and qualities as gurmukh. Although his relationship with Jahangir had deteriorated, as indicated by his imprisonment, when Jahangir fell ill, and his advisors told him that he could only be cured by the prayers of a holy man, it was Guru Hargobind to whom he turned. Guru Hargobind held no ill will and prayed for a year at Gwalior. The example of the Guru emphasized his 'saintliness'.

As a result of this Jahangir offered to free Guru Hargobind. Also being held prisoner were fifty-two Hindu princes, around 1612 or 1619 (dates vary according to different records). He responded that he would leave only if he was allowed to take the princes with him. Jahangir compromised out of respect for the Guru and said that he would be allowed free with as many princes as could hold his coat as he left.

The Guru had a coat made with fifty-two tails, and thus when he was released he had the fifty-two Hindu princes holding on to his coat-tails, and thus all were freed. This is celebrated as Bandi Chhor Divas (The Day of Liberation). It is said that when he was freed, he was welcomed home to Amritsar with deva lamps; and the festival of lights became a celebration of liberation and freedom.

Central to all of the efforts of the Gurus in Sikhism is the teaching that all are equal in the sight of Waheguru. As such, in the words of Guru Nanak, 'There is no Hindu or Muslim.' All are interconnected through the Divine:

> No one is my enemy, and no one is a stranger. I get along with everyone. (Guru Granth
> Sahib 1229)

The lives of the Gurus provide great examples of people who lived to build up all sections of society and humanity. Foremost in Sikh teaching is the equality of all; the Gurus, and in this case especially Guru Hargobind, showed their willingness to offer support and care without fear or favour. In one conversation with Jahangir Guru Hargobind taught this truth by quoting Kabir:

God first created light, All men are born out of it. The whole world came out of a single spark; Who is good and who is bad? The Creator is in the creation, and the creation in the Creator, He is everywhere. The clay is the same, the potter fashions various models. There is nothing wrong with the clay or the potter. God the true resides in all. (Pruthi, 2004, 76–7)

Those attitudes that would trample on the rights of one religion can be used to restrict the rights of all. As such the Gurus taught about, and fought for, the rights of all people. They recognized that humanity could not be uplifted if one portion of it is subject to ill-treatment. This event is deeply reminiscent of the story associated with Guru Nanak and the freeing of the prisoners held by Emperor Babur. The stories of Guru Nanak and Guru Hargobind are contiguous in standing up against oppression, irrespective of whoever it is directed against and whoever does it.

## The last years of Guru Hargobind

When Emperor Jahangir died in 1627, his son Shah Jahan succeeded him. The detente that existed between the Sikh Panth and the empire seemed to deteriorate after this. In 1628 when Shah Jahan was hunting in the area around Amritsar, his retinue clashed with some of the retainers of Guru Hargobind. Shah Jahan sent people to arrest Guru Hargobind; unable to find him, the emperor's men began to steal from the Guru's property, at which point the Guru's guards fell on the robbers, and some were killed. This was the first of many clashes with the forces of the empire. He moved his headquarters to Kiratpur in 1634 to avoid the harrying of the empire's troops. This was to be his home until his death in March 1644.

His choice of successor was made more difficult because of the deaths of three of his sons, and one his grandsons, Dhir Mal, turned against him. Of his remaining two sons, Suraj Mal seemed to be disinterested in the affairs of the Panth, and Tegh Bahadur had become meditative and reflected the meaning of his name 'master of renunciation'. Before his death, Guru Hargobind named his grandson Har Rai, through Gurditta, as the seventh Guru in human form.

## Thoughts for the classroom

There are many aspects of the life of Guru Hargobind that could form the basis of exploration in the classroom. The most obvious, and perhaps the most often used, is the perceived militarization of the Panth, signified by the adoption of the two swords of miri-piri. This is an interesting development, and its exploration in light of the teachings and examples of the previous Gurus would be very interesting. Sometimes, Guru Hargobind may be seen to be diverting from the path of Guru Nanak, but that misses the point within Sikhism that the Gurus are 'one' and of the same light. How the life and work of Guru Hargobind continue the work of previous Gurus is a far more interesting question.

Building on this, it is of note that Guru Hargobind, despite teaching and living the equanimity of miri and piri, has come to be known as a proponent of only one of these. This imbalanced view is useful to explore the one-dimensional view of people from history that is often portrayed. Care should be taken not to overemphasize aspects to provide a caricatured view of a person's life.

Noting the focus on the Adi Granth, the focus on Gurbani is incredibly important in the classroom. It is during the time of Guru Hargobind that the term 'dharmsala', which referred to the places of worship of Sikhs, was gradually replaced in the nomenclature by the term 'gurdwara', a word that is normally translated as 'door/abode of the Guru'. This is the term that is in use today. It would be interesting for pupils to explore if there is any change of focus reflected in this change. It coincided with the installation of the knowledge of the Gurus through the compilation of the Adi Granth, and if a place held the words of the Gurus, then the change in nomenclature reflects this changing emphasis and function of the place of worship. An interesting point is that the term 'guruduara', transliterated as 'gurdwara' from Gurmukhi, is potentially better translated as 'Guru's grace' (see Fenech and McLeod, 2014, 133). This may suggest a higher purpose for the gurdwara, as a source for the Guru's grace – not only through the place where the Gurbani is read, and the Guru is found, but where, in sangat, people can experience the grace of the Guru.

The events of the compilation of the Adi Granth provide a linear explanation that pupils could begin to understand, certainly in terms of the herculean task that this was. There are many aspects of Guru Hargobind's life that find resonance in the life and practice of a Sikh today. To explore Sikhism without reference to the Harmandir Sahib, the Akal Takht and the Adi Granth would miss much of its richness; and reference to these without a recognition of Guru Hargobind would be incomplete. A further teaching opportunity is Bandi Chhor Divas celebrated at the same time as the Hindu festival of Diwali. The events, and celebration, of this festival are an important aspect of recognizing the equality of all and the need to oppose injustice against all people.

## Guru Har Rai/Nanak 7 (1630–61)

Puran Singh (1926, 56) suggests, 'After the passing of Har Gobind a calm ensued, for the Sikhs were, by nature, peace-loving and fond of celestial contemplation.' This may be an overstatement, but there seems to have been some kind of rapprochement with Emperor Shah Jahan. This could have been Guru Har Rai's initial decision to locate at Kiratpur, and then, within a year, to remove his court to a small village in Sirmoor state. This removal of the centre of the Sikh Guru out of the immediate area of the emperor will perhaps have made them seem less of a threat. It might also be because the emperor realized that making an enemy of the Sikhs was not the wisest move, and he may have had other pressing issues. Guru Har Rai continued to keep upto 2,200 armed retainers, and so it is incorrect to suggest that after a period of martial development, Sikhs reverted to a 'more spiritual' bent. Guru Har Rai continued to wear the swords of authority of both miri and piri.

Stories associated with Guru Har Rai show his continuation of the work of the previous Gurus. At one point, Dara Shikoh the son of Emperor Shah Jahan, was dying from the effects of poison, and the only things that could cure him were medicinal herbs which were provided by Guru Har Rai from the hospital centre he had developed. It may seem surprising for a person to help someone who had tormented his grandfather so. However, the actions of the Guru should be unsurprising as one who makes no distinction and offers the Guru's grace to all.

## Consolidating the Panth

The distance between Guru Har Rai and the main centres of Sikhs had consequences for the development of Sikhism. For the most part, the Panth was held together by the masand system that was still in operation, and had many who were still loyal to the Guru. Problems arose with Prithi Chand and his followers establishing themselves in Amritsar. To combat the influence of Minas, Guru Har Rai reformed existing centres and established more centres and manjis throughout Punjab to serve as a link with the various communities.

Guru Har Rai did undertake journeys to visit the previous centres of the Panth, such as Amritsar and Kiratpur. He would seek to develop relationships with Sikhs and spread the message of Sikhism and consolidated aspects of the Panth.

## Gurbani

One of the teachings that Guru Har Rai is remembered for is his focus on the Adi Granth and the Gurbani. One example tells the story of him being asked if it was worthwhile to recite the bani, even if one did not believe. He replied in the affirmative:

> Just as grease sticks to the pot even when it is emptied, so does the Guru's Word stick to the heart. Whether you understand it or not, the Word bears the Seed of Salvation. Perfume persists in the broken pieces even after the vase that contained it has been shattered. (K. Singh, 1999, 66)

This story is told in a different way on SikhNet (n.d.):

> Someday the sunlight of knowledge will come to our minds and then, just like this ghee, it will melt ... and the Gurbani in our hearts will turn to wisdom.

The impact and importance of the Gurbani is shown in this and in a further story associated with the Guru. Guru Har Rai's eldest son, Ram Rai, had been sent to the emperor's court in his place. Ram Rai was found at the emperor's court as a result of another power struggle on the death of the emperor. When Emperor Shah Jahan died, both Aurangzeb and his brother Dara Shikoh vied for the throne. Aurangzeb tended towards a hardline

Muslim view that precluded religious tolerance, whereas it would appear that Dara was more open-minded. It is suggested that the Guru would have tended towards the claim of Dara, but whatever the views of the Guru, it is true that when Dara fled north, he called on Guru Har Rai for assistance. It is not known what assistance was given, but it was sufficient that Aurangzeb would see the Guru as overstepping the mark and becoming an enemy. Once hostilities with his brother had ended, Aurangzeb summoned Guru Har Rai to court to answer the charges. Perhaps emphasizing that he was not subject to the emperor, and certainly not at the whim of his summons, Guru Har Rai sent his son.

Ram Rai had been reminded to be true to the Guru's words. It would appear that reports of Ram Rai's acquiescence to the emperor and the seeking of his favour reached his father. One such event surrounds Ram Rai's reading of a bani of Guru Nanak:

> The clay of the Muslim's grave becomes clay for the potter's wheel. Pots and bricks are fashioned from it, and it cries out as it burns. (Guru Granth Sahib 33)

Perhaps mindful of his audience, Ram Rai edited the Gurbani to 'The clay of the faithless' grave'; with a Muslim emperor who was unsympathetic, or even opposed, to other religious groups, this may have been understandable, but it went directly against Guru Har Rai's instructions and suggested that Ram Rai was not an appropriate choice to replace him as Guru when the time came. Guru Har Rai is reported to have reacted to the above incident by proclaiming:

> The Guruship is like tiger's milk which can only be contained in a golden cup. Only he who is ready to devote his life thereto is worthy of it. Let not Ram Rai look on my face again. (Cole, 2010, 140–1)

Although Ram Rai apologized and tried to make amends, as he was dying Guru Har Rai nominated his other son, Har Krishan, as his successor. The choice of Har Krishan angered Ram Rai and also Emperor Aurangzeb, who felt he could control the Sikh Panth through a patronage of Ram Rai. A rival group did arise, in no small part due to the lands gifted to Ram Rai by the emperor. However, it is to Guru Har Krishan to whom the Guruship was passed, at the tender age five.

## Thoughts for the classroom

Guru Har Rai was Guru for a period of seventeen years. During this time, there were divisions and consolidations of the Panth. In comparison to the developments of the previous two Gurus it was a relatively quiet time. It was, however, a time for the Panth to regroup and breathe. The further development of the concept of miri-piri is important when considering the contiguous nature of the Gurus and the Panth more widely.

In the classroom, it is possible to use Guru Har Rai's focus on the teachings of the Gurus to help pupils understand the significance of the bani to Sikhs today. Owen Cole (2010) uses the experience of Ram Rai at the court of Aurangzeb as an example to illustrate the importance of the Gurbani and the imperative not to change or ameliorate their message for greater acceptance. The teachings of the Gurus are of central importance and should not be apologized for. The imagery evident in 'tiger's milk' as something difficult to attain, and then to treasure, would be a useful metaphor to explore in understanding Sikh attitudes to Gurbani.

# Guru Har Krishan/Nanak 8 (1656–64)

Being installed as Guru at the age of five, it is no understatement to say that the Guruship of Guru Har Krishan was beset by opposition from rival claimants (including Ram Rai) and also from the emperor. It would appear that Aurangzeb summoned Guru Har Krishan to ostensibly mediate between the Guru and his brother. The Guru did not go for a period of four years; later, on arriving at Delhi he was struck down with smallpox and was thus unable to meet with the emperor. Guru Har Krishan would die in 1664 from smallpox. On his deathbed he eschewed the claims of his brother and others and instead uttered the word 'Baba Bakale', indicating that the next Guru would be an elder to be found in the village of Bakale. It was thus that the Guruship passed to his great-uncle, and surviving son of Guru Hargobind, Guru Tegh Bahadur.

## Thoughts for the classroom

When learning about the Gurus in the classroom, it is perhaps the result of a Western mindset to question why a Guru would be chosen at such a young age, especially as Guru Har Krishan was only to live for a short time. The youth of Guru Hargobind or of Guru Gobind Singh is rarely questioned, and so it would appear that it is the relatively short period of Guru Har Krishan that leads to most questions. He is remembered for his purity, humility, service and knowledge. There are many stories of him conversing with Hindu holy men about spiritual topics; he also contracted smallpox while ministering to the many who came to him in Delhi for refuge and blessings. For Sikhs, he is truly an example of selfless service. Trilochan Singh (1981, 93), his modern biographer, comments:

> With cautious and enlightened foresight, Guru Har Krishan ignored the self-propagated popularity of Aurangzeb and Ram Rai and won the hearts of Hindus, Muslims and Sikhs alike by his matchless humanity and spirituality.

The influence of the young Guru continues today as Sikhs try and emulate his spirituality and selflessness.

# Guru Tegh Bahadur/Nanak 9 (1621–75)

Guru Tegh Bahadur was born Tyag Mal (master of renunciation), the youngest son of Guru Hargobind and Mata Nanaki, in 1621. His early life was spent in Amritsar where he learned languages, Gurbani and the martial arts of swordsmanship, horsemanship and archery. At the age of thirteen he accompanied his father into the battle of Kartarpur. Tyag Mal excelled in battle and was renamed, in honour of his prowess, Tegh Bahadur (brave/ best sword wielder).

Following these events, the future Guru Tegh Bahadur began to immerse himself in meditation and study, living up to his birth name as the 'master of renunciation'. When his father, Guru Hargobind, named Guru Har Rai as the next Guru, he asked Tegh Bahadur to move to the town of Bakala with his wife and mother. It is reported that, at this time, Guru Hargobind told Mata Nanki that Tegh Bahadur would one day be Guru and have a son that would become famous in fighting for justice. While at Bakala, the future Guru, Tegh Bahadur, devoted himself to meditation, some suggesting that he spent most of his time in a dark cellar in meditation of the naam.

When Guru Har Krishan died and indicated his successor would be found in Bakala, it was not as simple as people automatically assuming the Guru would be Tegh Bahadur. However, there is a tradition narrated by Ranveer Singh (2021) that the words of Guru Har Krishan were actually far clearer than that the next Guru would be found in Bakala. Rather, he suggests, drawing on *Guru Kian Saakhian: Tales of the Sikh Gurus*, that Guru Har Krishan named the next Guru:

> 'After me, the Guru for the Sikh Congregations will be my Baba, who is at the town of Bakala, (You) have his Darshan. Diwan Jee, you better take this material to the village Bakala and present it before Sri Guru Tegh Bahadur Jee. From now on the Satguru of the Sikhs is Baba Jee at the town of Bakala. People should go and have his Darshan.' And after saying so, Guru Jee was immersed in the name of the Omnipotent. (Bindra, 2005, 69–70)

Ranveer Singh suggests in his translation that the identifier was 'my Baba', referring to his great-uncle by relationship rather than name. Although this tradition is of interest, and would be a sensible narrative, there are alternative traditions that suggest the original words may have been ambiguous and only became clearer later.

The story is told of twenty-two members of the Sodhi family (the family of Guru Arjan) travelling to Bakala and claiming to be Guru. A wealthy Sikh merchant named Makhan Shah was sailing in a violent storm and prayed that if he were saved and made it to port, he would give 500 gold coins to Guru Har Krishan. Having made it safely to port, Makhan Shah began travelling to the Guru; on hearing of the Guru's death and also his words about Bakala, Makhan Shah changed direction and travelled to Bakala. To each of the claimants to the Guru's throne, he gave two gold coins, and each was pleased with the gift from the merchant. Prior to leaving the village, he was approached by a child who told him of a meditative figure who was in an underground room. Makhan Shah visited Guru Tegh Bahadur and gave him two gold coins. The Guru replied to the effect; 'You have broken your promise. When you were on the ship you promised to give 500 gold coins to the Guru if you were saved.' Makhan Shah was filled with joy and noised abroad that the True Guru had been found, and that Sikhs should come and receive blessings from him.

## Opposition

The story of Makhan Shah did not eliminate all sources of opposition or division in the Panth. One of his main opponents was Dhir Mal, the grandson of Guru Hargobind, who had been a thorn in the side of Guru Har Rai during his Guruship. He claimed the Guruship on the death of Guru Har Krishan, and his claim was strengthened in the eyes of some because he held possession of the original Adi Granth. Following the installation of Guru Tegh Bahadur as Guru, there was an attempt on his life arranged by Dhir Mal.

The humility of Guru Tegh Bahadur infuriated both Ram Rai and Dhir Mal; this humility in pressing his case as Guru won many of the Sikhs to support him as Guru. Although he was Guru with the sovereign aspects that came along with the darbar of the Guru, including a retinue of armed guards, he lived a simple, austere life. Recognizing the importance of the Sikh cities, especially Amritsar, shortly after his installation Guru Tegh Bahadur made his way to Amritsar.

On his arrival at Amritsar, the members of the Sodhi family and the masands who had occupied Harmandir Sahib refused Guru Tegh Bahadur entrance and shut the doors on him. Many of those within the Darbar Sahib had accepted the claims of Prithi Chand to be Guru, in the absence of Guru Har Rai and Gur Har Krishan. This was on the instructions of Hajri, the son and successor of Prithi Chand. Guru Tegh Bahadur waited at what is now called Thara Sahib (pillar of patience). He retired to the nearby village of Wala, where the women of Amritsar came out to beg forgiveness for the actions of the masands of Amritsar. These events laid the basis for the recognition that the masand system was subject to corruption, and the actions of the masands may have led to the ultimate disbanding of the system under Guru Gobind Singh.

## Journeys

Unable to gain access to Amritsar, Guru Tegh Bahadur built a town on a nearby hillock and named it Anandpur (haven of bliss). He was hoping to find peace in this 'haven'; however, he was harried by opponents, many of whom were family members. To find peace, and to spread the message of Waheguru, Guru Tegh Bahadur decided to travel and leave Punjab for a while. On these journeys he visited Sikh centres in Sondip, Chittagong, Sylhet and Assam. While in Dacca he received word that his son, Gobind Rai, had been born on 26 December 1666. After three years of travel, during which he was acclaimed as Guru by the Sikhs everywhere he went, Guru Tegh Bahadur returned to Patna to join his family. His visits to Sikh centres and communities strengthened people in their sense of belonging, and also in their understanding of the message of the Gurus. These were important in the expansion and consolidation of the sangat.

During these years, Emperor Aurangzeb had embarked on a series of measures that were in opposition to those who were non-Muslim. It was a nervous and tense time for the Hindus and Sikhs of Punjab; there were reports of destruction of temples, forced conversions and the charging of taxes for Hindus to visit places of pilgrimage. It is reported that those who had pressed their claims to be Guru had remained remarkably quiet, and so in 1671 Guru Tegh Bahadur embarked on journeys around Punjab to strengthen and help those who were feeling targeted. He travelled from village to village preaching the importance of *dharam* and of standing firm. This was a direct challenge to the oppression and suppression of non-Muslim religion from the Mughal Empire. A warrant for the Guru's arrest was issued, but he was able to evade arrest and returned home to Anandpur.

## Martyrdom

The religious persecution of non-Muslims did not stop. In 1675, a delegation of Brahmins led by Kara Ram came to visit the Guru. They complained to him of the treatment of Hindus and the forced conversions that were being undertaken and attempted. The brahmins knew of the history of the Gurus in standing up for justice and the rights of all. As such, they were asking Guru Tegh Bahadur to intervene on their behalf.

The Guru knew that to do so would be to risk his own death. He would be challenging the very authority of the emperor. His response to the brahmins was for them to return home and to tell their persecutors that they would have no objection to conversion to Islam, on the condition that Guru Tegh Bahadur converted or was pressed to convert first. This was a challenge to the edicts of the emperor and a symbol that argued for the rights of non-Muslims to live as they chose. This was not a choice that he made lightly; he knew that he might be courting death in a similar way to his grandfather, Guru Arjan. His ten-year-old son, Gobind Rai, supported the decision and recognized the martyrdom that might result.

Prior to his leaving Anandpur, on 8 July 1675, Guru Tegh Bahadur nominated and installed his son as the next Guru. On 11 July, Guru Tegh Bahadur and some attendants left Anandpur to plead the case of non-Muslims in front of the emperor, knowing full well that this might be his last act.

He was arrested with his companions near Ropar and then, three months later, transferred in an iron cage to Delhi to the court of the emperor. He was held in prison in Delhi for eight days under the supervision of Qazi Abdul Wahab Vora. He was asked to either perform a miracle or convert to Islam. His nephew, Ram Rai, had performed miracles at the court of Aurangzeb, which was one of the reasons Gur Har Rai had lost confidence in him. It was unbecoming of a descendant of the Gurus, and to perform a miracle would have been an act of ego, something that Guru Tegh Bahadur could not countenance. Without a miracle or willingness to convert, his two companions, Mati Das and Sati Das, were sawn in half in front of him.

None of this could convince him to convert. He was willing to sacrifice much, not least his ego, for others. On 11 November 1675 Guru Tegh Bahadur was beheaded at Chandni Chowk. In the eyes of Sikhs, this saintly Guru was martyred for the rights of others. This fact was elucidated by his son, Guru Gobind Singh, in the Dasam Granth:

> He protected the forehead mark and sacred thread (of the Hindus) which marked a great event in the Iron age. For the sake of saints, he laid down his head without even a sign. For the sake of Dharma, he sacrificed himself. He laid down his head but not his creed. The saints of the Lord abhor the performance of miracles and malpractices. Breaking the potsherd of his body head of the king of Delhi (Aurangzeb), He left for the abode of the Lord. None could perform such a feat as that of Tegh Bahadur. (Dasam Granth 117)

This understanding of the martyrdom of Guru Tegh Bahadur is written in the way that Sikhs understand it. He was a willing martyr to protect the rights of not just the Panth but also Hindus. He was willing to die to protect the rights of all people. The eulogy of Guru Gobind Singh, above, makes this clear. The events of the death of Guru Tegh Bahadur and Persian Muslim sources place a different slant on events, while it might be important for us to note that here what is significant is how this event is interpreted by Sikhs today.

## Thoughts for the classroom

The life of Guru Tegh Bahadur is a fusion of the principles of miri-piri in a way that is perhaps more obvious than in lives of others. For most of his life, he lived in quiet contemplation. Where relatives opposed the succession of Guru Har Rai and Guru Har Krishan, Guru Tegh Bahadur followed his father's instructions and quietly led a life of meditation and family life. He did not leave the temporal world, he was fully involved in life but meditated on the naam. In his early life, he fought to protect the Panth. In his later life, he was able to fight for the rights of the Panth through non-violent resistance. His preaching and travels throughout Punjab were in direct opposition to the emperor and reiterated the sovereignty of the Sikh Panth. The life that he led is full of stories and experiences that reiterated the principles that had been taught and lived by previous Gurus. The stories associated with Guru Tegh Bahadur are full of potential for an exploration of the teachings of Sikhism.

The patience that he showed with those who opposed him is inspiring. As such, using the examples from Guru Tegh Bahadur's life can provide a springboard for an exploration of principles that should find expression in the lives of Sikhs today.

Within modern Sikhism, Louis Fenech (2000) has suggested that there is a focus on martyrology. He is not convinced that the deaths had the same meaning at the time as they do now. Wherever the truth of this lies, the martyrs (shahids) are important in establishing aspects of Sikh identity. The inclusion of the examples of Guru Arjan and Guru Tegh Bahadur is important in establishing the lack of ego and attachment to the world that is evidenced in the life of someone who is gurmukh. The importance is that the events of the martyrdom show people, without thought for the self. These examples are important for the classroom and also for an understanding of concepts within Sikhism such as equality, sewa and the living of the Five Virtues (all to be explored in subsequent chapters).

# Guru Gobind Singh/Nanak 10 (1666–1708)

Guru Gobind Singh was born Gobind Das (later Gobind Rai) to Guru Tegh Bahadur and Mata Gujri, in Patna, on 22 December 1666. As noted earlier, his father was away when he was born and, indeed, was martyred when Guru Gobind Rai was only nine years old. As with all of the Gurus in human form, he was of the same light and continued the work that they had begun. Bhai Nand Lai suggests his importance as the tenth and final Guru in human form in relation to the others:

> He was the one to exhibit the panorama of the nine-lighted torches displaying the 'truth'
> and annihilating the night of darkness of lies and untruths. (*Ganjnama*, 104)

His teachings and developments made brighter the truths and work of the previous nine Gurus in human form.

One tradition, following the martyrdom of his father, holds that Bhai Jata rescued Guru Tegh Bahadur's head and brought it to Guru Gobind Rai, who was able to honour his father with a cremation (the rest of his body had been rescued and cremated by Lakhi Shah). This event may take on added meaning when we explore the events of Baisakhi in 1699 and the founding of the Khalsa.

There are generally seen to be six major phases in the life of Guru Gobind Singh (see Kaur Singh, 2005). This will provide a structure against which we will explore his life and his contributions to the development of the Panth and Sikh identity. The six phases are:

- Patna (1663–73): he was born and spent his early childhood in Patna.

- Anandpur (1673–82): here he continued with his learning in many areas of life. It was in Anandpur that he learned of the martyrdom of his father and was installed as Guru. He was also married to his first wife, Mata Jito, just north of Anandpur.

- Paonta (1682–8): a phase of the Guru's life where literary interests were foremost in his court; he also continued martial exercises. His eldest son, Ajit Singh, was born here in 1687. The mother of Ajit Singh was the Guru's wife Mata Sundari. Most Sikhs would suggest that Mata Sundari was the same person as Mata Jito, only she had changed her name. There is an alternative view that some would describe as beyond the pale – that Mata Sundari was the second wife of Guru Gobind Singh (e.g. see Singh and Singh (2006), who speak in a very matter-of-fact manner about the birth of children to both Mata Jito and Mata Sundari). The Guru also engaged in the Battle of Bhangani in 1687.

- Anandpur (1689–1705): this may be seen to be the most eventful phase of Guru Gobind Singh's life. He built forts at Lohgarh, Anandgarh, Keshgarh and Fategarh, and this period was characterized by many sieges and battles. His three sons from Mata Jito were born in Anandpur: Jujhar Singh (1691), Zorowar Singh (1696) and Fateh Singh (1699). It is during this period that his sons were killed. It is also during this time that the Khalsa was formed in 1699. He was married to Mata Sahib Kaur in 1700.

- Damdama (1706): he established court at Damdama which became known for its literary focus. Mata Sahib Kaur and Mata Jito joined him at Damdama, and this would be important for the development and security of the Khalsa following the death of the Guru.

- Nander (1707–8): he started a friendship or alliance with the new emperor, Bahadur Shah. Here, he was murdered on 7 October 1708. It is generally believed that the day before his death, he installed Guru Granth Sahib as the Eternal Guru for Sikhs.

This overview provides a sketch of the events of the life of Guru Gobind Singh. We will now explore the main developments of Sikhism within the time of Guru Gobind Singh, some of which will necessitate a greater exposition of the events described above.

## Literary culture

Although it is possible to say that Guru Gobind Singh is remembered more for the establishment of the Khalsa and martial involvement and development, these are only part of his multifaceted life. One of the major aspects of life in the court of Guru Gobind Singh was his focus on the literary arts. Particularly prolific periods of literary developments were during his residency in Paonta and the second Anandpur period. It is reported that there were fifty-two court poets and that Guru Gobind Singh invited many to come to his court. Some of these were responsible for the translation of classic Puranic tales such as those featuring Chandi, Rama and Krishna. In elements of Guru Gobind Singh's own writing there are retelling of tales that include references to deities found in Hinduism, such as Chandi and Rama. This will be explored in further detail in Chapter 5, where we discuss the Dasam Granth, but to provide a background, Gurinder Singh Mann and Kamalroop Singh (2011) would suggest that such passages should be read within the context of the Guru's constant affirmation of Ikonkaar (the One). In a similar vein to Guru Nanak using a variety of names from Hindu and Muslim backgrounds to describe Waheguru, so too does Guru Gobind Singh. This does not mean, for Sikhs, that Guru Gobind Singh worshipped Shakti (the divine feminine) or other deities; rather the stories helped show aspects of the way that Sikhism should be lived, and were always placed in a Sikh context and the purpose of life for those following the Sikh Panth.

The Guru's poetry and writings are seen to reflect his multifacetedness. Devinder Pal Singh (1999, 38) has suggested:

All of Guru Gobind Singh' works reveal the power of his poetic imagination and his mystical intuition. They, also show the amazing range of his learning and knowledge in the fields of mythology, metaphysics, astronomy. Human psychology, geography, botany, ayurveda and warfare ... He possessed an uncanny mastery over the magic of words. He used them with natural ease to render a variety of moods, scenes and sounds.

His patronage of poetry reportedly led to the creation of a large body of work known as the *Vidya Sar* or *Vidya Sagar*, the weight of which was nine maunds (350 kilograms). This entire work was lost during the evacuation from Anandpur in December 1705; however, some elements of it survive.

As teachers we may be tempted to just focus on the aspects of Guru Gobind Singh's life that have always been explored, namely, his institution of the Khalsa. But a focus on his writing and poetic pursuits helps us understand his teachings about how to seek union with Waheguru and the nature of existence and reality. As we read the works of Guru Gobind Singh it provides a different perspective and helps us understand the contributions that he made to the understanding of the teachings of the previous nine Gurus in human form. Returning to the imagery of Bhai Nand Lai in *Ganjnama* earlier, he was the light by which the teachings of the other Gurus in human form were illuminated. One example that will be developed in Chapter 5 surrounded his emphasis on the feminine and masculine elements of the divine. It is easy to focus on particularly masculine elements of Waheguru, and while Waheguru is without gender, Guru Gobind Singh used examples of Shakti to illustrate the points that enable a balance in the understanding of Akal Purakh.

Many writings of Guru Gobind Singh continue to be used by Sikhs today. For example, *Jaap Sahib* is the Gurbani that forms the first part of the Dasam Granth. It is one of five Gurbanis (the first being the *Japji*) that many Sikhs recite each morning and is also recited at the preparation of the *amrit* on the occasion of the *amrit sanskar*. The *Jaap Sahib* is a meditation on the nature of Waheguru, both in praise and description; the first few lines are:

> He who is without mark or sign, He who is without caste or line.
> He who is without colour or form, and without any distinctive norm.
> He who is without limit and motion, All effulgence, non-descript Ocean.
> The Lord of millions of Indras and kings, the Master of all worlds and beings.
> Each twig of the foliage proclaims: 'Not this Thou art.'
> All Thy Names cannot be told. One doth impart Thy Action-Name with benign heart.
> Salutation to Thee O Timeless Lord!
> Salutation to Thee O Beneficent Lord!
> Salutation to Thee O Formless Lord!
> Salutation to Thee O Wonderful Lord!
> Salutation to Thee O Garbless Lord! (Dasam Granth 1)

This recitation has been described as reflecting 'aesthetic idealism' which places an 'emphasis on aesthetic communion and its result Wismad – wonder. Music, consequently, plays a great part in this system. It is the poetry and the music of the contents of the Granth revealing simple and direct truths which charm a reader of Gurbani ... [and] bring peace to the soul' (Singh, 2003, 51–2). Through the bani of Guru Gobind Singh and all Gurus, a person is able to experience the Divine and feel a greater connection to, and awareness of, the naam.

Further exploration of the bani of Guru Gobind Singh, especially the Dasam Granth, will be done below, when discussing the martial spirit of the Guru, and in Chapter 4, when we focus on the structure, place and use of the Dasam Granth in history and today.

## The martial spirit

Throughout Guru Gobind Singh's early years, alongside the literary pursuits that we have just explored, the Guru was involved in martial exercises. In line with previous Gurus, Guru Gobind Singh continued to receive offerings of arms and horses. This, combined with visitors from the different Sikh centres, made Paonta a busy village, with its own armed force that was loyal to the Guru.

This martial spirit, and perhaps intimidating presence, led to the local chieftains in the surrounding hills developing jealousy and also a sense of worry and foreboding. Inspired by petty jealousies, two of the local hill chieftains, Bhim Chand and Fateh Shah, created an alliance of a large number of hill chieftains and determined to attack Guru Gobind Singh and the Sikh forces. The Guru, himself, describes the attack to be unprovoked: 'On this the king Fateh Shah become angry and fought with me without any reason' (Dasam Granth 129). In the Battle of Bhangani in 1688, the Sikh forces were heavily outnumbered by the local hill forces, and the fighting lasted over the course of a day. Despite being outnumbered, and receiving many casualties and fatalities, the forces of the Guru won the day.

There are many things that are evident from the accounts of the Battle of Bhangani. Firstly, it established or enacted an important feature of a war for Guru Gobind Singh – that of *dharam yudh* (variously translated as 'war of righteousness', 'war fought in the defence of righteousness' and 'war of justice'). A dharam yudh in the Sikh context is a war that is fought to protect the rights of people, for self-defence, when other solutions have failed, and should be fought honourably. Within the Battle of Bhangani it is possible to see that it was not a battle of an aggressor but was fought in self-defence. It is also noteworthy that in his recitation of the events, Guru Gobind Singh celebrated the conduct and valour of people on both sides. The idea of a person conducting themselves honourably is also shown in a future battle at Anandpur, where the Guru received complaints from some of his soldiers that Bhai Kanhaiya was sharing water, from what little they had, with some of the enemy forces. On being asked by the Guru for his response to these accusations, Bhai Kanhaiya admitted that this is what he had been doing, but said he was following the teachings of the Guru that all were equal, and that while they could destroy the enemy with the sword, they could also destroy enmity with compassion. Guru Gobind Singh commended Bhai Kanhaiya for being the one among his forces who understood the message of Gurbani. He then reminded his forces of the bani of Guru Arjan:

> I have totally forgotten my jealousy of others, since I found the Saadh Sangat, the Company of the Holy. No one is my enemy, and no one is a stranger. I get along with everyone. Whatever God does, I accept that as good. This is the sublime wisdom I have obtained from the Holy. The One God is pervading in all. Gazing upon Him, beholding Him, Nanak blossoms forth in happiness. (Guru Granth Sahib 1299)

The life of Guru Gobind Singh may have been permeated with battles, but his conduct and writings show that his approach to war went hand in hand with Gurbani, and that war must not be for profit but for the purpose of protecting others and their rights.

With the confidence that the Sikh community gained through this first battle, Guru Gobind Singh moved to Anandpur, where he began to build fortresses. Around 1691 (dates vary according to source) the Battle of Nadaun was fought when Bhim Chand and other chieftains, against whom the Guru had fought in 1688, approached him for help against the Mughal Empire, whose local representative had been unsuccessfully trying to collect taxes. This is, again, narrated in the Dasam Granth:

> Much time passed in this way, Mian Khan came (from Delhi) to Jammu (for collection of revenue). He sent Alif Khan to Nadaun, who developed enmity towards Bhim Chand (the Chief of Kahlur). Bhim Chand called me for assistance and himself went to face (the enemy). Alif Khan prepared a wooden fort of the hill of Navras. The hill-chief also prepared their arrows and guns. (Dasam Granth 135–6)

The hill chieftains, supported by the forces of Guru Gobind Singh, were victorious, and an agreement of friendship was established between them. Despite this friendship, the Guru continued with his building and arming of forts.

Throughout the remainder of his life, there continued to be battles, including:

- The Battle of Guler (1696)
- The Battle of Anandpur (1700)
- The Battle of Anandpur (1701)
- The Battle of Nirmohgarh (1702)
- The Battle of Basoli (1702)
- The First Battle of Chamkaur (1702)
- The First Battle of Anandpur (1704)
- The Second Battle of Anandpur (1704)
- The Battle of Sarsa (1704)

- The Second Battle of Chamkaur (1704)

- The Battle of Muktsar (1705)

While each of the battles was significant for different reasons, there are two that stand out in Sikh history and identity. Firstly, in the Second Battle of Chamkaur, the two elder sons of Guru Gobind Singh, Ajit Singh and Jujhar Singh, were killed. Secondly, and prior to this, during the battles of Anandpur, the two youngest sons of Guru Gobind Singh, Zorowar Singh (aged eight) and Fateh Singh (aged five), were also killed along with the Guru's mother, Mata Gujari. Despite receiving the promise of safe passage for Sikhs leaving Anandpur from Emperor Aurangzeb, Mughal forces took two groups of Sikhs captive, and in one of these were the Guru's two youngest sons and mother. The boys were killed by burying them alive in a wall.

All of these deaths were to have a deep impact on Guru Gobind Singh. After the deaths of Fateh and Zorowar, he wrote a letter to Aurangzeb that is titled *Zafarnama* (the epistle of victory), so named to reflect the spiritual victory of the Guru and the moral failures of the emperor. The *Zafarnama* is found today in the Dasam Granth. In this letter, Guru Gobind Singh was able to fuse the aspects of his literary and spiritual genius, with a focus on the moral and martial aspects of leadership and war.

## The *Zafarnama*

The *Zafarnama* forms part of the Dasam Granth and will explored as part of that in Chapter 4, but at this point in the discussion of the life of Guru Gobind Singh it has an important place in the narrative. The emperor, Aurangzeb, and his forces had made promises to the Guru and to the Sikhs, and as was evident from the deaths of his younger children and mother, the promises were not honoured. The *Zafarnama* is a letter that was sent in 1705 by the Guru to Emperor Aurangzeb.

The letter is written in the tone of addressing an inferior and highlights the sovereignty of the Guru. Essentially, it condemns Aurangzeb that although he and his forces were victorious, the victory was hollow because of the immoral way in which the war was fought and because the promises made on the Qur'an were broken. The letter has 111 verses, and a substantial number (up to 34) deal with the praise of Waheguru. Guru Gobind Singh also recounts events of the Second Battle of Chamkaur where his elder sons were killed. Others respond to the emperor's invitation for the Guru to meet with him; instead Guru Gobind Singh issues an invitation to Aurangzeb, promising him safe passage. Many parts of the letter reprove Aurangzeb for the actions of his forces, for the breaking of oaths:

> He, who follows his faith with sincerity, he never budges an inch from his oaths. I have
> no faith at all in such a person for whom the oath of the Quran has no significance. Even
> if you swear a hundred times in the name of the Quran, I shall not trust you any more.
> (Dasam Granth 2752)

There are sections that praise the Emperor:

> You are a clever administrator and a good horseman. With the help of your intelligence
> and the sword, you have become the master of Degh and Tegh. (Dasam Granth 2755)

The moral high ground is firmly established by Guru Gobind Singh. The theme throughout
is the need for a person's actions to match their words. It is interesting that despite the
emperor's positive attributes, Guru Gobind Singh suggests that no previous good can
justify a person who does not act as they should. The victory that is alluded to in the title
of the letter is the spiritual and moral victory of the Guru who has kept his word and his
relationship with Waheguru. The message of maya and the rejection of the ego are also
developed in this letter, both of which Aurangzeb had broken through his actions:

> You are proud of your kingdom and wealth, but I take refuge in the Non-Temporal Lord.
> Do not be careless about this fact that this saraae (resting place) is not the permanent
> abode. (Dasam Granth 2757)

The Guru is able to combine this message with a justification of the need to take up
arms: 'When all other methods fail, it is proper to hold the sword in hand' (Dasam
Granth 2750).

The response of the emperor is well documented; such was the righteousness of
Guru Gobind Singh's message that Aurangzeb was overcome with remorse. By this time,
he was ninety-one years old and worried about the end of his life and what awaited
him. Recognizing the injustice that had been done to the Guru, Aurangzeb withdrew all
warrants against him and sought to meet with the Guru to seek redemption. Before the
Guru was able to meet him, Aurangzeb died.

The need to not hold grudges and to move forward is exemplified in the life of Guru
Gobind Singh as he began to support Emperor Bahadur Shah, shortly after Aurangzeb's
death. It was this closeness or conciliatory attitude between the Guru and Bahadur Shah
that led Nawab Wazir Khan to send soldiers to kill Guru Gobind Singh. It is said that one
night when he was resting, the Guru was stabbed in his side, and despite killing one of
the men as they fled (the other being killed by other Sikhs in the camp), his wounds were
fatal, and he died on 7 October 1708 (dates differ and may be 17, 18 or 21 October).

The timeline of Guru Gobind Singh is fluid in this chapter, and having explored the
events of his death, it is important to return to two important events in his life, where he
was able to lay the foundation for the leadership and continuation of the Panth after his
death. The first of these is the establishment of the Khalsa; the second, the installation of
Guru Granth Sahib as the Living/Eternal Guru.

## Khalsa

There are many stories of the events in the lives of the Gurus that are essential to
understand the development of Sikhism. We have looked closely at the river experience

of Guru Nanak, the installation of Guru Angad as Guru, the martyrdom of Guru Arjan, the adoption of the two swords of miri and piri by Guru Hargobind and many others. It can be argued that among these 'essential' stories is that of the establishment of the Khalsa at Anandpur in 1699. Sainapat, in *Sri Gur Sobha*, writing three years after the Guru's death, describes the events in a succinct manner:

> On the auspicious occasion of Baisakhi ...
> As the Divine Guru revealed the creation of Khalsa Panth,
> He eliminated all the (earlier) entanglements ...
> One the bank of the sacred river Satluj.
> Many joined the Khalsa Panth after listening to Guru's words. (K. Singh, 2004b, 59)

The background to the events surrounding the creation of the Khalsa, which will be explored below, were much more complex than the Guru calling people together to Anandpur for the celebration of Baisakhi in 1699. This had been a tradition dating back to the time of Guru Amar Das (see above).

The first impetus was the divine 'call' of Guru Gobind Singh. This is evident in *Bachitra Natak*, where Guru Gobind Singh describes the purpose of his life as instructed by Waheguru:

> I have adopted you as my son and hath created you for the propagation of the path (Panth). 'You go therefore for the spread of Dharma (righteousness) and cause people to retrace their steps from evil actions.' I stood up with folded hands and bowing down my head, I said: 'The path (Panth) shall prevail only in the world, with THY ASSISTANCE.' (Dasam Granth 122)

Although this passage does not specifically mention the Khalsa, it is evident from the life and writings of Guru Gobind Singh that his understanding of his role was to develop the Panth. In some ways it can be seen that Guru Gobind Singh developed the other side of the coin to Guru Nanak; where Guru Nanak propagated good (which Guru Gobind Singh continued), Guru Gobind Singh lived in a world and context where he also needed to condemn evil. Thus, Guru Gobind Singh's life, and especially his creation of the Khalsa, is seen to be a natural development of Sikhism for his time and the future.

The second impetus to the founding of the Khalsa was the place that the Panth found itself in in establishing itself in conflict with, and in the context of, the Mughal Empire. As discussed above, the relationship with the Mughal emperor was always precarious and had become increasingly so since the time of Guru Arjan. The sovereignty of the Sikh Panth was seen to be a threat to the empire both militarily and religiously. There had been examples of the jealousies of people like Ahmad Shah and Diwan Chandu Shah, who viewed Sikhs with mistrust and motivated the emperors to act against the Panth. The precarious position was highlighted throughout the Guru's life; and to fulfil the impetus established by Guru Hargobind of an emphasis on miri-piri, there could be seen to be a need to form a community of Sikhs that would establish a distinct Sikh identity and group that would defend the Panth and stand against injustice.

The third impetus to the creation of the Khalsa was the disunity that could be found within the Panth. The masand system that had been responsible for the spread of Sikhism and also for the collection of dasvandh and other offerings to the Guru was seen to have become corrupt. The system had served its purpose well in the beginning, but over time some of the masands had become corrupt and set themselves up within the local community as if they were the Guru; they were also misappropriating funds meant for Guru Gobind Singh. Prior to 1699 there were examples of many complaints against masands, and some had needed to be disciplined by the Guru. It is evident from the Dasam Granth that Guru Gobind Singh was aware of the self-aggrandizement of some masands:

> Who squanders his belongings to Sannyasis in the name of Dutt, Who on the direction of the Masands (the priests appointed for collections of funds) takes the wealth of Sikhs and gives it to me, Then I think that these are only the methods of selfish-disciplines I ask such a person to instruct me about the Mystery of the Lord. He, who serves his disciples and impresses the people and tells them to hand over the victuals to him. And present before him whatever they had in their homes. He also asks them to think of him and not to remember the name of anyone else. (Ang 1325)

For some in the Sikh Panth who had approached the Guru about the masands, they had been asked to bring their offering directly to the Guru at Baisakhi in 1699. It was, perhaps as a part of this that the Guru realized the issue was systemic and unfixable as the Panth had grown so large. In this way the replacement of the masands was an important factor in the creation of the Khalsa.

With this as a background a large number of Sikhs gathered at Anandpur for Baisakhi in 1699. Although the narrative is essentially the same, there are slight variations in the recorded events. After the morning services, the Guru stood in front of the assembled congregation with his sword held high. He asked if any of the people assembled would be willing to give their head for their faith/to him. Some narrations have him asking for five from the outset. This request would have had added meaning for Guru Gobind Singh, and also for those who knew him, as he had received the head of his father, Guru Tegh Bahadur, after his martyrdom. A hush fell over the congregation when the request was made. Eventually, one man came forward and was taken into the tent with the Guru. The Guru emerged with a bloodied sword, and the man was nowhere to be seen. This was repeated a further four times.

One important aspect of the story concerns the identity of the five who came forward to offer their heads:

- Daya Ram, a Jat from Lahore
- Dharam Das, a Jat from Hastinapur

- Muhkam Chand, a cloth printer from Dwaraka

- Himmat, a water bearer from Jagannath

- Sahib Chand, a barber from Bidar

These five represented different castes and would form the basis of the Khalsa. The number five had been significant throughout different points in Sikh history. Guru Arjan had been accompanied by five Sikhs as he went to his death at Lahore. Guru Hargobind gave these five Sikhs a company of one hundred men to command. Guru Gobind Singh's grandfather was also accompanied by five Sikhs on his way to Delhi where he would be executed. Five had also been important in the ceremony of *charan pdhul*, an initiation ritual that had its beginnings with Guru Nanak (following aspects of existing Hindu customs). In this ceremony, developed further by Guru Amar Das, a person would be offered water which had been poured over the toe of the right foot of five chosen Sikhs.

Returning to the narrative of Baisakhi, after the fifth had been taken into the tent, Guru Gobind Singh emerged hand in hand with the five Sikhs, each of them dressed in new robes and neatly tied turbans, both in saffron. These events are interpreted in different ways by Sikhs. For some, it was a miracle: the heads of these men had truly been chopped off, and they had been healed by the Guru's grace. For other Sikhs, the blood had come from the killing of goats. In some ways, the source of the blood may be immaterial as it is the faith of five, the *panj pyare* (five pure ones), which was most important. They had been willing to give their lives for their faith and for devotion to the Guru.

What followed, for each of the five, was the ritual of *khande di pahul* (pahul by the khanda or the double-edged sword) which is more commonly known today as amrit sanskar. In an iron bowl, Guru Gobind Singh and his wife, Mata Sahib Kaur, mixed amrit with a sword while repeating Gurbani. The amrit had been mixed with steel, perhaps symbolizing the sweetness of the Gurbani and the steel of the sword and the extension of miri-piri.

Following the repetition of Gurbani, Guru Gobind Singh sprinkled amrit into the eyes of each and anointed their hair with it. The Guru gave the amrit to each of the panj pyare, and they each drank from the same bowl. Again, breaking down the barriers of caste, drinking from the same vessel shattered any illusion of caste distinction. Each was given the surname 'Singh' (lion), and later women would receive the surname 'Kaur' (princess). In this ceremony the common identifiers of caste, family, occupations and beliefs were replaced by their belief in Waheguru and their commitment to the Panth.

The panj pyare and, by extension, the future members of the Khalsa were give five symbols to represent their place as Khalsa:

- *Kesh*: All Khalsa Sikhs were to keep hair anywhere on their body uncut.

- *Kangha*: A wooden comb was always to be carried.

- *Kachera*: A pair of breeches/shorts were to be worn by soldiers.

- *Kara*: A steel bracelet/bangle was always to be worn.
- *Kirpan*: A sword was always to be carried.

Collectively, these are known as the 5Ks (*panj kake*); their symbolism and use today will be explored in Chapter 7. The Khalsa also received four rules of conduct (*rehit/rahat*):

- Not to cut hair on any part of their body.
- Not to smoke, chew tobacco or consume alcoholic drinks.
- Not to eat an animal that had been bled to death (as was the rule for slaughter of animals by Muslims in a halal way).
- Not to engage in molestation of Muslim women (later extended to not committing adultery).

It may appear that the ritual of khande di pahul and the attendant symbols and rehat separate Sikhs from Hindus and Muslims. In the address that Guru Gobind Singh gave in establishing the Khalsa, he made it clear that there is only one way of Waheguru that destroys all differences of religion, there is no caste with all being encouraged to mix and work together, and places of pilgrimage for Hindus and the worship of the images of deities is outlawed.

It should be noted that the obligation to adopt the 5Ks and live the four rehat may not have been as formalized at the time of the Guru and in the years afterwards as they are perceived today. This is not to negate that they were encouraged and even prescribed; just that their adoption by all Sikhs was not as wholesale as might be suggested by some books and narrators. Indeed, the Singh Sabha movement can be seen to have 'reclaimed' these elements of Sikh identity, and the previously accepting attitudes in the intervening years were cast aside. More exploration of this will be undertaken in Chapter 7.

After initiating the panj pyare into the Khalsa, the Guru greeted them and the Panth with the words:

Waheguru Ji Ka Khalsa Waheguru Ji Ki Fateh
The Khalsa belongs to Waheguru; the victory belongs to Waheguru.

This is now the greeting when members of the Khalsa meet one another.

The panj pyare were the first members of the Khalsa, the first to go through the amrit sanskar. This, perhaps, would have been sufficient to establish the community of Sikhs who were willing to signify their faith through the wearing of new clothes and the taking of amrit, but it was followed by an event that was as challenging to Sikhs as the challenge to caste may have been. Singh Mandair (2013, 65) has described what happens next as constituting 'an excessive violence where the Guru sacrifices his transcendence/authority and therefore does violence to the very order of sacredness, and empowers the Khalsa'.

Guru Gobind Singh knelt before the panj pyare and asked them to initiate him into the Khalsa. The five initially refused, but on the repeated entreaties of the Guru, they relented and gave amrit to the Guru in the same way that he had administered it to them. It was at this point that, in concert with the panj pyare, he renounced all vestiges of caste and family and replaced his name Rai with 'Singh'. The image of the Guru kneeling, and perhaps in obeisance to the Khalsa would have been disturbing to the gathered Sikhs. Guru Gobind Singh was their Guru; he was the divine light to whom they looked for leadership and guidance. It has been suggested, and this might be a later interpretation, that the Guru was passing on the leadership of the Panth to the Khalsa. In a similar way that Guru Nanak had installed Guru Angad as his successor, the humility of Guru Gobind Singh in acknowledging the authority of the Khalsa prepared a way for the leadership of the Panth to be in the hands of the Khalsa. This authority would be combined with and be under the sovereignty of Guru Granth Sahib (see below).

Following the first six initiations into the Khalsa there are reports that twenty thousand Sikhs received amrit at Anandpur and, as word spread, many more throughout the Panth. This spiritual yet militant spirit within Sikhs was a challenge to the traditional leadership of the Khatri Sikhs, who had been the main source of masands, and also to the surrounding peoples. These would form the basis of future conflicts involving the Panth.

It is important at this point to note a tendency that can be found in textbooks, conversations and other writings of both Sikhs and non-Sikhs. The tendency is to use the word 'baptism' to describe amrit sanskar, or to speak of Amritdhari Sikhs, or Sikhs who have taken amrit, as 'baptized Sikhs'. Even though this is found within the conversation and writings of Sikhs, I believe that this is a colonial hangover and, as already mentioned, an effort on the part of Sikhs to make their beliefs and practices understandable to non-Sikhs and Western Christians in particular. The same tendency is found in the naming of gurdwaras as temples. I think it is important for all people, and teachers especially, to utilize terminology that is accurate and reflects the authenticity of a religion. It is not a Sikh's responsibility to change their terminology for my benefit, but it is my responsibility to understand the terminology of Sikhs. There are similarities and differences between the understanding of baptism in Christianity and amrit sanskar in Sikhism. As a teacher we might use one as a springboard to understand the other, but we should emphasize the distinctiveness of each. We should not make the two synonymous in meaning or in expression.

## The living Guru

As will be explored in Chapter 4, there were different versions or recensions of the Adi Granth in existence throughout the Sikh Panth. There were inconsistencies because of additions and edits that were made in copies, or because of the active intervention of people like Prithi Chand. With this as a background, and also the unwillingness of those in possession of the Kartarpur Bir, and this also being in the possession of descendants of Dhal Mal, who are alleged to have taunted the Guru when refusing to give it to him with the words: 'If you are a Guru, make your own', Guru Gobind Singh determined to make an authoritative version of the Adi Granth.

Tradition holds that in Damdama Guru Gobind Singh recited the whole of the Adi Granth to Bhai Mani, who wrote it down. As part of this process, Guru Gobind Singh added bani of his father, Guru Tegh Bahadur. It is this version that is seen as Guru Granth Sahib today.

It may seem 'incredible' for the whole of the Adi Granth to be recited, but as it was Guru Gobind Singh, in the Sikh worldview, this becomes completely credible.

On the day before his death, recognizing that the end was near, Guru Gobind Singh installed the Adi Granth as the Living and Eternal Guru, Guru Granth Sahib. Reports indicate that he went through the same process as previous Gurus in taking a coconut and five paise and prostrating himself before the Guru. The spiritual authority of the Panth lay now with Guru Granth Sahib, and the Khalsa with the obligation to interpret it and lead in the temporal world.

The line of Gurus in human form had ended, but the installation of Guru Granth Sahib meant that the same light that was part of the previous Gurus was to be found in the Eternal Guru. More about the place of Guru Granth Sahib will be explored in the next chapter. With the Panth established, it is seen as a natural development that the guidance that had been manifested in the lives and bani of the Gurus in human form would find its fulfilment in the imbuing of Guru Granth Sahib with that same authority.

## Thoughts for the classroom

As has already been mentioned, Guru Gobind Singh is one of the two Gurus in human form who are most often explored in the classroom. In so doing, the focus is usually on the formation of the Khalsa, and therefore, we may be reducing his influence and legacy to one story. This is not to say that this story is not important; indeed, its significance will be explored in depth in Chapter 7. The identity of Sikhs as Khalsa is central in today's world, and arguably since 1699. When we explore his life, however, we should use elements of his writing alongside the fusion of the spiritual with the temporal. The reduction of Guru Gobind Singh as someone who militarized the Panth misses the central aspect of his life as a Guru who embodied the light of Waheguru. One illustration of this is the response of Aurangzeb to the *Zafarnama*; this was an embodiment of the teaching to explore all other means before resorting to violence. There would not have been many who would have blamed Guru Gobind Singh had he launched a retaliatory offensive against the Mughals, but instead he wrote a letter that fused the principles of Sikhism in praising Waheguru, and the way of a gurmukh, with a condemnation of false living. It enabled Aurangzeb to see the error of his ways, and potentially stave off further suffering.

Every aspect of Guru Gobind Singh's life seems to be filled with heartbreak and martyrdom. Beginning with his father, continuing with his four sons and his mother, he experienced great loss in the harshest of circumstances. Yet in the midst of all of this he prepared the Panth for an existence beyond one entailing the presence of Gurus in human form. He recognized the importance of sangat and of the Khalsa and the Gurbani in sustaining and defending Sikhism. There are many stories and writings that can be used to explore his life and legacy.

## Storytelling

For each of the Gurus there are a multitude of stories that could form the basis of an exploration of Sikh beliefs and values in the classroom at all stages of education. Storytelling lies at the heart of understanding Sikhism. It has to be utilized correctly and enthusiastically by the teacher.

To an extent, stories lie at the heart of religion, especially Sikhism. The stories of the Gurus can be used to frame morality, teachings and also the boundaries of Sikhism. Trevor Cooling (2002, 45) suggests that stories are 'big ideas sometimes referred to as a metanarrative, which express our whole understanding of the whole world and help people to make sense of their lives'. This is just so with Sikhism. As we reflect on some of the stories of the Gurus, whether it is the river experience of Guru Nanak, the compilation of the Adi Granth or the story of the creation of the Khalsa at Baisakhi, they can help us understand the important aspects of Sikhism. We can understand the nature of Waheguru, a Guru in human form, of maya, of existence through a utilization of stories of the Gurus in the classroom.

Robin Mello (2001) explains that learning can be deepened with the use of stories. They also have many levels of understanding that need to be analysed and studied for academic understanding. The stories that are told help us understand what was important for Sikhs then and today. Miller Mair (1989, 257) suggests that this is so: 'All our stories are expressions of ourselves even when they purport to be accounts of aspects of the world. We are deeply implicated in the very grounds of our story telling.' Sikhism can thus be experienced through its stories. Whatever the age of student we are working with, using the stories of the Gurus can help them understand more deeply not just the life of the Gurus but also the teachings of Sikhism and their importance to Sikhs today.

## A warning

I am convinced that a focus on the Gurus in human form is essential to understand the development and teachings of Sikhism. In focusing on these Gurus there is the possibility that our teaching of Sikhism becomes a history lesson, and while there are many interesting events and developments, that is only a small part of the story. What is central to the lives of each of these Gurus is the worship of Waheguru, the realization of the naam within and the true nature of existence. The lives of each of the Gurus in human form should be explored in a way to understand their impact on the teachings of Sikhism, the lives of Sikhs at their time but, most importantly for our classrooms, the lives of Sikhs today. I have necessarily taken a large portion of this book to explore their lives and teachings. I hope to combat the proclivity to just focus on Guru Nanak and Guru Gobind Singh, as important as they are. The other Gurus are similarly ways to help people understand the divine.

They are important as manifestation of the attributes of Waheguru; they are also contiguous with one another to recognize the light that is passed from one to the next. In the context of this, for Sikhs, their continuity is automatically accepted. The message was not changed by any of the Gurus, just that it was developed in light of the growing needs of the sangat and the contexts in which it found itself. As we move on in the following chapters to exploring expressions of Sikh spirituality and devotion, they will necessarily refer to the Gurus, and it hoped that this background will help teachers approach the way that Sikhs live with a grounding in the example and teachings of the Gurus.

# Chapter 4

# Guru Granth Sahib

It could seem incongruous for a book that, in the previous chapter, was at pains to point out the contiguous nature of the line of the Gurus in human form to suddenly change tack and dedicate a chapter to the eleventh Guru, Guru Granth Sahib. Although there is a necessary chapter break, this is not to indicate any discontinuity between the message of the Gurus in human form and the message and importance of Guru Granth Sahib. Prior to his death, Guru Gobind Singh installed Guru Granth Sahib as the 'Living' or the 'Eternal' Guru. It is in the pages of Guru Granth Sahib that *Gurbani* is to be found; the same light that imbued the teachings of the Gurus from Guru Nanak to Gobind Singh is on every page and every recitation of the hymns that it contains. Consider comments from Sikhs today about the place of Guru Granth Sahib:

> Guru Granth has the same importance as the Ten Gurus in how I live my life.
> Guru Granth Sahib is the core guiding light now and the go to source in case of any question. (Holt, interview)

In Chapter 3, we explored how Guru Granth Sahib was compiled by Guru Arjan and then later by Guru Gobind Singh. In this chapter, we will consider the contents as well as how the Guru is and has been used in the lives of Sikhs throughout history and today.

## A holy book?

In a world religions paradigm one of the traditional hallmarks of a religion would be a holy book or scriptures. In this way, if a grid is compiled under this section heading, proudly written by pupils would be the name 'Guru Granth Sahib'. In some way, however, in describing Guru Granth Sahib as 'just like' any other holy book, we lose the unique view of the Guru that Sikhs have in comparison to other books. Guru Granth Sahib is seen to be a reflection of that same light as the Gurus in human form:

> This Holy Book is the home of the Transcendent Lord God. (Guru Granth Sahib 1226)

> The light of the Ten Gurus shines in Guru Granth Sahib. (Ardas Prayer)

The installation of Guru Granth Sahib as Guru did not end all attempts at establishing further Gurus in human form. It was in no small part due to Mata Sundari, the widow of

Guru Gobind Singh, that the pre-eminence and authority of Guru Granth Sahib became firmly established in the *Panth*. She sent out *hukamnamas* in her own name, reinforcing and emphasizing the wishes and teachings of her husband. When faced with claims of a further Guru outside of Guru Granth Sahib, she said:

> Khalsaji, you must have faith in none other except the Timeless One. Go only to the Ten Gurus in search of the word. Nanak is their slave who obtain their goal by searching the Word? The Guru is lodged in the Word. That One Itself merged with the Guru who revealed the Word. The Word is the life of all life: through it we meet with the ultimate One. (Singh, H. 1983b, 108–9)

Mata Sundari's description helps us understand that Guru Granth Sahib is more than a holy book. It is imbued with the same light as each of the ten Gurus in human form. Throughout Chapter 3, the contiguous nature of each of the Gurus in being of the same light was emphasized. In the Sikh worldview, this is so with Guru Granth Sahib, who is the Living or Eternal Guru. Pashaura Singh (2014b, 134) notes this when he explains:

> The ultimate authority in the Sikh tradition … lies in Guru Granth Sahib. In a certain sense, the Sikhs have taken their conception of sacred scripture further than other 'text-centred communities' such as Jews and Muslims.

This is highlighted in the way that the Guru is spoken about and treated within the Sikh community, and especially the gurdwara today. Guru Granth Sahib, when it is not in the *diwan* (court of the ruler) hall, has its own room in the gurdwara (or in the Akhal Takht for Guru Granth Sahib at Harmandir Sahib) known as *sach khand*, or the realm or court of Waheguru. The identification of this room as sach khand, as explored in Chapter 2, indicates the way that the Guru is viewed and held in high esteem. Guru Granth Sahib is placed in a room so named to indicate the union that the Guru enjoys with Waheguru. As mentioned above, the Guru is of the same light as the human Gurus, who were *braham-giani* from birth, and it is in this manner that Guru Granth Sahib is viewed and treated.

Each morning, Guru Granth Sahib is 'awoken' and processed through the gurdwara to the *takht* (throne) at the front of the diwan hall. The Guru is raised above the heads of those who carry it, Gurbani is sung and, in the words of one Sikh, 'there is a lot of razaamatazz' (Holt, interview) that accompanies the installation of the Guru in the morning. Those in its presence should have their heads covered and feet bare. The Guru is treated as royalty. Once placed on the takht, the Guru is covered often with, firstly, a white sheet and then with a highly decorated *ramalla* (robes). Above the takht will be a canopy just below the ceiling. Everything about the treatment of Guru Granth Sahib reinforces its place as the Living Guru and as royalty. The highly decorative ramalla is reminiscent of the robes of those of high esteem. When the Guru is read, the *granthi* (reader of scripture) waves a *chauri* or a fan made of metal with, traditionally, yak hair. This is waved out of respect for the Guru and is seen to be an act of sewa (see Chapter 6) and is, again, reminiscent of the treatment of the Guru as royalty. It is tradition within the gurdwara that a person should not turn their back on Guru Granth Sahib.

The installation is revered at night, when the Guru is returned to sach khand and the *manji* (bed). The manji should be at least 12 inches in height, 36 inches in width and 18 inches in depth, and a canopy should be above it, just below the ceiling. The Guru is again covered with a simple white sheet, with more ornate ramallas of differing thicknesses depending on the season. The same rituals are followed as in the morning.

Similar morning and evening rituals are carried out in gurdwaras around the world, and live streams are available of these events at the Harmandir Sahib. Each element of the treatment of Guru Granth Sahib shows its importance and identification as the Eternal and Living Guru. This view stands in contrast to the view of the holy books in other religions. At one and the same time it is correct to describe Guru Granth Sahib as the scripture of the Sikhs, but to do so gives the wrong impression. The Guru is so much more than a 'mere' book, even one that contains the words of God. Each *shabad* is imbued with the light of Waheguru.

One further note that highlights the way Guru Granth Sahib is viewed is the concept of *beadbi*, or acts of sacrilege performed against Guru Granth Sahib. They range from a person having their head uncovered in the presence of the Guru, to much more nefarious acts such as tearing a page from the Guru or burning it. Following one such event, where a lit cigarette was thrown onto the page being read at the Takht Anandpur, Nihang Sikhs killed the man who had desecrated the Guru. One Nihang Sikh suggested in its aftermath:

> But lately beadbi has become a common practice with instances of Guru Granth Sahib Ji's pages being torn, even burnt. Unfortunately, nothing has been done in this matter. 'Sade Guru di raksha appa jaan de kiti hai, Sikhi sanu saukhi nhi mili asi kamai hai' (We always laid our life for Guru, we have earned Sikhi with many sacrifices and it was not easy). (Singh and Brar, 2021)

This act of retaliation was condemned throughout the worldwide Sikh community and is seen to have gone too far. However, it does show the way Guru Granth Sahib is seen. Acts of violence towards it are viewed as acts against living beings. Again, this is an extreme and unacceptable act of violence but shows the way the Guru is treated.

## Editions

As noted in Chapter 3, the composition of the first Guru, the Adi Granth, and latterly Guru Granth Sahib was under the direction, and had the involvement, of the Gurus in human form. Guru Arjan worked with Bhai Gurdas to compile the Adi Granth to ensure that everything that was contained therein was Gurbani, designed to teach the truth of Nanak Panth and how to seek union with Waheguru. This process was repeated in the final composition of Guru Granth Sahib where Guru Gobind Singh worked with Bhai

Mani Singh to produce the authoritative version of the Guru. There have been, however, different versions of the Adi Granth that are of note:

- Kartarpur Vaali Bir: This was the original version of the Adi Granth compiled by Guru Arjan. As noted in the previous chapter, this copy was held by Dhir Mal at the time of Guru Tegh Bahadur's installation. His descendants are still in possession of this copy of the Adi Granth.

- Bhai Banno Vaali Bir: This was the copy made by Bhai Banno when he was made responsible for having the Adi Granth bound. In this copy there are additions that were not approved by Guru Arjan. This version is in the possession of his descendants and may be housed at Gurdwara Banno Sahib in Kanpur.

- Damdama Vaali Bir: This is the version that was written by Bhai Mani Singh and dictated by Guru Gobind Singh. In addition to the Adi Granth, Guru Gobind Singh added Gurbani from Guru Tegh Bahadur. In installing this version as Guru, Guru Gobind Singh closed the canon where nothing else could be added. This is the version of Guru Granth Sahib that is used throughout the Sikh Panth.

Perhaps, due to the widespread nature of the Panth and the difficulty of reproducing Guru Granth Sahib, in the years following the establishment of Guru Granth Sahib as Guru, there were versions of the Kartarpur Bir, and especially the Banno Bir, that were used by Sikhs. Indeed, Pashaura Singh (2014a) suggests that the Banno Bir was the most commonly used. He argues that it was during the time of Ranjit Singh that the Damdama Bir became the version that was used throughout the Panth. He employed scribes with the specific task of making copies of the Damdama Bir, which were then gifted to all of the Takhts and to many gurdwaras. This revival of the Damdama Bir was firmly established upon its first printing in 1864 and its adoption by the Singh Sabha movement. The printing of Guru Granth Sahib also meant that its pagination could be standardized.

## English translations

There were two translations into English of elements of Guru Granth Sahib in the late nineteenth and early twentieth centuries. Each of these have shortcomings, but they can help us understand how Sikhism was developing, and how it was viewed within the British Empire, to whom Singh Sabhas were responding with their articulation of Sikh beliefs (see Chapter 9).

The first translation, published in 1877, was by Ernest Trumpp, a German philologist who travelled to Punjab to begin work on translating Guru Granth Sahib. In his first meeting with Sikhs,

he told them that he was a Sanskrit scholar, that he understood their sacred writings better than they did themselves, and by way of emphasising his remarks, pulled out his cigarcase and perfumed with it the *Adi Granth* which was lying on the table before him. (Singh, 2004, 51)

Trumpp saw Sikhism as just another form of Hinduism and considered Guru Nanak a Hindu teacher. Indeed, as he read Guru Granth Sahib, he noted:

> We need hardly remark, that this whole definition of the Supreme is altogether Pantheistic. The Hindu way of thinking comprehends in the Absolute both spirit and matter, as the creation of material bodies out of nothing is totally incomprehensible to the Hindu mind. (Trumpp, 1877, c)

Trumpp's translation was problematic in many ways. The promulgation of a Hindu pantheism with elements of a monotheism was reductive in terms of the understanding of Sikhism. It also framed the discussion for future translations and the responses of those within the Sikh Panth. Arvind-Pal Singh Mandair (2005, 253) has suggested that Trumpp's translation 'remains historically the most influential document concerning the question: "What is Sikhism?"' What he seems to be suggesting is that in articulating their 'theology', Singh Sabhas and others accepted the framework within which Trumpp worked – that of Western philosophy and Orientalism. To articulate Sikh belief, a person needed to explain how it differentiated itself from prevailing Hindu norms.

The second translation was that of Max Macauliffe, who tried to rectify some of the assumptions and errors of Trumpp. He admits in his introduction that one of his purposes was to 'endeavour to make some reparation to the Sikhs for the insults which [Trumpp] offered to their Gurus and their religion' (Macauliffe, 1909b, vii). Macauliffe used the *Janamsakhi*s to highlight the contributions and demarcation of Sikhism from Hinduism. Where Trumpp was dismissive of Sikhism, Macauliffe was equally harsh on Hinduism in the context of Sikhism. He delineated Sikh beliefs and practices, however, by referencing Sikh similarities to Protestant Christianity (Shani, 2008). Indeed, again in his introduction, he highlights the comparative virtues of 'philanthropy, justice, impartiality, truth, honesty, and all the moral and domestic virtues known to the holiest citizens of any country' (Macauliffe, 1909b, xxiii).

Other English versions build on these translations and are used by many Sikhs in Britain today. Both of these editions, along with some of the inheritors of their translation traditions, highlight the care with which Guru Granth Sahib should be read. All translations and interpretations of scripture reflect a particular cultural context of the translator and the writer. Both Trumpp and Macauliffe, while writing from different perspectives and understandings of Sikhism, were still writing from a Western Protestant Christian perspective. As such, some words are translated with specific meanings and understandings attached. As we saw in Chapter 1, the *Mool Mantar* is hard to render in an English translation, as the words mean more than can be captured in one word, or their meaning is changed by a definite article. Teachers should be aware that the way that students read Guru Granth Sahib may produce unintended readings that reflect the readers' worldviews. Similarly, when a Sikh reads Guru Granth Sahib in English, it should be with the understanding that it may not capture the context and message of the original shabad.

Within the classroom, a focus on the skill of hermeneutics in reading Christian and Muslim scripture has begun. One such project is Texts to Teachers, and their findings suggest:

> Sacred text scholarship allows students to investigate the layers of meaning that people find significant. In making the hermeneutical process more explicit teachers help students become conscious of the process of reading sacred texts, and the place of the reader in making sense of a text, as well as the senses held by communities, and those held at different times and places. This may apply to all religions and worldviews. (Bowie, Panjwani and Clemmey, 2020, 10)

It could be argued that we are using a Christian approach to scripture to understand how to read Guru Granth Sahib. The practice of hermeneutics is prevalent within Sikh studies already, for example, Nikky-Guninder Singh in various publications has engaged in feminist readings of events and scriptures.

## Authors and structure

In exploring the composition of the Adi Granth, it was noted that the volume of Gurbani contained the writings of the first five Gurus in human form, along with Sufi and Hindu sants whose teachings reflected the truth of a person's search for Waheguru. In his recitation of the Adi Granth, Guru Gobind Singh added in teachings of his father, Guru Tegh Bahadur. As such, the contributors to the final Guru Granth Sahib are listed in Table 4.1. The hymns are arranged in a specific order focused on three sections (see Chapter 3):

- The first section contains hymns that would be used in the daily personal worship of a Sikh. It begins with the *Japji* (which in turn begins with the *Mool Mantar*), then *Rahiras* (supplication; which has nine hymns) and, finally, the *Sohila* (praise; which consists of five hymns). Sikhs recite the *Japji* at sunrise, the *Rahiras* at sunset and the *Sohila* just before going to sleep at night.
- The main section begins with the hymns of the first five Gurus in human form, with the writings of Guru Tegh Bahadur inserted where they were felt important by Guru Gobind Singh. Then comes the writings of the sants and saints.
- The final section has a collection of writings that are sometimes described as 'miscellaneous', maybe because they are couplets or writings that are not used with specific rags.

The hymns of Guru Granth Sahib are designed to be sung. The musicology of the hymns was specifically designed by Guru Arjan, and Guru Gobind Singh continued this

**Table 4.1** Contributors to Guru Granth Sahib

| Gurus in human form | |
| --- | --- |
| Guru Nanak | 974 hymns |
| Guru Angad | 62 couplets |
| Guru Amar Das | 907 hymns |
| Guru Ram Das | 679 hymns |
| Guru Arjan | 2,218 hymns |
| Guru Tegh Bahadur | 59 hymns and 56 couplets |
| **Bhaktas (Hindu sants/poets from the Bhakti tradition) and Sufi saint poets** | |
| Kabir | 292 hymns |
| Farid | 4 hymns and 130 couplets |
| Namdev | 60 hymns |
| Ravidas | 41 hymns |
| Jaidev | 2 hymns |
| Beni | 3 hymns |
| Trilochan | 4 hymns |
| Parmananda | 1 hymn |
| Sadhana | 1 hymn |
| Ramananda | 1 hymn |
| Dhanna | 4 hymns |
| Pipa | 1 hymn |
| Sain | 1 hymn |
| Bhikhan | 2 hymns |
| Sur Das | one line |
| Sundar | 1 hymn |
| Various Bhatts | 123 swayyas (verses) |
| **Sikhs** | |
| Mardana | 3 couplets |
| Satta and Balvand | 1 hymn |

expectation. Indeed, for the singing of the hymns and to create the correct mood and approach there are instructions and guides; these rules are often known as *gurbani kirtan* or *gurmat sangeet*. The use of music in teaching the Guru's shabad or Gurbani was begun by Guru Nanak. As already noted, when Guru Nanak travelled he was accompanied by Bhai Mardana, who was a *rababi*. The musicality of the Gurbani are an integral part of their message.

# Guru Granth Sahib in worship and Sikh life today

The exploration of how Guru Granth Sahib is treated in terms of the morning and evening rituals, as well as its place in the diwan hall, is indicative of how it is used in worship and life. These, and *nitnem* (daily routine/habit) of the various Gurbani (see Chapter 7), are central to the collective and individual worship of Sikhs. The communal worship of Sikhs usually takes the format prescribed by Article XV of the *Rahit Maryada*:

> Ceremonial opening of Guru Granth Sahib, Kirtan, exposition of scriptures, expository discourses, recitation of Anand Sahib, the Ardas, the raising of Fateh slogan and then the slogan Sat Sri Akal and taking the Hukam.

In addition to the recitation or reading of Guru Granth Sahib by a granthi at the front of the diwan hall, there are other examples of how the Guru is used in worship.

## Kirtan

In addition to the *langar* and personal meditation, Sikh worship in the gurdwara usually focuses on *kirtan* or the singing/recitation of Gurbani from Guru Granth Sahib. The singing is usually based on the rags suggested alongside the Gurbani. The musical mode has been specifically designed to reflect the mood and focus of the shabad. Examples of the moods associated with rags are:

- *Soohi* – joy and separation
- *Bilaaval* – happiness
- *Gauri* – seriousness
- *Aasa* – making effort
- *Bhairaagi* – sadness
- *Tukhari* – beautification
- *Malaar* – separation
- *Vadhans* – *vairaag*, loss
- *Parbhati* – bhakti and seriousness

Singing kirtan is at the heart of Sikh devotion as they are seen as essential for union with Waheguru:

> At the Gurdwara, the Guru's Gate, the Kirtan of the Lord's Praises are sung. Meeting with the True Guru, one chants the Lord's Praises. (Guru Granth Sahib 1075)

Singing kirtan can allow the discovery of *naam* within the worshipper. Involvement in kirtan requires the mind, words and actions. The focus during kirtan should be on Waheguru and the shabad that helps a person find union. Kirtan is an immersive experience that enables Sikhs to experience Gurbani.

Kirtan in the diwan hall usually involves a group of musicians seated to the side of Guru Granth Sahib. Traditional instruments include the dilruba, the sarangi, the esraj and a form of pakhawaj (a precursor of the tabla):

- The dilruba is a large string instrument, with a big resonance box.
- The sarangi is a short-necked string instrument.
- The esraj is similar to the dilruba but is a modern version.
- The pakhawaj/tabla is a two-headed drum.

Other instruments can be played, but it is important within kirtan that the music takes second place to the singing of the Gurbani. The music can create a mood, but the Gurbani will have the impact on a person. In Britain it has become common to project the words that are being sung onto large screens. The words are in Gurmukhi and also in English, so that those who are not fluent in Gurmukhi can understand what is being sung, and it can have impact on a person beyond its musicality.

## Akhand path

*Akhand* is generally seen to mean 'uninterrupted', and *path* means reading. Therefore, an *akhand path* is an uninterrupted reading of Guru Granth Sahib. It usually takes place in the gurdwara over a period of forty-eight hours. The continuous reading is not carried out by one person but by a series of people who overlap in reading a few words so that there is no interruption.

Akhand paths are important and usually mark important festivals, or events in a person's life. In some gurdwaras there may be weekly akhand paths to try and build an ongoing connection between the devotees and the Guru. The akhand path is opened with a short service and ended with a similar service that includes shabads being sung and *ardas* (prayers) being offered, as well as the offering of *karaprasad*. During the actual reading of the akhand path, kirtan should not be sung.

Tradition holds that akhand paths began with Guru Gobind Singh. Following the completion of his recitation to Bhai Mani Singh, the Guru asked five of his companions to read it to him without interruption. Also, there were akhand paths before Banda Singh

Bahadur was sent to meet the emperor's forces and even before Guruship was bestowed on Guru Granth Sahib.

People who attend, but are not reading, can come and go as they please, but they are expected to sit in silence as they listen to the Gurbani being read. The connection that the akhand path brings between Waheguru and those who listen should not be underestimated. It is a deeply sacred event that enables a person to experience the Gurbani.

## Birth rituals

Prior to giving birth, a pregnant woman, in the final few months, may begin to sing kirtan or meditate on the naam and recite shabad. It is possible that the woman may listen to, rather than recite, the *bani*. Both of these practices place Gurbani and the message of Guru Granth Sahib at the centre of a child's earliest development. It is a belief among many Sikhs that it is never too early to begin the spiritual development of a child; and listening to Gurbani and the naam cannot help but point the child in the right direction.

Article XVII of the *Rahit Maryada* outlines the various rites and steps included in naming rituals. There is some discussion as to whether the formal Sikh rituals existed before the late nineteenth or early twentieth century (see Chapter 9), and there is a high degree of conformity in their practice. It is important to note that Guru Granth Sahib, as the Eternal Guru, plays a crucial role in the naming of a child (*naam karan*).

- After the birth of a child, when the mother has had her bath and is comfortable moving around, the family and relatives go to the gurdwara with karaprasad that they have prepared, or that has been made in the gurdwara.

- In the presence of Guru Granth Sahib, various shabads that express joy and thankfulness (such as Angs 628 and 396) are recited.

- *Hukam* is then taken. This is the opening of Guru Granth Sahib that begins the reading from the top of the left-hand page.

- Using the first letter of the Hukam, the granthi suggests a name, and when it is accepted, the name is announced. It is becoming more common nowadays for the parents to choose the name themselves, but it is still announced by the granthi. Interestingly, first names within Sikhism are not specific to one gender and can be used for both boys and girls. The name 'Singh' is appended to a boy's name and 'Kaur' to a girl's.

- The *Anand Sahib* (see Chapter 7) is recited.

- It should also be noted that there is no concept of pollution or uncleanness attached to giving birth. 'The birth and death are by His ordinance; coming and going is by His will. All food and water are, in principle, clean, for these life-sustaining substances are provided by Him.'

## Amrit sanskar

The *amrit sanskar* was explored slightly in Chapter 3 when looking at the events surrounding the founding of the Khalsa. This rite continues today, as it did then, as a person's initiation into the Khalsa; and the rite tries, as much as possible, to replicate the initiation of the initial *panj pyare* during Baisakhi in 1699. In Chapter 3, it was mentioned that many Sikhs now use the shorthand of 'baptism' or 'baptized Sikh' to denote the amrit sanskar or being *amritdhari*. Although the *Rahit Maryada* uses such terminology, I think it is important to enable Sikhs to be understood on their own terms, rather than in a way that is understandable to Christians. I will avoid such terminology as an attempt to slightly decolonize the way that Sikhism is taught within the classroom.

In exploring how amrit sanskar should be carried out, the first thing to note is that, in the same way as in naam karan, kirtan and the *anand sanskar* (see below), the service has to take place in the presence of Guru Granth Sahib. Just as the panj pyare took amrit in front of Guru Gobind Singh, so too people today take amrit in front of the Living Guru. The second requirement for the *sanskar* is that in addition to the person taking amrit, there be six amritdhari Sikhs in attendance: one to read Guru Granth Sahib and the other five to represent the panj pyare. The rite has certain aspects that have been outlined in the *Rahit Maryada*:

- The person taking amrit should be of sufficient age, maturity and understanding.
- Taking amrit is available to all regardless of gender, age or caste.
- Each of the six and the person to be initiated should have bathed and washed their hair prior to the ceremony.
- Guru Granth Sahib should be opened. Any man or woman of any country, religion or cast who embraces Sikhism and solemnly undertakes to abide by its principles is entitled to ambrosial baptism.
- The person taking amrit will wear the 5Ks and stand facing the Guru, with their hands folded.
- If a person is seeking to retake amrit, they should be chastised by the panj pyare in front of the congregation.
- The panj pyare explain the principles of Sikhism to those taking amrit.
- This will be concluded with the question: Do you accept these willingly?
- With an affirmative response, one of the five will perform the ardas and take the Hukam.
- The five prepare the amrit. The bowl should be of steel and placed on a clean support. Clean water and puffs of sugar are placed in the bowl, and the five should sit around it. They will be seated in the *bir* position (sitting, the body rests on the right leg with the right calf and foot inward, and the left leg up to the shin is vertical).

- The five will recite the *Japji*, the *Jaap*, the *Ten Sawayyas*, the *Bainti Chaupai*, the first five and the last verses of the *Anand Sahib*.

- One of the panj pyare, while reciting the Gurbani, will hold the edge of the bowl with their left hand and stir the amrit with a double-edged sword held in their right hand. This should be done with full concentration.

- The four remaining panj pyare will hold the edge of the bowl with two hands and focus their attention on the amrit.

- One of the panj pyare will perform the ardas.

- Those being initiated will also sit in the bir posture. They put their cupped right hand in the cupped left hand and drink the amrit five times. The panj pyare who pours the amrit into the cupped hands says: 'Say, Waheguru ji ka Khalsa, Waheguru ji ki Fateh!' The initiate recites this back after drinking the amrit.

- Five handfuls of nectar are sprinkled into the eyes, and then another five into the hair of the person receiving amrit. Each of the sprinklings is accompanied by the person sprinkling repeating 'Waheguru ji ka Khalsa, Waheguru ji ki Fateh', and the initiate responding in kind.

- Any amrit remaining should be drunk by all amritdhari Sikhs present.

- The panj pyare recite the *Mool Mantar*.

- One of the panj pyare instructs those who have taken amrit in the responsibilities of the Khalsa (see Chapter 7). The rebirth into the Khalsa is highlighted:

Today you are reborn in the true Guru's household, ending the cycle of migration, and joined the Khalsa Panth (order). Your spiritual father is now Guru Gobind Singh and spiritual mother Mata Sahib Kaur. Your place of birth is Kesgarh Sahib and your native place is Anandpur Sahib ... You have become the pure Khalsa, having renounced your previous lineage, professional background, calling (occupation), beliefs, that is, having given up all connections with your caste, descent, birth, country, religion, etc. ... You are to worship none except the One Timeless Being – no god, goddess, incarnation or prophet.

- One of the panj pyare will perform the ardas.

- The Sikh reading Guru Granth Sahib will take the Hukam.

- If the person receiving amrit had not been through the naming ceremony, they renounce the previous name and are given a new name beginning with the first letter of the Hukam.

- Karaprasad is distributed, and the new Khalsa Sikhs will eat together from the same bowl.

The focus at this point in the book is the centrality of Guru Granth Sahib in the life and worship of Sikhs. As such, the responsibilities of Khalsa Sikhs will be explored in Chapter 7.

## Marriage/*anand sanskar* (joyful ceremony)

As with all important life events, the involvement of the Guru is paramount in the anand sanskar. Since the time of Guru Ram Das, *lavan* hymns have been traditionally recited during the wedding service. Article XVIII of the *Rahit Maryada* outlines various stipulations in terms of conduct and preparation:

- Sikhs should consider the caste and background of potential partners (the implications of such in terms of the belief in no caste distinctions is explored in Chapter 5).

- A Sikh woman should marry a Sikh man (the issue of this requirement in terms of gender equality will be explored in Chapter 5).

- A Sikh should be of marriageable age and married according to the *anand* rites.

- Horoscopes should not be required to determine an auspicious time. Following the example of Guru Nanak, all days are auspicious, and therefore the day should be fixed by mutual consent.

- Elements that are found in Hindu wedding ceremonies, such as red threads around the wrist and performing havans (sacred fires), should not be performed.

- The two sides of the marriage party greet each other by singing shabads and with the traditional greeting of 'Waheguru ji ka Khalsa, Waheguru ji ki Fateh'.

- All should be in the presence of Guru Granth Sahib.

- Singing of shabads should take place.

- Sitting facing the Guru, the bride will be to the left of the groom.

- The officiator will seek the permission of those assembled, and then ask the bride and groom to stand with their parents and offer the ardas to begin the wedding ceremony.

- The duties of a married couple will be explained by the officiator.

- The officiator explains the concept of a 'single soul in two bodies' and how it is a prelude to union with the Divine.

- The couple bows before the Guru to symbolize their acceptance of the duties of a married person.

- The bride's father (or closest relative) helps her take hold of the groom's sash, which is over his shoulder. The granthi reads the lavan shabads, and the couple circumambulate the Guru, while the congregation (or *ragis*) sing the appointed parts of the lavan.

- There will be four circumambulations of the Guru while the verses are sung. After each round, the couple will bow before Guru Granth Sahib.

- After the fourth circumambulation the couple will be seated. The officiator will recite the first five and last verses of the *Anand Sahib*.

- The ardas will be offered to end the ceremony, and karaprasad will be distributed.

Other prohibitions or things of note include that a non-Sikh cannot be married in the anand sanskar; there should be no dowry; remarriage following the death of a spouse is accepted; a man should 'generally' only be married to one wife; and it is an Amritdhari man's responsibility to have his wife take amrit.

The anand sanskar is much focused on Guru Granth Sahib and the Gurbani. The Guru is at the centre of all of the commitments that are made. It enables a person to be married in front of their Guru. Aspects of the requirements outlined by the *Rahit Maryada* for marriage will be discussed in relation to other aspects of Sikhism below.

## Death rituals/*antam sanskar*

Death is a natural part of the cycle of birth, life, death and reincarnation, the Gurus did not hesitate to talk about it. It is a reminder of the shortness of life and of the presence of *maya* in the world. A person should seek for a true perspective on death and its place in the search for union with Waheguru. The Gurus speak of it rather matter of factly, and Guru Nanak speaks of it as the ninth and tenth stages of a person's life:

> Ninth, he turns grey, and his breathing becomes laboured; Tenth, he is cremated, and turns to ashes. His companions send him off, crying out and lamenting. The swan of the soul takes flight, and asks which way to go. He came and he went, and now, even his name has died. After he left, food was offered on leaves, and the birds were called to come and eat. O Nanak, the self-willed manmukhs love the darkness. Without the Guru, the world is drowning. (Guru Granth Sahib 137–8)

As is evident from this bani, Sikhs will be cremated rather than buried. Article XIX of the *Rahit Maryada* outlines the rites associated with a funeral:

- The body of a dying or dead person should not be taken off the cot/bed/bier and placed on the floor.
- Those who are left behind should not engage in 'breast-beating'; rather, accepting the will of Waheguru, a mourner should recite Gurbani or repeat 'Waheguru, Waheguru, Waheguru'.
- A person should generally be cremated, but if this is not possible, then there is no problem for a body to be buried in another way.
- A cremation can take place at any time.
- The body is bathed and clothed, including in the wearing of the 5Ks.
- Prayers should be offered, and shabads may be sung.
- While the cremation takes place, those gathered should listen to kirtan or continue with the singing of shabad.
- The *Kirtan Sohila* (see Chapter 7) should be recited and prayers offered.

- At the home, or in the gurdwara, there should be a reading of Guru Granth Sahib, the *Anand Sahib* repeated and prayers recited, and karaprasad offered.

- The reading of the Guru should be completed on the tenth day (though this is flexible).

- The ashes should be dispersed in flowing water or buried at that place. A monument should not be erected.

Although there are many stages, the funeral service is very simple. Gurbani plays an important part at each stage of the mourning process. It remind those left behind of the temporality of life but also of the comfort that can come through the words of the Guru.

# Thoughts for the classroom

It is evident through an exploration of all of the rituals of Sikhism that Guru Granth Sahib plays an important role in each of them. Guru Granth Sahib is the Living Guru, and its presence at the important stages of a person's life is essential. In this chapter, we have explored how it is used within the gurdwara, along with the life-cycle rituals. The *Rahit Maryada* makes clear the centrality of such:

> The essential components of all rites and ceremonies in Sikhism are the recitation of the Gurbani (Sikh Scriptures) and the performing of the Ardas. (Article XXII)

When we explore Guru Granth Sahib, its place and use within the Sikh Panth, it is important to study how it is different from other holy books. It is viewed and treated very differently. To use it in the classroom as just a series of proof texts to illustrate beliefs is not sufficient to understand its role in the lives of Sikhs today.

There are many activities that we could have students undertake within the classroom with regards to Guru Granth Sahib. Exploring how it has been, and how it is, read will be of immense importance to recognize its contribution to Sikh life and identity. I am reminded of the comment of one Sikh:

> Having access to Waheguru directly through Guru Granth Sahib Ji is a never ending blessing. (Holt, interview)

It is possible, depending on the age of the students we teach, that an interrogation of hermeneutics may not be the best use of our time, and we might focus on how it is used in worship. What is key, however, is that we as teachers challenge the assumptions that we have. With a greater understanding of its place in Sikhism we can teach more authentically and provide a more accurate experience of the way that Sikhs live today.

# The Dasam Granth

For the vast majority of observers of Sikhism, the only 'holy book' or 'sacred writing' that they will be familiar with in Sikhism is Guru Granth Sahib. As was discussed in Chapter 3, there is also the Dasam Granth, which is believed to be the writings of Guru Gobind Singh that were collected together by Bhai Mani Singh after the Guru's death. From the time of Guru Gobind Singh until the nineteenth century, it would appear that the Dasam Granth was accepted as the writings of Guru Gobind Singh without question. Indeed, in many gurdwaras it was installed alongside Guru Granth Sahib, being described as the 'little brother' in contrast. We will discuss issues surrounding its acceptance as Gurbani, but first let us explore its contents, as some of these are questioned in terms of their validity. The eighteen sections of the Dasam Granth are:

- *Jaap Sahib*: a prayer describing the attributes of, and worship of, Waheguru. The *Jaap* is used in the daily prayers of Sikhs (see Chapter 7).
- *Akal Ustat*: in this section, the *Akal Purakh* is praised and the numerous names attached to the divine used, including reference to Hindu deities and Muslim descriptions. Although recognizing the universality of Waheguru, Guru Gobind Singh rejects an overemphasis on ritual.
- *Bachittar Natak*: an autobiography that begins before his birth in the court of Waheguru where the purpose of his birth is discussed.
- *Chandi Charitar*: mainly an exploration of the divine feminine using Durga, in the form of Chandi, as the focus of discussion. It is based on Markandeya Purana, a Hindu text.
- *Chandi Charitar II*: a further exploration of the divine feminine in the form of Chandi.
- *Chandi di Var*: a ballad of Durga, and the text suggests that it is based on *Durga Saptasati*, a Hindu text. The opening verses are often used in prayer.
- *Gyan Prabodh* or 'the awakening of knowledge': this text praises Waheguru; it uses many Hindu characters, including references to the Mahabharata.
- *Chaubis Avtar*: an exploration of twenty-four avatars of Vishnu.
- *Brahma Avtar*: an exploration of seven incarnations of Brahma.
- *Rudra Avtar*: an exploration of Rudra (Shiva).
- *Shabad Hazare*: nine hymns set to different rags. The sixth is full of grief and is believed to have been written after the death of his four sons.
- *Savaiye*: thirty-three verses that praise Waheguru, with reference to the Puranas, the Qur'an and the Bible.
- *Khalsa Mahima* or 'praise of Khalsa': in this, the Guru explains why offerings are given to Khalsa soldiers.

- *Shastar Naam Mala* or 'garland of weapon names': containing 13,000 verses, this section celebrates various weapons.
- *Sri Charitropakhyan*: this section tells tales that illustrate noble or weak behaviour. Some of these tales include descriptions of sexual exploits of characters.
- *Chaupai Sahib*: the last part of *Sri Charitropakhyan*.
- *Zafarnama* or 'letter of victory': a letter written to Emperor Aurangzeb admonishing him for reneging on promises. A celebration of Waheguru.
- *Hikayat*: twelve tales similar to *Sri Charitropakhyan*.

In discussing its authenticity as the writings of Guru Gobind Singh, Gurinder Singh Mann and Kamalroop Singh (2011) suggest that it was not doubted until the nineteenth century with an analysis by Cunningham (1915). Prior to this, writers such as John Malcolm (1812) identify it as a work of Guru Gobind Singh. Malcolm describes its place in the Sikh Panth:

> This volume, which is not limited to religious subjects, but filled with accounts of his own battles, and written with the view of stirring up a spirit of valour and emulation among his followers, is at least as much revered, among the Sikhs, as the Adí-Grant'h of Arjunmal. (51–2)

Although Malcolm may be overstating its status alongside Guru Granth Sahib, it is interesting that as an observer he sees them as being treated on a par. On observing worship at Harmandir Sahib, Malcolm further states:

> When the chiefs and principal leaders are seated, the Adí-Grant'h and Dasama Pádsháh ká Grant'h are placed before them. They all bend their heads before these scriptures, and exclaim, Wá! Gúrúji ká Khálsa! Wá! Gúrúji ki Fateh! (120)

Guru Granth Sahib and the Dasam Granth are placed in front of the congregation, and to his eyes, both are afforded the status of scripture.

A suggestion is made by Cunningham that elements of the Dasam Granth were composed by some of the poets in Guru Gobind Singh's court. There is no supporting evidence for this, aside from the seeming incongruity of Hindu deities and themes. There is the possibility that following the Anglo-Sikh wars, when the Khalsa had been forced to lay down their weapons, it suited British purposes to play down the more militaristic elements of Guru Gobind Singh's writings. The suggestion is that in so doing they were able to funnel Sikh soldiers, who were seen to be a 'martial' race (see Streets, 2004), into the army of the empire.

The elements of Hinduism were also a concern of elements of the Singh Sabha, which may have resulted in not as much emphasis being placed on the Dasam Granth as had previously been done. One element of Singh Sabha was to remove any vestige of Hinduism from the practice of Sikhism. As Mann and Singh (2011) suggest, there are parts of the Dasam Granth that are difficult to understand in terms of the symbolism and status that is afforded. The difficulty, in their view, is not a reason to dismiss the Dasam Granth as Gurbani. A study of it and of Guru Granth Sahib takes effort; in their view,

> people don't have the patience or feel they have time to have Santhia of Sri Dasam Granth and as a result the Internet becomes a substitute for their needs. The daily comments from self-proclaimed experts ... influences people's ideas on the Dasam Granth. (39)

Despite all this, the Dasam Granth has always retained its stamp of authenticity; there was even the Sodhak Committee in 1897 that found the Dasam Granth was indeed written by Guru Gobind Singh. This was reiterated in a hukamnama in 2000, 2006 and 2008 that there should cease to be a debate about the authorship of the Dasam Granth (66).

It is still the case that the Dasam Granth is not used in a significant way in gurdwaras; but its status should not be in doubt for Sikhs. It is used and referred to by individual Sikhs in striving to understand Guru Gobind Singh and elements of Sikhism.

## Thoughts for the classroom

It is interesting that the Dasam Granth is not really found within the classroom until Key Stage 5. There may be mention of *Zafarnama* at GCSE as it impacts on Sikh views on war, but the richness of its teachings is not really explored. Neither is its place within the Panth. There are many elements of it that might present a mixed view of Sikh teaching. This is not in itself problematic as we are striving to teach pupils about the different ways to be Sikh. However, even within the Panth the way to understand the Dasam Granth is seen to be difficult. It does not have the same straightforwardness of Guru Granth Sahib, but elements could be used to explore the teachings and place of Guru Gobind Singh. As mentioned in Chapter 3, if all we focus on is the creation of the Khalsa and his militaristic efforts, then we are doing him, and his legacy, a disservice. The Dasam Granth refers to different religious figures, and these may serve as a springboard for how Sikhs view other religions. Using the texts of Hinduism to illustrate the teachings of Sikhism enables a person to see how Sikhism was helping people of the time understand how that which they had grown up with could be repurposed to understand Waheguru. This approach, in itself, is also a challenge to an understanding of Sikh views of Hinduism.

# Chapter 5

# Equality

An outworking of the Sikh beliefs about the nature of humanity, and one of the main themes of the Gurus, is the teaching of equality. This is, perhaps, one of the most known teachings that is found within the *Panth* and in the teachings of Guru Nanak and his successors. According to the teachings of Sikhism there is to be no division among humans because of gender, religion, race, caste and any other contracted notions that people use to cause division and treat others differently. In this chapter, we will explore the nature of equality in the teachings and examples in the lives of the Gurus. We will also look at how that equality may or may not have been shown within the history of Sikhism and the reality of equality today in the Sikh Panth.

## Equality at the time of Guru Nanak

Bhai Gurdas suggested:

> He preached in this darkage (kaliyug) that, saragun (Brahm) and nirgun (Parbrahm) are the same and identical. Dharma was now established on its four feet and all the four castes (through fraternal feeling) were converted into one caste (of humanity). Equating the poor with the prince, he spread the etiquette of humbly touching the feet. Inverse is the game of the beloved; he got the egotist high heads bowed to feet. (Bhai Gurdas, Var I:23)

### Caste

From the earliest times of Guru Nanak there has been a rejection of caste within Sikhism. The establishment of *langar* by Guru Nanak is evidence enough of his radical egalitarianism where he mandated that all should eat together at the same table. By this one act, he established a practice that challenged the core of the concept of caste that lay at the foundation of many aspects of Indian society. This, combined with a belief in the spark of divinity within all, ensures that the message of Sikhism is one that rejects divisions within society.

When we look at the lives of the Gurus, it is easy to see the equality they taught. Guru Granth Sahib is clear on the rejection of all caste distinctions and discrimination:

Pride in social status is empty; pride in personal glory is useless. The One Lord gives shade to all beings. (Guru Granth Sahib 83)

God does not ask about social class or birth; you must find your true home. That is your social class and that is your status – the karma of what you have done. (Guru Granth Sahib 1330)

The idea that a person can be unclean or impure because of their identity is against the central teachings of the Gurus; only that which they do can make a person impure:

If one accepts the concept of impurity, then there is impurity everywhere. In cow-dung and wood there are worms. As many as are the grains of corn, none is without life. First, there is life in the water, by which everything else is made green. How can it be protected from impurity? It touches our own kitchen. O Nanak, impurity cannot be removed in this way; it is washed away only by spiritual wisdom. The impurity of the mind is greed, and the impurity of the tongue is falsehood. The impurity of the eyes is to gaze upon the beauty of another man's wife, and his wealth. (Guru Granth Sahib 472)

That this ideal was not followed by all Sikhs is evident in the life of Guru Gobind Singh. Approximately two hundred years after the institution of the langar, the Guru introduced the *amrit* ceremony for entrance or initiation into the Khalsa. As already mentioned in Chapter 3, the *panj pyare* were representative of different castes. That they would drink from the same bowl used the same symbolism as that of the langar. This symbolism suggests that the rejection of caste, for some Sikhs, was a 'nice' teaching as long as it did not require any change to their behaviours. Indeed, in response, many Khatri Sikhs refused to take amrit claiming to be following the teachings of Guru Nanak. Singh Mandair (2013, 62) suggests that the establishment of the Khalsa and its attendant rites and obligations was seen to be an act of 'destructive violence'. The first act of destruction was in the social structures that provided status to the Khatris; this position in society would be lost if the *amrit sanskar* was fully implemented and its implications lived. The second act of destructive violence was the wearing of weapons.

It is suggested that in the eighteenth and nineteenth centuries, Khatri Sikhs continued to coexist alongside Khalsa Sikhs, but as the Khalsa fought for survival against the Mughal Empire, the Khatri Sikhs assumed a leadership role in the Panth. This was made possible by their gaining control of many gurdwaras throughout India. These Khatri Sikhs were also known as 'Sanatan Sikhs', and it is possible to see that in addition to their following of the teachings of Guru Nanak, they were determined to rise above the practices of the Khalsa and maintain their position in the social hierarchy. It is against this background that the Singh Sabha movement arose in the nineteenth century, and there was a renewed focus on *Tat Khalsa* or the 'true Khalsa'. As noted in Chapter 1, there are varying views on the contiguous nature of this approach and the desirability of an 'orthodox' Sikhism.

It is interesting to note that in contrast to the message of the Gurus, division on the basis of caste still persisted. This is more of a reflection of the way that caste was fully embedded into many aspects of Indian society. While a rejection of caste would be attractive to many who found themselves lower down in society, for those who held a privileged position, it was a direct challenge to the power they held and the influence they had. In the classroom, we quite rightly teach that the message of Sikhism, and particularly of the Gurus, is one of shattering all artificial divisions in society. We can use examples from the lives of the Gurus and the various periods in the history of Sikhism to explore fully how the teachings were lived.

The history of Sikhs in Britain can also show how when the community was small, the focus on the unity of Sikhs was important, but as the community grew, it became 'important' to reassert aspects of diversity. Darshan Singh Tatla and Gurharpal Singh (2006, 74) illustrate this by reference to the development of gurdwaras in Birmingham:

> Castes and sects that were initially together in the founding gurdwara have gone on to establish their own institutions, either because of discrimination or because of a desire to preserve a distinctive sub-identity.

Gurdwaras in Birmingham were subsequently developed by the Bhatra community, Angaria Sikhs, Ravidasi Sikhs (who perhaps are now no longer Sikhs) and Ghumar Siktr Sikhs. Similar sequences of events can be found in London and Leicester, which underline the 'evolution of both denominational and caste pluralism and factional rivalries' (74).

It is not just in history that we can explore the absence of caste in the Sikh Panth. While recognizing the importance of a casteless society, there are indications that living up to the ideal is still problematic. Tatla (2008) suggests that Sikhism in the modern world has thirty social groups that could be described as part of a caste. He suggests that of the total Sikh population, approximately two-thirds are Jat, one-tenth are Ramgarhia or Rahitia, with Dalits at approximately 15 per cent and Khatris at about 5 per cent. One response to the question 'How is equality shown in your community and in Sikhi more widely?' indicates that there are still residual caste distinctions in aspects of Sikh practice:

> It is not, we are Jatt and only associate with other Jatts. Our Gurdwara is Jatt only, an unnamed but 100% followed rule. All Gurdwaras in India and the diaspora continue to follow this. Large disconnect between theory and practice. (Holt, interview)

Recognizing that there is a disconnect between theory and practice is an important first step, but it also shows that there is a way to go before the theory is realized.

McLeod (2007) suggests that during the time of the Gurus, and prior to the Singh Sabha movement in the nineteenth century, the rejection of caste was based on *varan* (varna). In this the Gurus rejected the idea that people were born higher or lower, but there was an acceptance of jati, meaning the groups within which people are born, to give them a sense of identity and idea about their roles in society. McLeod suggests that

> the Sikh notion of caste (in theory at least) requires the elimination of the varan differences. Note this is not saying that Sikhs reject the jati concept, only the varan. The varan concept remains but it is shorn of all differences of status. (112)

He further argues that in striving to remove all vestiges of Hinduism from Sikhism, the Singh Sabha movement removed all aspects of jati, which had never been the Gurus' intentions. Many within the Sikh community would reject this and suggest that from the time of the Gurus, all concepts of caste were rejected. This would be supported by the commentary of observers who noted the rejection of caste within the Panth. Jagjit Singh (1996, 356) has suggested that 'the greatest social achievement of the Sikh revolution is that it severed connection of the Sikh Panth with the Indian caste system'. To suggest otherwise, he argues, is to ignore the reality of Sikhism and the tendency to view all of the societies of India as the same.

It could be seen to be the nature of humanity to seek the company of people who are seen to be similar; however, any worldview that seeks to divide and discriminate is rejected by the Sikh belief that the *naam* is within all. The *sangat* transcends all divisions, and this is a goal towards which all Sikhs are working as they strive to be *gurmukh*.

## Thoughts for the classroom

When we teach about the rejection of caste in Sikhism, it is important to establish what the Gurus taught and what the practices of Sikhs reflect. There is an undoubted equality; the design of Harmandir Sahib with its four doors that all join a single causeway is a physical reminder to all people that everyone is welcome, and they have the same path to Waheguru. Whatever the age of the students we teach, it is important that we recognize this basis. Also important, however, as students increase in their understanding is to explore the lived experiences of people and Sikhs today. This may seem to be challenging, both to the teacher and also to the message of Sikhism. It does, however, reflect the reality of life in the Sikh Panth. It is only through recognition of such disconnects that the 'messiness' of religion can be recognized. Teachers and pupils can begin to recognize the challenges of belief and the many influences that come into play when exploring a person's individual worldview. There is no doubt that caste is rejected, but sometimes actions suggest otherwise.

It is for this reason that I think, in this area and many others, that the use of authentic voices is crucial in the classroom. Listening to the voices of Sikhs as they articulate what they believe and how they live their lives enables the true experience of Sikhism to be reflected. A 'chocolate box' approach to Sikhism would teach this equality and leave children with the suggestion that every Sikh lives this perfectly. A messy or worldviews approach helps pupils recognize the challenge of faith.

## Gender equality

The place of women in Sikhism and in Gurbani is one of total equality with men. There is no difference among those who seek union with Waheguru. Guru Nanak taught:

> From woman, man is born; within woman, man is conceived; to woman he is engaged and married. Woman becomes his friend; through woman, the future generations come. When his woman dies, he seeks another woman; to woman he is bound. So why call

her bad? From her, kings are born. From woman, woman is born; without woman, there would be no one at all. (Guru Granth Sahib 473)

A woman's role and the basis for her equality is not relational in Sikhism. Rather, she is able to experience the Divine as a reflection of the naam that is within her. There are many examples throughout Gurbani and the lives of the Gurus that show the complete equality of men and women. The outlawing of sati, the appointment of women as *manji/puris* and many other aspects reflect this equality.

However, as may have been noted, in our recitation of the lives of the Gurus in Chapter 3, it was very much told in the traditional way, focusing on the experiences of the men in the narrative. Only occasionally did we pause to consider the contribution of women. This could be seen to be a shortcoming of the history that has been told. To fully articulate Sikh history and life in a way that is authentic to the egalitarian message of the Gurus, we need to hear the voices of women. In terms of an exploration of the Panth today, this may be straightforward in that we can include the experiences of Sikh women, and also avoid an overemphasis on the male experience; and we certainly do not portray the male experience as the normative expression of Sikhism. In terms of history, this is more difficult, but people like Nikky-Guninder Kaur Singh have begun this discussion. In exploring the events in *The Birth of the Khalsa*, she has suggested:

> In our re-memory we look not just for invisible women but also look for the invisible womb of men. We must, of course, discover the feminine voice of hidden women. But I want to go even further and find the hidden feminine voice in Guru Gobind Singh's text. (2005, 4)

She continues that there is a danger in only reading the texts and history of Sikhism with a patriarchal background and voice. It distorts the message of the Gurus and erases the experiences and importance of women within the Panth:

> How do we find female themes and motifs here? The task is undoubtedly daunting. But it is critical, because generations of Sikhs have been fed on this overly 'patriarchal' discourse, producing and reproducing male dominant structures in their society. The Khalsa has remained a brotherhood, almost a militaristic fraternity, from which women have been pretty much excluded. (5)

Some Sikhs today recognize this as an important issue facing the legitimacy of the Panth to live up to the teachings of the Gurus. Consider the following statements:

> Gender equality is words only!
> We talk the talk but don't fully apply [equality] in everyday life.
> There is no inequality in Sikhi. Sikhi is a path. People practise inequality based on the worst aspects of our nature in every community.

These reflect the tension within the Sikh Panth with regards to the realization of equality and the equal treatment of women. When we return to the concept of worldviews described in the introduction to this book, it is important to note that Sikhism is a Panth that is not resistant to cultural influences. This may well be the case in terms of the issue of gender equality within Sikhism; some of the Sikhs involved in discussions in the development of this book suggest that Sikhism is equal, but aspects of Punjabi culture take precedence in some aspects of Sikh living. It is very difficult to extract cultural influences from decades or centuries of religious living, but many Sikhs do and live the full realization of the message of the Gurus.

In aspects of the practice and belief of some Sikhs, there is a way to go. Jakobsh (2006b) notes the great emphasis that is placed on the role and status of women in Sikhism, particularly in comparison to other religions. She uses a popular website from the Institute of Sikh Studies to highlight the prominent place women have in the sangat:

> A Sikh woman has equal rights to a Sikh man. Unlike Christianity, no post in Sikhism is reserved solely for men. Unlike Islam, a woman is not considered subordinate to a man. Sikh baptism (Amrit ceremony) is open to both sexes. The Khalsa nation is made up equally of men and women. A Sikh woman has the right to become a Granthi, Ragi, one of the Panj Pyare (5 beloved) … Christian women must change their names after marriage. The concept of maiden and married names is alien to Sikh philosophy. (188)

Certainly, this is the teaching of Sikhism and also the practice in some Gurdwaras. Indeed, this approach builds on the teachings and example of the Gurus; for example, Guru Amar Das, in appointing the manjis throughout the Sikh Panth, drew on both women and men. Their qualifications were their knowledge of Gurbani and their trustworthiness, rather than any issue of gender. Jakobsh then compares this passage outlining the opportunities afforded to women in Sikhism, with the reality of her observations. She suggests that, in contrast to this ideal:

- It is rare for women to be *granthi*s or panj pyares.
- A married woman seeking to take amrit will usually be asked to have her husband accompany her.
- Women are able to cook, clean and serve as part of langar but are often unable to enter the room housing Guru Granth Sahib.
- In Harmandir Sahib, women are never a part of the panj pyare in the distribution of *karaprasad*. This is where the first five are given the food before it is offered to the rest of the assembled community.

There is also the example given by Nikky-Guninder Kaur Singh (2000) where she attended the funeral of her father. According to tradition, it is the son who has the honour of lighting the funeral pyre. Her brother had been unable to attend the funeral, and instead of Kaur Singh, as his closest relative, lighting the fire, the honour was given to a male non-family member. This disconnect between the teaching of gender equality and the traditions/expectations of the community leads her to the conclusion that women have come to rely on men in their communication with the divine … instead of searching within. They do not publicly question women's omission from Sikh rites of passage, nor do they celebrate women's affirmation in their sacred literature. (7)

There are indications, however, of the reclamation of the views of the Gurus in terms of gender equality when exploring the lives of British Sikhs today. It might be possible to suggest that the clash of culture with Western British society has actually facilitated a deeper exploration of issues of gender. Singh and Tatla (2006, 178) suggest that the picture in Britain today has begun to break out of the cultural norms, at the same time as the rise of powerful and self-sufficient women who challenge these norms and stereotypes:

The traditional Punjabi machismo, still so faithfully replicated in bhangra and Punjabi media, appears to be losing its hegemonic position as new expectations and practical necessities demand the recognition of equality.

Although precipitated by engagement with wider British society, this is entirely congruent with the message of the Gurus. Equality is one of the hallmarks of Sikhism, and while it may have been fully lived up to during some periods of history, it is possible to see a reclamation of female Sikh identity in light of the examples and teachings of the Gurus and many women of the Panth.

Two ways that gender equality is expressed in the Panth today is through the example of women in history and society today, and a reclamation of imagery and teachings that seemed to be reflective of the patriarchal discourse evident in society.

There are many Sikh women, throughout history and today, who can be used as inspiration for all members of the Panth in exhibiting how to live the life of someone seeking to embody Sikh principles and become gurmukh.

## Mata Khivi (1506–82)

Mata Khivi was the wife of Guru Angad. When we explored the life of Guru Angad, his propagation of the teachings of Guru Nanak and development and regulation of the langar were emphasized as important contributions. This was only part of the story as in both of these developments Mata Khivi made a significant contribution. She was one of those responsible for the spread of Sikh teachings, and she also took responsibility for the development and supervision of the langar. The care she took in preparing the langar meal showed the selfless service required of all Sikhs, and it came to be referred to as 'Mata Khivi Ji da Langar' (Mata Khivi Ji's langar). Her loving kindness and service is described in Guru Granth Sahib:

Balwand says that Khivi, the Guru's wife, is a noble woman, who gives soothing, leafy shade to all. Today, Gurdwaras serve millions of people every day and serve as her legacy. She gave the message of equality which makes all the children of God entitled to food. (Guru Granth Sahib 967)

It is important to note that Mata Khivi is not inspirational purely because of her relationship to the Guru, but her inspiration is all her own. This is an important aspect of any teacher's exploration of gender issues in the classroom. A woman's importance is not because of her relationship with a man. After the death of Guru Angad, she continued to live a life of compassion and love for a further thirty years. Sikhs follow her example even today in the joyful and compassionate service of langar.

One specific example of her love of the *bani* and of the Guru relates to her son, Datu. Recognizing his hurt feelings at being passed over as Guru, he was encouraged by friends to declare himself his father's successor. At the same time as he was planning to do so, he developed headaches. Mata Khivi encouraged him to seek reconciliation with the rightful Guru, Amar Das, and took him to meet the Guru. Guru Amar Das came out of his house to meet him, and they were reconciled. Mata Khivi was the catalyst in preventing a schism in the Panth at this early stage.

The life of Mata Khivi is an example of the importance of telling the full story when reciting events from the Guru's lives. As far as is possible we should include the contributions and influence of women. A further example of how this can happen is exemplified in the story of Baisakhi 1699. In the classroom the story can often be told without reference to gender. The role that Mata Sundari played in this story is an important aspect of the retelling of the story, as are the many women who took amrit at the time of the founding of the Khalsa.

## Mai Bhago (Kaur) (1666–unknown)

Mai Bhago is an inspirational Sikh woman, who, through her example and devotion to the Guru, is remembered for the rallying of Sikhs who had lost heart. She lived during the time of Guru Gobind Singh, when the Panth was subject to harrying by, and battles with, the Mughal Empire. The Guru had built a series of fortresses, and with his soldiers, he was forced to move between the different fortresses, and, at times, they were subsisting on the bare minimum of rations. After many months of this kind of living, forty of his retinue left the Guru and the Khalsa to return to a more normal and stable life in 1705.

One of the forty was Mai Bhago's husband. Her act of challenging not just the deserters but also her own husband is a symbol of courage. She also rallied the women of nearby cities and convinced the women in the cities to refuse hospitality to the forty. She also set about organizing an army of forty women to replace the deserters. The forty men were shamed, and they agreed to join with Mai Bhago and rejoin the struggle and renew their commitment to the Khalsa.

Thereafter, when the forty-one (the forty men and Mai Bhago) were on their way to request forgiveness of the Guru, and permission to take amrit again, it was discovered that the Mughals were in the process of laying siege to the Guru's fortress. With the Sikhs being outnumbered, the forty-one rushed forward to cut the Mughals off. They fought with valour, defending the Khidrana reservoir, and set ambushes for the Mughals. Along with the actions of the Gurus' existing forces, the Mughals had no choice but to withdraw. Of the forty-one, only Mai Bhago survived, and the forty are now known as *challi mukta* (forty liberated ones).

A greater example of the devotion to the Guru required of a member of the Khalsa perhaps finds no greater expression than in the life of Mai Bhago. Of course, the story of Sikhism can be told without her, but it would be much poorer and miss the equality of all that is inherent in the Khalsa.

## Inderjit Kaur (1923–2022)

Inderjit Kaur was a woman of many accomplishments. She became the first female vice-chancellor of a North Indian university, when she was appointed at the Punjabi University in Patiala. She had also served as the first woman on the board of Khalsa College in Amritsar. She was born in pre-partition Punjab, and when Partition happened she was part of a group that set up a charitable organization, Mata Sahib Kaur Dal. This helped over four hundred refugee families at Patiala. The work of the charity was collecting clothes for refugees. It also set up Mata Sahib Kaur Dal School, Patiala, for children of refugees. Inderjit Kaur also set up, and participated in, self-defence training for female refugees and topped the shooting competition.

There are many other examples of Inderjit Kaur's accomplishments, but as a more modern example of a Sikh woman who accomplished much she could serve as an example of the equality and opportunities available within the Panth. This is not to say there are no obstacles, but changes come incrementally, and there are many women today grabbing those opportunities. Within each local community there will be women who are doing tremendous things, and by seeking to use their stories the importance and power of women within Sikhism can be fully expressed.

## Prakash Kaur (1951–)

One final example is that of Prakash Kaur, who is head of a foundation called the Unique Homes Foundation, which in turn is run by a trust named after Bhai Ghanayya, a companion of Guru Gobind Singh. Prakash Kaur was abandoned as a child, and this led her, in 1993, to establish a home for children rejected by society. The foundation, based in Jalandhar, provides a home for sixty girls to receive the care that they need to have the life opportunities they were denied in being abandoned.

## Language and symbols

The overwhelming image of a Sikh that can be found throughout society is of a bearded Khalsa Sikh man. This perpetuates the myth in wider society that only men are Amritdhari or Khalsa Sikhs. It is interesting that the language and examples that are used unknowingly perpetuate this narrative. One such example is the Twitter account 'LookASingh' with the idea of publishing Sikh appearances in the media. The intention of the account seems to be very positive about the recognition of Sikhs in the media, and images show both men and women; but in the use of the terminology 'Singh', it appears that Sikhs are Singhs, rather than both Singhs and Kaurs. The view may be that women can be Sikh, but that, perhaps, the obligations of the Khalsa are only incumbent on men. This is far from the truth, and as is evidenced by the examples of many women today and throughout history, the Khalsa is available to all. It could be suggested that this is an inheritance of the reformation and formulations of the Singh Sabha movement in the nineteenth and early twentieth centuries. Interestingly, however, the 2020 British Sikh Report indicates that women are far less likely to be Amritdhari than men. Nikky-Guninder Kaur Singh (2005) suggests that the perceived norm of Khalsa identity has been reinforced throughout history and society. Part of this is being overcome through the example of many female Khalsa Sikhs. It is also being reclaimed by a reinterpretation of the language that is used to explore issues within the Panth.

In terms of language, Nikky-Guninder Kaur Singh suggests, in light of the Gurbani that emphasizes equality, that by 'focusing on the feminine dimension, we discover that Sikh literature is replete with rich feminine symbols and imagery' (1993, 3). Kaur Singh (2005) has also discussed the appropriation language and symbolism. One of the most fundamental reclamations would be the language that is used around the Divine or Waheguru. I have tried to be very conscious to avoid the male pronouns when referring to Waheguru. Indeed, the use of the word 'God' may lend itself quite naturally, because of a Western inheritance, to the use of 'he', 'him' or 'his' in describing the Divine. It is evident from the *Mool Mantar*, and many other teachings of the Gurus, and particularly, Guru Nanak, that Waheguru is without gender, indeed Waheguru is both mother and father:

> I am a child – You cherish and sustain me. You are the Great Primal Being, my Mother and Father. (Guru Granth Sahib 1319)

The recognition of the genderless nature of Waheguru, and including the feminine aspects of the Divine, rather than an overfocus on male metaphors, can help Sikhs, and observers of Sikhism, fully realize the importance of the feminine. Tracing the presence of the divine feminine in the writings of the Gurus, and linking it with how women are respected, Nikky-Guninder Kaur Singh (1993, 244) suggests:

> She is mata the creator, the preserver, and the nurturer; she is mati, the epistemological ingredient; and she is nadar, the benevolent glance necessary for our salvation. The birth of all life begins with her raktu (menstrual blood).

These expressions of femininity may be alien to some, but the reclamation of the feminine in understanding the nature of Waheguru is important for understanding the role and importance of women. Men and women can both find themselves in Waheguru, just as they can both find Waheguru within themselves. Waheguru is genderless but can also be experienced as both. The problems of inequality arise when one is given precedence.

One further example that Kaur Singh uses is that of the sword as a male image illustrating how a non-gendered, or perhaps more specifically a bi-gendered, object has fed a patriarchal narrative. However, it is possible to return to the ways that the Gurus understood the symbol to revitalize the feminine in Sikh language, belief and practice. This is entirely congruent with the nature of existence and the nature of Waheguru. In Sikh teaching, there is both unity and duality; Waheguru is self-existent and One but is at the same time both 'mother' and 'father'. To overly focus on one element of existence is to miss the point of Sikhism. The gendered discourse of Sikhism can be seen to be needing to be addressed to ensure that the entire nature of existence of Waheguru can be experienced and understood.

Returning to the symbol of the sword mentioned above, it is possible to view this image as non-gendered, though it is traditionally seen to be male. Nikky-Guninder Kaur Singh (2005) suggests that the sword is both a male and female image, but only its male overtones are focused on. It is, in tandem with its destructive potentiality, also a creative force shown throughout the Dasam Granth, but also through its use in the birth of the Khalsa. The mixing or creation of amrit is only possible when the sword is utilized. Without recognizing the femininity of the sword as 'an inspiring symbol for creativity with the capacity to function like a pen or paintbrush', its power is lost. It 'ends up merely as an intimidating sign of male power' (7). Recognizing its militaristic and creative applications in Sikh teaching will help recapture Sikh identity as one of celebrating the equality of the feminine.

## Thoughts for the classroom

There is an inherent equality in Sikhism and its practices. The *Rahit Maryada* makes clear that the rites of Sikhism, including amrit sanskar, are available to all regardless of gender. The recalibration of Sikhism in the nineteenth century regarding the condemnation of female infanticide and sati, practices condemned by the Gurus, highlights that cultural practices and norms should not replace the central teachings of Gurbani.

In the classroom it is important to note the differences between religion and culture, and also that cultural expressions of religion are important to explore. This, as has been noted, is an important tenet of a worldviews approach. Exploring the 'theory' alongside the 'practice' enables students to be able to explore the lived reality of a religion. As suggested in this section, there are many examples within Sikhism of women who have lived lives that can be used as examples of the principles of Sikhism. It is important that we enable women's voices to be heard. Part of this is to use authentic voices; what are the experiences of female Sikhs today? How do their experiences marry up with the teachings and examples of the Gurus? We need to explore representation in the classroom. How many of the pictures and examples that we use are male? We can be guilty of perpetuating the patriarchal view of Sikhism.

Some teachers may be concerned with articulating the view that women may not always find full equality in the Panth. This is why the use of authentic voices is key. This is not just the teacher's opinion; rather, we are using examples from within the community to explore any disparity. Nikky-Guninder Kaur Singh is an important writer in exploring the feminine within Sikhism, and using voices from within the Panth enables a level of criticality that is important in presenting a Sikhism that is far more than a neatly packaged chocolate box.

## Religious freedom

A major theme that arises when the lives of the Gurus are explored as a complete narrative is the focus on the importance of fighting for and protecting the rights of all people. The most compelling example is the martyrdom of Guru Tegh Bahadur, where Sikhs see his martyrdom as a result of his protecting the religious freedom of the Hindus who sought his help. This event is celebrated each year as Bandi Chhor Divas and is a reminder of the importance of this principle. The focus on Sikhism is the way that a person lives:

> One who practices truth, righteous living, charity and good deeds, Has the supplies for God's Path. Worldly success shall not fail him. (Guru Granth Sahib 743)

This suggests that of utmost importance for the Sikh is the provision of the circumstances where a person can perform good deeds, regardless of religion.

The declaration of Guru Nanak that there is no Hindu or Muslim illustrates the fruitlessness of religious argument; there is only one Waheguru who should be sought. A passage in Guru Granth Sahib reads thus:

> The world is going up in flames – shower it with Your Mercy, and save it! Save it, and deliver it, by whatever method it takes. (Guru Granth Sahib 853)

Some translations have 'through whichever door (religion) humanity approaches' at the end suggesting that there is efficacy in each religion. One Sikh has suggested that the four doors of Harmandir Sahib may also be symbolic of four paths to Waheguru – Sikhism, Buddhism, Hinduism and Islam (the four that were most known in India at the time). This is not an interpretation found anywhere officially, but it does reflect the Sikh attitudes to religion – that Waheguru is variously described (a fact found throughout Guru Granth Sahib and the Dasam Granth) but that all are striving to understand their relationship with the same naam. One example is found in relation to Islam in Guru Granth Sahib:

> Let mercy be your mosque, faith your prayer-mat, and honest living your [Qur'an]. Make modesty your circumcision, and good conduct your fast. In this way, you shall be a true Muslim. Let good conduct be your Kaabaa, Truth your spiritual guide, and the karma of good deeds your prayer and chant. Let your rosary be that which is pleasing to His Will. O Nanak, God shall preserve your honour. (Guru Granth Sahib 140)

The Gurus take the principles found in 'other' religions and repurpose them to help people understand how they can truly be on the path to becoming gurmukh.

This does not mean that there is no falsity; indeed *maya* can obscure the search for Divine by placing illusory obstacles in the way. These may be seen to include what could be described as 'empty' rituals as shown in the writings and experiences of Guru Nanak and the other Gurus. The emphasis is, however, that all have the opportunity to discover the naam within, and the good deeds and beliefs of others can lead people to Waheguru.

## Thoughts for the classroom

The importance of religious freedom is found, but sometimes it can be overemphasized to provide an overly positive view of Sikhism. While the Gurus were able to recognize the positive aspects of religious living, they would also reject empty ritual, or concepts such as caste, that were seen to be in direct contradiction to the Sikh message. Indeed, elements of the Khalsa are to distinguish Sikhs from people of other religions. The command to abstain from meat killed in a halal way or to avoid wearing of the veil stand in direct contrast to Islam, while the prohibition against piercing and the use of images of deities contradict Hinduism. Indeed, the nineteenth-century book *We Are Not Hindus* shows the desire to stand apart from other religions. This dichotomy is of interest to explore in the classroom.

The main focus for positive aspects of religious freedom would begin with Guru Tegh Bahadur. The accessibility of Bandi Chhor Divas at different levels for different ages provides an entry point for discussion of religious freedom and the Sikh Panth. The use of the 'other' religious parts of Guru Granth Sahib and the Dasam Granth is equally interesting in the classroom to see how religious beliefs can be repurposed to help present the message of Sikhism.

## Living in sangat

*Sangat* is a word that is roughly translated as 'fellowship' or 'community'. Two other variations are often used:

- Sadhsangat, meaning a fellowship or group that is seeking the truth

- Satsangat, meaning 'true fellowship' or community

Although having slightly different meanings and emphases, these terms are often used interchangeably to refer to a group or community of Sikhs. This can be a small group, a large community or the worldwide community of Sikhs (this book has tended to use the word 'Panth' to indicate the worldwide community, but 'sangat' is also appropriate). The purpose of sangat is to bring together people who can help each other on their spiritual path to union with the Divine.

> The True Guru is found in the Sat Sangat, the True Congregation. Day and night, praise the Word of His Shabad. (Guru Granth Sahib 22)

The first sangat was established by Guru Nanak at Kartarpur. Bhai Gurdas highlights the importance of living in sangat:

> The true Guru Nanak Dev inspired people to remember the true name of the Lord whose form is truth. Founding dharamsala, the place for dharma, at Kartarpur, it was inhabited

by the holy congregation [sangat] as the abode Word Wahiguru was imparted (by Guru Nanak) to the people. (Bhai Gurdas Var XXIV)

As with the sangat at Kartarpur, the sangat today is open to all regardless of gender, caste or any other distinction. Being together, seeking to understand Waheguru inspires and strengthens people.

These communities have had different manifestations throughout history, such as with the *masand* system. Today there can be informal gatherings of Sikhs or more commonly the formal gatherings of Sikhs in the gurdwara. As the world changes, there are many different ways of meeting in sangat, some of which may now be virtual. These can occur in chat rooms, on social media, over video calls and via email chains. It is important to recognize that sangat is not just a community of friends, rather it is about the search for truth. Guru Granth Sahib recognizes that in sangat Waheguru can be found:

Joining the Sat Sangat, the True Congregation, I ask about the Path to God. In that Congregation, the Lord God abides. (Guru Granth Sahib 94)

Without sangat, it is impossible for a person to experience the Divine and become gurmukh (see Guru Granth Sahib 266 and 282). The influence of maya is increased when one does not have the companionship of like-minded people who are seeking Waheguru. People may not notice the negative or positive impact of the company they are keeping for a long time; but the concept of sangat helps a person develop those qualities that reflect that of being gurmukh. Guru Granth Sahib teaches:

Kabeer, the mind has become a bird; it soars and flies in the ten directions. According to the company it keeps, so are the fruits it eats. Kabeer, you have found that place which you were seeking. You have become that which you thought was separate from yourself. Kabeer, I have been ruined and destroyed by bad company, like the banana plant near the thorn bush. The thorn bush waves in the wind, and pierces the banana plant; see this, and do not associate with the faithless cynics. (Ang 1369)

The concept of sangat helps a Sikh understand that it is a person's actions that reflect whether they are gurmukh or *manmukh*, rather than the circumstances of birth, gender, caste or anything else that seeks to differentiate humanity. A Sikh should live in *satsangat* and feel the presence of Waheguru, not least through the presence of others.

## Thoughts for the classroom

Sangat is an area that is rich for the exploration of concepts of equality, support and friendship. The strength of the community or fellowship comes from the desire to work towards the same goal – that of union with Waheguru. In addition to seeking the companionship of those who will build up and strengthen an individual in this search, it is incumbent on the individual to be that type of person for others. The responsibility of the focus on sangat is on everyone, to provide an environment and community that helps.

Central to this concept of sangat is the equality of all; as mentioned, the community at Kartarpur set the example of sangat as the Abode of the Creator. This is, in the end, the purpose of sangat.

It would be interesting in the classroom for teachers to explore the various ways that a community can be with, and strengthen, each other. The world has changed significantly since the time of the Gurus in human form, and as such so have the opportunities for sangat. The benefits of such 'virtual' places might be that the ideal of equality can be lived up to, as they 'exist on neutral ground and serve to level their guests to a condition of social equality' (Oldenburg, 1999, 6). This links, very well, with the way the people all around the world keep in touch and develop that sense of community.

# Chapter 6

## Sewa

*Sewa* (shortened from '*karasewa*' meaning 'selfless service') is arguably one of the most identifiable characteristics of a Sikh, and of Sikhism more broadly in the modern world. Guru Granth Sahib outlines the importance of sewa as a way of seeking union with Waheguru:

> One who performs selfless service, without thought of reward, Shall attain his Lord and Master. (Ang 286)

> You shall find peace, doing seva (selfless service) … In the midst of this world, do seva, And you shall be given a place of honor in the Court of the Lord. (Ang 25–6)

Sewa lies at the heart of Sikhism and what it is to be Sikh. In the true action of sewa a person is able to combine selfless service with a remembrance of the Divine. Guru Granth Sahib teaches that a person who performs sewa (*sewadar*) should focus on Waheguru:

> Centre your awareness on seva-selfless service-and focus your consciousness on the Word of the Shabad. Subduing your ego, you shall find a lasting peace, and your emotional attachment to Maya will be dispelled. (Ang 110)

The act of sewa is an act of worship. To an observer this may not be immediately observable, but in serving others the spiritual and the temporal can find true expression. A Sikh is able to be selfless and reject ego through a focus on the needs of others and the remembrance of Waheguru. Returning to the nature and purpose of existence explored in Chapter 2, we are able to see how *maya* is overcome or reality is brought into focus by focusing less on the self and the ego. The service that is given is of great importance for those who are served, but in an irony that we have already observed, as a person seeks less of the self they find the true nature of the self, and are a step further towards union with the Divine.

The concept of sewa, as well as building on Sikh beliefs about reality, also builds on the expressions of sewa that are found throughout the Guru's lives. As we explore the expression of sewa today, we will necessarily build on the example of the Gurus. There are seen to be three main forms of sewa:

- *Tan* (the physical aspect of sewa)
- *Man* (the mental aspect of sewa)
- *Dhan* (the material aspect of sewa)

# Tan

Tan is the physical aspect of sewa, where a person does something to help or serve someone else. This is perhaps the highest form of service, being seen in some societies as the lowest form of work. The Gurus sought to highlight the value of both the spiritual and the physical. In the society in which Sikhism developed, some of the most physical tasks were carried out by those who were considered the lower castes. Physical/manual work was sanctified by the Gurus and finds its expression in the key expression of sewa: *langar* (see below). The act of peeling onions or cleaning tables expresses humility but also enables a person to overcome the ego that may consider such work beneath them. In considering some work as beneath them, it is possible that a Sikh is reflecting on how they will be affected or viewed, rather than the service this gives to other people and to Waheguru.

The manual labour or work reflected in tan extends far beyond the langar. Any aspect of physical work can be considered sewa, if it is not done in expectation of reward; this could include shopping for someone else, babysitting and countless other activities. The reading, or fanning, of Guru Granth Sahib can also be seen to be an act of physical service.

# Man

'Man' is the mental aspect of sewa. This is the utilization of a person's talents to help the Sikh and wider community. Every person has different talents and abilities, and these can be used in many different ways. In the Sikh community in Southall, there are examples of 'Sunday Schools' where there are classes to learn Punjabi and Sikhism. The teachers donate their time freely to help the younger members of the community.

Other examples in the UK include the Guru Nanak (Gravesend) Football Club, attached to the Guru Nanak Gurdwara. Established in the 1950s, they are a non-league football team that have players and coaches from different cultures and backgrounds. They also include children's teams; those who give sewa as part of the football club are sharing their talents and highlight that they are striving to develop every aspect of a child's life, in terms of mental and physical health.

These examples show that in 'man' there is little limit to the expression of sewa. Each individual has talents that they can develop and share to help others. Those 'others' may be individuals or groups. There may also be some who do not have the physical ability to help others or the financial circumstances to do so; 'man' is the expression of sewa that can be practised by all.

# Dhan

Dhan is the material aspect of sewa, where a person donates or gives something in an act of sewa. This may be goods or money. In terms of the langar (discussed below) a person may give produce that can be used or money to purchase the produce. *Dasvandh*, or the giving of 10 per cent of one's wealth, falls into the category of dhan. In today's world, material wealth may be seen to be the main distraction from Waheguru; it provides the distraction outlined in Chapter 2 that highlights the material world as maya. When a Sikh focuses on their ego and the accumulation of material wealth as the end purpose, they see no need to seek the *naam* within. The giving of material wealth helps dissolve the ego and keeps a Sikh centred on what is important. Examples throughout the history of Sikhism in Britain highlights the sacrifices of people in the Sikh community to build and maintain gurdwaras.

One key aspect of the British Sikh Report 2020 was a focus on organ donation as an act of sewa. The suggestion was that over two-thirds of Sikhs considered organ donation to be an act of sewa. This is highlighted in the British Sikh community by the personalization of the issue in the Hope4Anaya campaign. Anaya Kaur Kandola was born with a condition called autosomal recessive polycystic kidney disease (ARPKD), which is both rare and complex. She required a kidney transplant as part of her treatment; the possibility of a donor match was greater within the Punjabi community. This highlighted to many in the Sikh community a person who was representative of so many in need. The example of organ donation typifies the nature of selfless service but also the fact that the conception of sewa is broad and can apply in all aspects of life. This type of sewa can also be seen in India where many Gurdwaras have medicine dispensaries building on the example of Guru Har Rai.

In some ways the division of sewa into tan, man and dhan is both helpful and unhelpful in exploring Sikhism. On the one hand, recognizing the three different types enables a person to see the different ways that they can seek to live the principle of sewa. The activities that Sikhs might consider as sewa include:

- supporting those in need, cooking, cleaning and serving in the langar;
- by realizing the Divine every breath becomes an act of sewa, and therefore, constantly serving Him and His creation;
- charity donations to hospices, Great Ormond Street Hospital, Khalsa Aid and so on;
- helping the homeless;
- with love, in any possible way presented by Waheguru.

On the other hand, they can be seen to be somewhat artificial separators; below we will explore the practice of langar as one of the most obvious examples of sewa in the Sikh community. This does not fit easily into one aspect and could be considered to be combine two or three of them. At the end of the day, it is sewa, and the categorization of it is immaterial.

## *Langar*

As we saw in Chapter 3, langar was established by Guru Nanak and then developed and utilized as a key principle by the succeeding Gurus in human form. The story associated with the founding of the practice of the langar is rich with meaning for Sikhs.

As a young man Guru Nanak was a source of concern for his father, Mehta Kalu. He was so distracted by spiritual matters that his father wondered how he would make enough money to be successful and feed his family. Determined to help Guru Nanak become a trader, he gave him twenty rupees to buy commodities such as salt and turmeric that he could then sell. It was a lesson in how to use money wisely and put it to good use. Guru Nanak's father even sent a servant with him to ensure that a good bargain was made.

After a time, Guru Nanak and his companion came upon holy men in a forest who were deep in meditation in yogic postures. They were ascetic and had taken vows of poverty. Guru Nanak decided to give the money to the holy men, who would then have be able to buy food and clothes. He felt that this was good use of the twenty rupees. Over the protestations of his companion, Guru Nanak placed the twenty rupees in front of the holy men. They refused the money but did agree that Guru Nanak could go to a local village and buy food for them as they had not eaten for seven days. So this is what Guru Nanak did and then watched gladly as the men ate the food.

Although he had experienced gladness in feeding the holy men, as he was returning home, he thought of the way his father would react. Instead of returning home, he sat under a tree on the outskirts of the village. Realizing that his servant had returned without his son, Mehta Kalu got the servant to tell his story. Despite the interventions of his mother and sister, Nanaki, Guru Nanak was subjected to his father's anger. It was, however, a lesson that the Guru learned, and passed on to his followers – that there is no greater use of wealth than to share food with those who are hungry.

This story laid the basis for the establishment of the langar at Kartarpur, where none were turned away and all ate together, male and female, regardless of caste. As has been noted, this was developed further by Guru Angad and Guru Amar Das. Though entirely congruent with Guru Nanak's message, there were two complementary aspects of the langar that continue to this day:

- to feed the hungry; and

- to share a communal meal.

These are not mutually exclusive, but they do show different benefits and emphases in the langar for Sikhs today, both reiterating key principles of Sikhism – that of sewa and care for the poor, and the importance of *sangat*.

One of the key features of a gurdwara today is the Guru's kitchen: the langar. It puts into action the principle of sewa and reflects the teachings and examples of the Gurus:

> The Langar – the Kitchen of the Guru's Shabad has been opened, and its supplies never run short. (Guru Granth Sahib 967)

In each gurdwara, there is a large kitchen and a langar hall where all sit on the floor to eat the meal together (there will be exceptions to sitting on the floor, except usually due to age and infirmity). All aspects of the langar are donated: the food (either directly or from a financial donation) and the preparing, cooking and serving. This service is also found within Harmandir Sahib, where thousands of meals are prepared each day; and the washing of the steel trays is said to produce a cacophony of sound.

The meal is available to all, and as such what is served is vegetarian so that all can join in the meal. The sewadars who are involved in this service can be seen to be showing aspects of 'tan' and 'man' in that they are sacrificing of material goods and their time. Each of these sewadars contributes this sewa willingly and happily. In some gurdwaras there are often waiting lists for the donation and service of langar.

The sharing of a meal enables a sense of community or of sangat to develop. As people eat together, any distinctions between people are broken down, and people, as they converse, recognize the light of the Divine within all. Eating together is an opportunity for service but also to build relationships through which the reality of existence can be found.

For some in the Sikh community, the communal aspect of the meal is that which is most often seen. Although all are welcome, there may be a limited ability to welcome those truly in need into the gurdwara. This is a reality of modern life in the UK, where people may not be willing to enter, or even know that they can enter a gurdwara. For some Sikhs, this has been unacceptable, and they have sought to find ways to extend the reach of the Guru's kitchen and the langar.

One such example is the charity Feed My City in Manchester run by Sikh Foundation Manchester. This is an emergency food charity that provides hot meals and dry food bags to those in need. All food is vegetarian and free of charge. A person can self-refer or refer others to receive assistance. Alongside this, there is a food truck that goes to places where there are people most in need, such as the homeless. This sewa is available to all regardless of race, religion and gender and is seen by its founders to be the true expression of the message of Guru Nanak.

## Thoughts for the classroom

Sewa is a principle of Sikhism that seems to bring together the teachings of the Gurus. As such, it is possible that its teaching will be found in all of the different key stages. In the earlier key stages pupils may explore the concepts of equality and sharing as shown in the practice of the langar. It is important, as children's understanding increase, that they make explicit links to the teachings of Sikhism and the examples of the Gurus to see the central importance of sewa to Sikh life and identity. Again, a utilization of authentic voices to describe their experiences and motivations is key in recognizing the way that sewa is underpinned by belief. Often, it is possible to teach sewa as a practice with no reference to the underpinning beliefs but it is inadvisable. For example, the service of all of humanity reflects the belief that the naam is within all.

Within the teaching of religion in schools, a focus on personal knowledge is important (Ofsted, 2021). In exploring sewa and associated practices, it is possible to begin with the children's own understandings of service, equality and sharing. Thereafter, having learned the Sikh principles and practices, it is important to return to the children's knowledge to understand what they have newly learned, and how they situate themselves in understanding a person's responsibility to serve and treat others equally.

# Chapter 7

# Expressions of Faith

In exploring expressions of faith by Sikhs in the way that they live their lives, it is important to bring together all of the elements that we have explored so far in the book. In essence we are beginning to look at the main expressions of a person's faith, or of their desire to become *gurmukh*. It might be true that when a person is developing in their understanding of Sikhism, either as a child, an older convert or someone who is returning to the *Panth* later in life, they will be fulfilling responsibilities and duties based on a knowledge only of what they are 'supposed' to do. The ideal, however, is that they express their beliefs through the actions and practices that are considered to be religious.

With this as a caveat, it is important to note that every aspect of Sikh belief will, in some way, find expression in the way that a Sikh lives their life. It is evident from the previous chapter that the practice of *sewa* expresses belief in the *naam* that is within all; in the Gurus and in following their example; and also in the concept of equality that lies at the heart of the message of the Gurus and the path to becoming gurmukh. While sewa might be a 'good' or 'nice' action without these beliefs, the beliefs are what make sewa intelligible and important in a Sikh worldview.

As we go through this chapter we will explore some key practices that lie at the heart of Sikh living today. Links will be made with beliefs that we have explored already, but there may well be links that are not made. This does not mean that they are not there, but it is just space that precludes a fuller exploration. It is hoped that individuals will begin to draw links for themselves between the beliefs and practices that we explore. Elements of Sikh expressions of faith have been described in Chapter 4 where the life-cycle rituals of birth, marriage, death and the *amrit sanskar* were explored in terms of the events that happen and also how they link to the importance of Guru Granth Sahib. These will not be repeated here, but they could be revisited by the reader as a way that the beliefs in Sikhism find expression to key events in a person's life.

Interestingly, if we were to look at the vast majority of classrooms that are teaching Sikhism within the UK, whatever key stage they might be, the expression of faith that will be most commonly explored (perhaps to the exclusion of others) is the 5Ks. I am not suggesting that they are not important, and indeed, they will be explored as an expression of faith later in the chapter. This approach, however, is a very reductive approach to Sikhism that perhaps reinforces a martial expression of Sikhism that misses the internal spirituality important within Sikh living. Just because it is the most noticeable identifier does not mean it is where should begin and end our exploration of Sikhism. The importance of the 5Ks will be explored, but what is noticeable for me, in my conversations with Sikhs, when we speak about the practices that are expressions of faith, is that they begin the discussion with *piri* – those parts which are focused on the spiritual. It is not that *miri* is not important but just that there is a balance to be struck, and for most Sikhs the spiritual is the main focus of everyday life. Consider the following activities that Sikhs have identified as important in their daily lives:

- Remember the Lord every second of the day, praise him and do good deeds.
- Strive to remember the Divine in all aspects of life. Reading the daily prayers is only a minute part of daily worship.
- Daily individual prayer and with *sangat* (congregation) at the gurdwara.
- Daily worship, morning and evening.
- *Naam japo, vand chhako, kirat karo.*
- Acceptance of the Divine through spiritual and physical practices. That is, acceptance of Divine presence in all beings and acceptance of nature's work through long, uncut hair.

These spiritual aspects will be explored in this chapter, along with the need to recognize the role of *tegh* and *degh*, alongside *miri-piri*, in striving to achieve justice and equality for all. All of these practices are fully rooted in the physical world identified in the time of the Gurus as the life of a householder, but combining them with a spiritual focus and impetus. The first three that will be explored have been variously described as the 'three pillars' of the teachings of Guru Nanak: naam Japo, vand chhako and kirat karo.

## *Naam japo*/naam simran/meditation on the *naam*

Although meditation on the naam could be seen to form part of the religious expression of a Sikh, it is inextricably linked with the nature of humanity and the ability to understand the true nature of existence, becoming gurmukh and the attainment of *sach khand*. As such it is important to explore this central feature of connecting and uniting with Waheguru. It is through *naam simran* that a Sikh is able to escape *haumai* and overcome the egocentric nature of *maya*. The importance of meditation on the naam is shown throughout Guru Granth Sahib:

> It is a good time, when I remember Him in meditation. Meditating on the Naam, the Name of the Lord, I cross over the terrifying world-ocean. With your eyes, behold the Blessed Vision of the Saints. Record the Immortal Lord God within your mind. Listen to the Kirtan of His Praises, at the Feet of the Holy. Your fears of birth and death shall depart. Enshrine the Lotus Feet of your Lord and Master within your heart. Thus this human life, so difficult to obtain, shall be redeemed. (Guru Granth Sahib 190)

Meditation on the naam is the way that a person receives the grace of the Guru, which enables the illusion of maya to be shattered and the reality of existence to be understood. Naam simran is often practised by the repetition of the name of the Divine. It is a practice that is 'commanded' in the *Rahit Maryada* – that a person should adopt this practice each day. Through this recitation a person is able to access the naam within and draw closer to Waheguru. Using the name of Waheguru as a focus for meditation means that a person is able to reflect on the qualities of the naam and purify their minds.

> Meditating, meditating, meditating in remembrance, I have found peace. I have enshrined the Lotus Feet of the Guru within my heart. The Guru, the Lord of the Universe, the Supreme Lord God, is perfect. Worshipping Him, my mind has found a lasting peace. Night and day, I meditate on the Guru, and the Name of the Guru. Thus all my works are brought to perfection. (Guru Granth Sahib 202)

Although, most common is the repetition of the name 'Waheguru', there are seen to be nearly 950 names of the Divine that are outlined in Guru Granth Sahib (Singh, 2006, 176). Individuals are able to vary the name of their meditation as all are the naam. This meditation is seen to inspire a person to action and to live the qualities of a gurmukh. Earlier, in Ang 202, Guru Arjan suggests: 'The giving of hundreds of thousands, billions and trillions in charity – these are obtained by those whose minds are filled with the Name of the Lord.' It is not purely an esoteric practice but a motivator that finds concrete expression in the lives of an individual and in the sangat.

There are specific *bani* that can be recited each day, which enable a Sikh to strive to find union with the Divine. These are called *nitnem* (daily routine/habit) and are usually recited in the morning, evening and just before retiring to bed. These are required of Amritdhari Sikhs, but many others similarly recite them with varying degrees of consistency.

## Morning prayer

From the time of the Guru, morning prayer or worship has been a hallmark of Sikh devotion. In the time of Guru Angad, after early morning devotions, Sikhs would engage in exercise, highlighting the importance of both aspects of Sikh life. The *Rahit Maryada* suggests:

> A Sikh should rise early, bathe and meditate on the one true God. (Section 1)

Today, the recitation of the five bani in the morning prayers is an essential part of striving to unite with Waheguru and also of preparing for the day ahead. The five bani that are recited as a part of the morning prayer are:

- *Japji*: this is the first teaching/hymn in Guru Granth Sahib covering Angs 1–8. The *Japji* is mainly written in praise of Waheguru, and as such its recitation reminds Sikhs of their relationship to the Divine, as well as the characteristics and ineffability of

Waheguru. See Chapter 1 for a greater discussion of the *Japji* and its description of Waheguru.

- *Jaap*: this is the first hymn of the Dasam Granth, composed by Guru Gobind Singh. It has been suggested that *Jaap Sahib* is to the Dasam Granth what the *Japji* is to Guru Granth Sahib (see Chapter 4 for a greater exploration of Guru Gobind Singh's composition). This, again, focuses on the qualities of *Satguru*. One excerpt highlights this:

Salutation to Thee O Omnipotent Lord!
Salutation to Thee O Doer Lord!
Salutation to Thee O Involved Lord!
Salutation to Thee O Detached Lord!
Salutation to Thee O Kindredless Lord!
Salutation to Thee O Fearless Lord! (Dasam Granth 5)

This being only a small part of the *Jaap Sahib* shows that the focus and time needed for a meditation on the naam is not insignificant. The time enables a Sikh to reflect on Waheguru, the qualities associated with the Divine and the desire to become gurmukh and attain *mukti*.

- *Tav-Prasad Savaiye* or *Sudha Ustat*: this is a composition of Guru Gobind Singh from the Dasam Granth. It is suggested that it was composed for Bhim Chand to highlight the fact that riches, soldiers and kingdoms do not enable a person to achieve union with Waheguru. It is a long passage but highlights the futility of human ego–focused action, and the blessings available to those who meditate on the naam. A sample from *Tav-Prasad Savaiye*:

But O King! Without the remembrance of the Name of the Lord, all this is of no account, being without an iota of the Grace of the Lord. The trained soldiers, mightly and invincible, clad in coat of mail, who would be able to crush the enemies. With great ego in their mind that they would not be vanquished even if the mountains move with wings. They would destroy the enemies, twist the rebels and smash the pride of intoxicated elephants. But without the Grace of the Lord-God, they would ultimately leave the world. (Dasam Granth 39)

The focus is always on the maya/illusion of ego-focused action and the reality of those able to access the truth through the Guru's grace.

- *Chaupai Sahib*: this is bani composed by Guru Gobind Singh. This recitation is an *ardas* (request) of Waheguru for protection. It begins:

Protect me O Lord! with Thine own Hands
all the desires of my heart be fulfilled.
Let my mind rest under Thy Feet

Sustain me, considering me Thine own.
Destroy, O Lord! all my enemies and
protect me with Thine own Hands.
May my family live in comfort
and ease alongwith all my servants and disciples.
Protect me O Lord! with Thine own Hands
and destroy this day all my enemies
May all the aspirations be fulfilled
Let my thirst for Thy Name remain afresh.
I may remember none else except Thee. (Dasam Granth 2743)

The recitation of this bani enables a Sikh to remember their dependence on Waheguru.

- *Anand Sahib*: this is one of the bani of Guru Amar Das. It is called *Anand* because it is believed that a person who recites this can receive *anand* (complete bliss or happiness). Beyond the morning recitation of bani, it is also recited at many Sikh religious rites and services. It is found in Guru Granth Sahib (1917–22) and is an emotive description of the bliss that Guru Amar Das found in his union with Waheguru. It begins thus:

  One Universal Creator God. By The Grace Of The True Guru: I am in ecstasy, O my mother, for I have found my True Guru. I have found the True Guru, with intuitive ease, and my mind vibrates with the music of bliss. The jewelled melodies and their related celestial harmonies have come to sing the Word of the Shabad. The Lord dwells within the minds of those who sing the Shabad. Says Nanak, I am in ecstasy, for I have found my True Guru. (Guru Granth Sahib 917)

  The words of Guru Amar Das serve as reminder of the bliss of union but also of how to attain that same union.

Each of these *Gurbani* used in the morning devotions helps a Sikh meditate on the naam and understand more the reality of existence and the nature of humanity, and it is hoped that through the recitations they can achieve union with Waheguru. Its placement at the beginning of day establishes its significance as the first thing that a Sikh will do and Waheguru being the first thought or remembrance of the day. One Sikh suggests that these prayers take approximately thirty minutes, and that it is important to remember them as a basis for the other aspects of life and the living of the other principles of Sikhism.

## Evening prayer

The evening prayer is known as *rehras*. These prayers take place at dusk as the day and night come together. Within the rehras are bani from five Gurus in human form: Guru Nanak, Guru Amar Das, Guru Ram Das, Guru Arjan and Guru Gobind Singh. The part from Guru Gobind Singh was added in the late nineteenth century. The Gurbani that are recited are:

- *sodar*, which is found in Guru Granth Sahib (8–10);
- *sopurkh*, which is found in Guru Granth Sahib (10–12);
- *Chaupai Sahib*, which is found in the Dasam Granth and is also part of the morning prayer; and
- *Anand Sahib* (6 *shabad*s), which is found in Guru Granth Sahib (917–22) and is also part of the morning prayer.

These prayers can be recited individually but can also be part of a family's devotion in the evening, following a day of work. The recitation of the evening prayers enables thanks to be given to Waheguru on the completion of the day but also helps reorient the mind from the day spent in the world of work and some of the mundane aspects of existence. Each of the shabads reminds the Sikh of the importance of meditation on the naam but also of the greatness of Waheguru. This is an important reminder and brings equanimity of mind. In the evening prayers, Sikhs

> pay homage to the Transcendent Reality, they sing praises of Divine Magnificence, they seek the protection and succour of the omnipotent Creator, and they express their joy on hearing the melodious Word within their inner self. (Kaur Singh, 2011, 84)

This passage from Nikky-Guninder Kaur Singh is a reminder that all elements of worship and devotion within Sikhism are opportunities for introspection and for a connection with the Divine within oneself.

## Night-time prayer

The night-time prayer is known as *Kirtan Sohila* and contains bani from Guru Nanak, Guru Ram Das and Guru Arjan and consist of five shabads, found in Angs 12–13 of Guru Granth Sahib. This prayer is recited before a person goes to sleep, sometimes while the person is sitting in bed. The five hymns explore different themes in a person's relationship with Waheguru.

- The first shabad compares death to the moving of a bride into the home of her husband. Death is spiritual joining of the individual soul to Waheguru. At this point, a devotee should remember the naam. It is perhaps the theme of this shabad that has led to the tradition that *Kirtan Sohila* is recited at funerals.
- The second shabad explores the nature of Waheguru in being a unity and diversity (see Chapter 1). The shabad uses metaphors to try and understand these aspects of Waheguru.

> There are six schools of philosophy, six teachers, and six sets of teachings. But the Teacher of teachers is the One, who appears in so many forms. O Baba: that

system in which the Praises of the Creator are sung-follow that system; in it rests true greatness. The seconds, minutes and hours, days, weeks and months, And the various seasons originate from the one sun; O Nanak, in just the same way, the many forms originate from the Creator. (Guru Granth Sahib 12–13)

- The third shabad is a hymn of Guru Nanak in praise and adoration of Waheguru.
- The fourth shabad explores the humility required of people before the Gurus and others in order to attain union with Waheguru.
- The fifth shabad pleads for spiritual effort in this life to attain mukti:

  Within the home of your own inner being, you shall obtain the Mansion of the Lord's Presence with intuitive ease. You shall not be consigned again to the wheel of reincarnation. (Guru Granth Sahib 13)

Each of these prayers focuses on an individual's relationship with Waheguru and is a way for a Sikh to meditate on the naam and the characteristics of Waheguru. Through this a person can begin to experience the naam and Divine within themselves.

The prayers themselves are an exercise in discipline, and an effort to remember Waheguru throughout the day. Although it is a requirement of Amritdhari Sikhs, many Sahajdhari Sikhs also strive to fulfil different elements of nitnem. One Sahajdhari Sikh suggested that while he will complete the morning prayers each day, his recitation of the evening and night-time prayers are less regular and that there are times that he will listen to them rather than recite them. In this way, he feels that he is doing his best in striving to become gurmukh.

## The *Ardas*

The ardas is a formal prayer of supplication that is used within Sikh life. The word is an amalgamation of two Persian words: *Araz* and *Daashat*. In putting these words together the resultant word becomes the petition of a slave to a master. As explored in Chapter 4, it is used in services in the gurdwara and also by an individual before or after undertaking a task. In some Sikh homes, the ardas is repeated before the eating of food. An individual recites it by standing with folded arms, whereas in communal worship one person will stand with folded arms while others stand with their hands placed together in prayer (though the *Rahit Maryada* suggests that they, too, should have the arms folded).

There are generally seen to be three sections to the ardas:

- The first part praises and reflects on Waheguru. The first line is:

  One Absolute Manifest; victory belongeth to the Wondrous Destroyer of darkness. May the might of the All-powerful help!

- The second discusses the example and sacrifices made by Sikhs throughout history. This highlights the importance of history for Sikh identity and practice today. The example of *shahidis* is a particular focus.

- The third section often changes and is where supplications are made on the basis of the occasion. Forgiveness is asked as part of the ardas.

In this prayer, Waheguru, the Sikh sangat throughout history, the congregation today and the individual are brought together. It unites the Panth and helps a Sikh understand aspects of their faith that will bring them closer to Waheguru. It also helps them understand that every aspect of life relies on Waheguru and their faith as a Sikh.

## Thoughts for the classroom

It is important to remember when teaching Sikhism within the classroom that there are many different ways to live as a Sikh. As such, while the remembrance of/meditation on the naam is a central aspect of Sikhism, there are many different ways to make this an aspect of daily life. Could there be an aspect of remembering the naam that manifests itself in vand chhako and kirat karo? The answer would be in the affirmative, even though an aspect of the naam is not recited. As pupils explore the nature of naam japo and the recitation of nitnem, it is important that the actual prayers are used to enable pupils to understand the purpose of prayer. There are aspects that are about petitions on behalf of the individual or of others, but the daily prayers that are prescribed are about reinforcing an understanding of Waheguru and the nature of humanity and existence. Only through this spiritual aspect of life can a person hope to find union with Waheguru in this life.

Naam japo is, however, only one of the three central pillars of Sikh teaching. In line with the teachings and examples of the Gurus, it is impossible for one solely focused on such activities to find union with Waheguru. The saintly life must be combined with that of a householder who lives as a part of the material world and puts into action the other aspects of Sikh teaching.

## *Vand chhako*

> Says Kabeer, listen, O my mother – the Lord alone is the Provider, for me and my children. (Guru Granth Sahib 524)

Waheguru is the source of everything in life. As such, nothing truly belongs to an individual, and a Sikh is to share that which they have. In this way, they focus less on the self and the ego (see Chapter 2) and are able to be selfless. The sharing of one's wealth takes place in community.

Within Sikhism there are many opportunities for a Sikh to share that which they have in selfless giving and service. Vand chhako links very closely to sewa, explored in Chapter 6. The various aspects of giving of oneself in terms of tan, man and dhan are described extensively in Chapter 6. The additional aspect of vand chhako is the giving of *dasvandh* in charity. Many Sikhs will also see the invitation to give one-tenth to extend to their time as well, whether that is in naam japo or sewa, they are giving of themselves in devotion to Waheguru.

Material wealth in itself is not bad, but when it becomes the focus of a person's life, they are mired in maya and allowing maya to disguise the truth of existence. Only through remembrance on the naam can a true perspective of material wealth be acquired. When a Sikh realizes this, they are able to share their wealth with others, as indicated by vand chhako.

## Kirat karo

Kirat karo is a central pillar of Sikhism that suggests a person should follow an honest living. Everything a Sikh earns should be earned honestly, and there should be no dissimulation in the way that they carry out their work. In seeking an honest living Sikhs are able to exercise the talents and abilities which Waheguru has bestowed on them. As such an important aspect of honest work is the remembrance of the naam.

> Those who have meditated on the Naam, the Name of the Lord, and departed after
> having worked by the sweat of their brows – O Nanak, their faces are radiant in the Court
> of the Lord, and many are saved along with them! (Guru Granth Sahib 8)

As already mentioned, in distinction to ways of renunciation, the way of the Guru is that of a householder. In kirat karo and other aspects of Sikhism, the physical and the spiritual merge. The one cannot be without the other. Just as Waheguru is *nirgun* and *sagun*, just as the Gurus wear the swords of *miri and piri*, so a Sikh should combine living in the world with a remembrance of the naam.

The importance of earning an honest living is told within a story of Guru Nanak. On approaching Eminabad, he was met by a poor carpenter, Lalo, who invited the Guru and Mardana to stay with him. The Guru agreed and spent a number of days with Lalo enjoying the hospitality and the 'simple' fare that Lalo served with devoted attention. While Guru Nanak was staying with Lalo, a rich man of the village, Malik Bhago, held a great feast to which he invited many people. However, Guru Nanak did not attend. This made Malik Bhago angry, and he confronted the Guru, essentially asking, 'Why do you refuse my food, yet eat the simple fare of a carpenter?'

In response, the Guru accompanied Malik Bhago to his feast saying that he saw no difference between the two men. He did, however, take some of Lalo's food with him. On arriving at the banquet, the Guru held Lalo's food in one hand and Malik Bhago's food in the other. When he squeezed each, milk ran out of Lalo's offering while blood flowed out of Malik Bhago's.

The Guru explained that Lalo made and served the food that he had worked hard for, and therefore it was clean. However, Malik Bhago's food was not clean because it was not earned by hard work; rather it was bought through work in which he was unkind and mean. That was why blood had come out of it, symbolic of the blood he asked of his workers and associates. The Guru told him to work honestly using his own hands.

## Thoughts for the classroom

In the way that religion is sometimes understood in the West, there are elements of a person's life that are religious and others that are seen to be separate. Within Sikhism this dichotomy is seen to be false. The 'three pillars' of Sikhism show that all aspects of a person's life are expressions of their faith. The way that a person remembers Waheguru in meditation and prayer; the way that they remember Waheguru through honest work combined with a meditation on the naam; the way that they use their wealth and serve other people. Each of these actions in turn is seen to reject the maya of ego and enable a Sikh to begin to recognize the naam within. It has been reiterated throughout this book that Sikhism is not a world-renouncing religion but a world-embracing one. Waheguru needs to be found in community and in the act of living.

The three pillars are of immense importance in helping students understand how every aspect of a person's life is lived in relationship with Waheguru. Utilizing, again, the authentic voices from Sikhs, the equanimity of mind and selflessness that such an approach brings is evident. It seems counterintuitive that thinking of Waheguru and others first would enable a person to live a happier and more fulfilled life. However, using the voices of Sikhs students would recognize the importance of following these principles and the effect it has on people's lives.

# Gurdwara

As noted in Chapter 3, the word 'gurdwara' is normally translated as 'door/abode of the Guru'. We also noted that it might be better translated as 'Guru's grace' (suggesting that a gurdwara is somewhere that the grace of the Guru can be experienced or received). This idea links with the concept explored in Chapter 5 of sangat. In the midst of the *sadhsangat* Waheguru can be found. Both of these understandings of gurdwara reflect the nature and purpose of the buildings today. Reiterating the discussion around the use of words such as 'baptism', I think it is important that as teachers we use the word 'gurdwara' instead of 'temple'. Again, this is a term that is used to help non-Sikhs understand the place and function of a gurdwara. The word 'temple' loses the focus of the gurdwara as the abode of the Guru.

It may appear odd to include a discussion of the gurdwara in a chapter on 'expressions of faith', especially as throughout this book we have explored various aspects of activities that take place within the gurdwara (see Chapters 3, 4, 5, 6 and earlier sections of this chapter). These activities might be better termed 'expressions of faith' rather than the gurdwara itself. The activities that take place in a gurdwara discussed so far include:

- langar,
- kirtan,
- meeting in sangat,
- naming ceremonies,
- marriages,
- amrit sanskar,
- funerals,
- the ardas and
- the procession of Guru Granth Sahib in the morning and evening.

Most of these activities are focused around Guru Granth Sahib and reflect its place as the Living Guru. There are many other beliefs that are reflected in both the design and the use of the gurdwara. As most of the activities have been explored, in this section, we will explore the design of the gurdwara and how this reflects Sikh beliefs and the practicalities of Sikh expression as a community.

Generally, the main features of a gurdwara are seen to be:

- Guru Granth Sahib,
- *diwan* hall with a throne for the Guru at the front;
- sach khand, or room for Guru Granth Sahib to rest;
- *Nishan* (flag) *Sahib* and
- langar kitchen and hall (sometimes called *pangat* (row)).

There will be ancillary features, such as shoe racks, washrooms and administrative offices, and some larger gurdwaras have sleeping places where travellers can stay. There is no set architectural pattern for gurdwaras, but they are often patterned after aspects of Harmandir Sahib in Amritsar; thus domes may often be found on purpose-built gurdwaras. In areas of small Sikh populations, gurdwaras may be found in converted homes. Indeed, these types of buildings were of the type used in the days when Sikhs were establishing their presence in the UK. It was in the 1960s and 1970s that purpose-built gurdwaras began to be seen in Britain as communities became more established and funds were able to be raised. The gurdwara became important as a community centre, a place where Sikhs could gather and develop their understanding and identity as Sikhs, in sangat.

Most of the features of the gurdwara listed above were discussed in Chapters 4 and 6. The feature that has not yet been discussed is the *Nishan Sahib*. This is the flag that is flown outside of every gurdwara to indicate to Sikhs and non-Sikhs that this place is a gurdwara. It is replaced each year at Baisakhi.

Nishan Sahib has its roots in the raising of a flag over Akal Takht by Guru Hargobind; this was originally a flag of *basanti* yellow. Guru Gobind Singh changed the flag to a blue

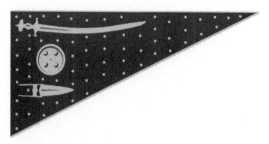

**Figure 7.1** Nihang Nishan Sahib (usually in blue and white colours). Copyright Charles Singh. This file is licensed under the Creative Commons Attribution-Share Alike 4.0 International Licence.

**Figure 7.2** Nishan Sahib (colours of saffron and blue) in the public domain.

colour, and the early flag had the three symbols of the *kattar* (dagger), *dhal* (shield) and *kirpan* (sword) (see Figure 7.1); this flag continues to be used by Nihang Sikhs today.

Sometime during the early nineteenth century, perhaps under the auspices of Maharaja Ranjit Singh, the Nishan Sahib was changed to saffron with the image of the *khanda*, similar to the one used by many Sikhs and gurdwaras today (see Figure 7.2). The flag itself can be seen to be a symbol and an expression of faith.

It is evident on closer examination that the three symbols from the earlier Nishan Sahib are replicated on the khanda. The dagger or two-edged sword in the middle, the kirpans around the outside and the dhal (circle) in the middle. The symbolism of each helps to understand aspects of Sikh beliefs and as such are expressions of faith.

The khanda (double-edged sword) reminds Sikhs of the birth of the Khalsa in 1699 as the *amrit* was, and is, prepared by stirring water and puffs of sugar with the double-edged sword. The right-hand edge of the sword symbolizes freedom and authority, which are supported and ruled by the moral and spiritual values of Sikhism. The left-hand edge is symbolic of Divine justice, where Waheguru issues justice to wrongdoers. It can also symbolize the destruction of all barriers that are used to divide people such as caste, gender and so on.

The chakra (circle) symbolizes *Ikonkaar*, the oneness of Waheguru who is without beginning or end. It recalls elements of the characteristics of Waheguru outlined in the *Mool Mantar*. It also symbolizes the oneness of creation and of humanity. The chakra was also used as a weapon against injustice.

The two kirpans symbolize the two swords of Guru Hargobind signifying miri-piri, the spiritual and temporal parts of life, and of the leadership of the Gurus. The kirpan on the left side signifies piri – the sword of spiritual sovereignty – and the kirpan on the right signifies miri – the sword of political sovereignty.

The Nishan Sahib is not only an indication of the gurdwara but also contains symbols of faith within the Panth. The beliefs that it draws together suggesting the oneness of Waheguru, the unity of humanity, the importance of Khalsa, the sovereignty of the Sikh Panth and the importance of fighting for justice. It encapsulates some of the essential aspects of Sikhism. Either consciously or subconsciously it serves as a reminder of the beliefs, the history and the responsibilities inherent in Sikhism.

Further exploration of the importance of the gurdwara as a centre of the community will be done in Chapter 10.

## Thoughts for the classroom

In the classroom, a staple of a world religions paradigm is a focus on places of worship. In some classrooms this type of activity will entail the labelling of the important parts of the layout of a gurdwara. This is fine as far as it goes, but it misses the importance of the gurdwara both as an expression of Sikh beliefs and as a place where Sikh beliefs can be expressed. For example, a mention of sach khand, the bedroom of the Guru, without reference to the wider understanding of sach khand as the court of Waheguru, would miss the centrality of the Guru as an expression of the light of Waheguru.

A labelling of the kitchen and the langar hall would miss this as an expression of the equality of humanity. Similarly, the Nishan Sahib could be copied and labelled, but without understanding the concept of symbolism its importance can be missed. Sometimes we can imagine that some elements are too complex for children to understand, but from an early age, they can engage with the why of religious belief and expression. One example is the series on TrueTube (www.truetube.co.uk), where Charlie and Blue visit a gurdwara. The puppet is able to ask questions about why things happen. Why do people sit on the floor? Why do people cover their heads? and so on. These actions may appear strange or alien, without understanding the beliefs that underpin them. The gurdwara provides many opportunities to explore not just the expressions but also the beliefs of Sikhism.

## Five Ks and the rules of the Khalsa

In Chapter 4 we explored the way that amrit sanskar is performed today. At one point in the ceremony, one of the *panj pyare* outlines the responsibilities of Khalsa Sikhs. These are very much based on the responsibilities outlined in the events of Baisakhi in 1699. The first of these responsibilities is the wearing of the *panj kakke* or 5Ks. It is interesting in observing the teaching of Sikhism in schools that possibly the most focused on aspect of Sikhism, whatever the age of the pupils, is the 5Ks. They help them remember promises they have made to Waheguru, as well as important events in the history of their faith. They are:

- *kesh* (uncut hair),
- *kangha* (comb),
- *kara* (steel wristband),
- *kachera* (shorts) and
- *kirpan* (ceremonial sword).

Kesh: This refers to uncut hair. Both male and female Sikhs believe their hair is given by Waheguru and is sacred, and therefore they never cut it. It can be seen to be a sign of holiness and a way to follow the example of the Gurus in human form.

Kangha: This refers to combs that are used to keep a Sikh's long hair tidy and clean and symbolizes cleanliness of body and mind. Sikhs believe that in looking after their hair, they are showing respect to Waheguru. They also believe that Waheguru gave them their bodies, so it would be disrespectful to let any part of this gift become untidy or dirty.

Kara: This is a metal wristband, often steel. This seems to have developed from a piece of forearm armour used when the Khalsa fought the rulers of India. It reminds Sikhs of the teachings of the Gurus and to discourage them from breaking the laws of the Khalsa. The wristband is circular, which represents the eternal nature and Oneness of Waheguru, who is without beginning or end. The kara is often worn by Sikhs who have not taken amrit.

Kachera: This refers to loose shorts that are worn under a Sikh's clothes. These shorts were comfortable for members of the Khalsa when they were riding their horses. They also provided great freedom of movement when fighting. In addition to being a reminder of the need to fight injustice, because of their positioning on the body, they are a reminder of moral cleanliness and sexual restraint.

Kirpan: This refers to a sword, once used by the Khalsa to fight against the rulers of India. It is to be used only in self-defence. Most Sikhs only wear a small decorative kirpan because the laws of some countries restrict the size of knives and swords that can be carried. It also reminds Sikhs that they should fight for those who are less fortunate.

It will be noted, and is often a surprise to students, that the turban is not one of the 5Ks. It is, however, integral to a Khalsa Sikh's expression of commitment. Indeed, for one group of Sikhs, the Akhand Kirtani Jatha, a small black turban (*keski*) is one of the 5Ks, replacing the kesh, though the uncut hair is observed.

So identifiable are the 5Ks of Sikhism that there are many Keshdhari and Sahajdhari Sikhs who adopt some or all of them as reminders of their commitment to Waheguru. One Sikh, who wears the 5Ks but has not received amrit, suggests that the emblems are important and 'part of the path of Sikhi and cannot be disregarded. I hope to find the courage and discipline to maintain the Punj Kakkar on my being one day' (Holt, interview). He suggests that the amrit sanskar, for him, is not to be taken lightly, saying: 'I am not capable of complying fully with the requirements of Amrit sanskar! I rather live a life of a Sikh without taking amrit.'

In addition to the 5Ks, and the expectations for all Sikhs outlined previously, such as the three pillars, a Khalsa Sikh commits to the following:

- They will worship only Waheguru. They will worship no statue, idol or other human being.

- Each day, they will offer the prayers required of a Sikh.

- They will only adhere to the teachings of Guru Granth Sahib and no other religious book. They will not associate with minas.

- Every male should add 'Singh' (lion) after his name and every female Khalsa should add 'Kaur' (princess) after her name.

- They must never remove hair from any part of their bodies.

- The use of intoxicants, drugs, smoking and alcohol is strictly forbidden.

- They will not pierce any part of their bodies.

- They will not eat meat of an animal killed by the draining of blood (mainly seen to be in a halal way, but it would also apply to kosher).

- Women will not wear the veil.

- They must never steal or gamble.

- Their dress should be simple and modest.

- When meeting another Khalsa Sikh, they should greet them with 'Waheguru Ji Ka Khalsa, Waheguru Ji Ki Fateh'.

If a Sikh commits any of the four taboos below, they should seek to go through the amrit sanskar again:

- cutting of the hair;

- eating the meat of an animal killed in a halal way;

- cohabiting with someone other than one's spouse; or

- using tobacco.

## Thoughts for the classroom

The restrictions or encouragements above are found in the *Rahit Maryada* which developed out of aspects of the Singh Sabha reform movement (see Chapter 9). There was a heavy focus within the late nineteenth and early twentieth centuries to distinguish Sikhism from Hinduism. Indeed, so much so that it led McLeod (1976) to suggest that even the 5Ks did not have the status they required until the late nineteenth century; he based this on manuscript evidence as well as observations from people like Cunningham

(1915) for whom they were a minor footnote in the events of the founding of the Khalsa in 1699. Jagtar Singh Grewal (1998, 303) suggests:

> McLeod is right that explicit references to 5 Ks are rather late. But to assume that the 5 Ks were introduced in the eighteenth century is wrong … The formulation came later but the substantive symbols were there from the time of instituting the Khalsa.

This raises the issues for teachers of teaching received tradition. We are teaching Sikhism as it is understood in the twenty-first century; as such we need to be conscious that there may be competing narratives of how the Panth and Sikh identity developed. This does not mean that we need to reject practices; indeed, we should not, because we are teaching Sikhism as it is understood and practised today.

However, the way that Sikh identity is expressed is not necessarily determined by the Khalsa ideal. Many see the Khalsa requirements as synonymous with being Sikh:

> The Amrit Sanskar is the moment you accept Guru Granth Sahib as your Guru. Without a 'teacher' you cannot be a 'student'. (Holt, interview)

However, others are more embracing in their understanding of the diversity of Sikh expression, suggesting:

> You can be a Sikh and not Amritdhari. However, we should all aspire to be Amritdhari. Khalsa, the Sant-Sipahi, is the full form of Guru Nanak Dev Ji Maharaj's Sikh.
> I know Sikhs who have not done ceremony but are very good Sikhs, and people who have done Amrit but behave in very bad ways. So yes, I suppose you can be, but they should really take Amrit. (Holt, interview)

In the British Sikh Report of 2020, a survey was completed with 2,700 Sikhs. In terms of being Amritdhari, only 11 per cent reported that they were, with 84 per cent saying they were not Amritdhari. There were other aspects of expression that required response:

- 27 per cent wore a turban;
- 82 per cent wore the kara;
- 84 per cent recited the prayers with varying levels of frequency; and
- 16 per cent never recited the prayers.

In light of this, it may be necessary for teachers to reorient the way that Sikhism is taught within the classroom. Although many Sikhs will see Amritdhari as the ideal, amrit is not taken by the vast majority of Sikhs in Britain. How can this be reflected in the classroom? One way this may be addressed is through the use of a social science lens. Reports such as the British Sikh Report help provide data that can be used to look at the Sikh experience in the UK. This should also be explored alongside authentic voices that might help students understand the way that a Sikh worldview is navigated against the Khalsa ideal. The use of people in the local community are particularly helpful to understand this diversity of expression. As a personal note I have learned most of my understanding of Sikh spirituality and expression by listening to members of local Sikh communities, whether they are Khalsa or non-Khalsa Sikhs. There are, however, authorial voices from a British Sikh perspective that can also be used to help provide first-person experiences in the classroom. One such author is Sathnam Sanghera, who has written *The Boy with the Topknot: A Memoir of Love, Secrets and Lies* (2012); *Marriage Material* (2022); and *Empireland* (2021). One further suggestion of a volume with different voices is Anita Goyal and Aastha Singhania's *Voices from Punjab: The Strength and Resilience of 15 Punjabi Women Living in the UK* (2019).

# *Gurpurbs*

*Gurpurb* (also Gurpurab) is a compound of the words 'Guru' and 'purab', meaning festival or celebration. In Sikhism a Gurpurb is a celebration of a Guru. There are other celebrations within Sikhism called *mela*s that are not associated with Gurus; in this section we will explore Gurpurbs as expressions of devotion to the Gurus. The reason for these, though recognition of Gurpurbs is not the original intention of the passage, is expressed in Guru Granth Sahib:

> The stories of one's ancestors make the children good children. They accept what is pleasing to the Will of the True Guru, and act accordingly. (Ang 951)

Gurpurbs have been increasingly more popular since the late nineteenth century, and celebrations differ from place to place and family to family. For most Gurpurbs there is an *Akhand Path* in the gurdwara (see Chapter 4) and Gurbani is read within the home. In some of these events, Guru Granth Sahib is taken in procession through the streets and celebrated. These events will be, at the same time, festive and devotional, individual and communal. They are an opportunity to celebrate the Gurus and also to remember their teachings and be inspired to live a more gurmukh life. Among the most celebrated Gurpurbs are:

- the birthday of Guru Nanak;
- the birthday of Guru Gobind Singh;
- the martyrdom of Guru Arjan;
- the martyrdom of Guru Tegh Bahadur;
- the nomination of Guru Granth Sahib as the Living Guru;
- Baisakhi, as the celebration of Guru Gobind Singh's creation of the Khalsa.

The celebrations are important to explore in the classroom as they highlight what is important in the Sikh Panth. As is evident from the list of Gurpurbs mentioned above, the lives of the Gurus are key to Sikh identity, as is Guru Granth Sahib and the concept of martyrdom. As we explore these concepts within the classroom we can link them to the Gurpurbs and help students understand the importance of the days, but also remembrance of the concepts.

## Summary

This chapter's focus on expressions of faith has utilized different examples and built on other expressions of faith described in previous chapters. This highlights the interconnectedness of beliefs and practices within Sikhism. They are intertwined in a myriad of ways, and it is difficult to separate them; and maybe we should not be trying, as Sikhism is a Panth that brings everything together, exemplified in the concept of Waheguru as nirgun and sagun. The one is not without the other. The organization of this book has brought necessary distinctions for the sake of organization, but the organization of a curriculum may not have these constraints. It is hoped with a background of Sikhism that a teacher can build a curriculum that authentically expresses the beliefs and lived reality of Sikhism.

# Part 2

# Contemporary Issues

# Chapter 8

# The Ethical Dimension

As we get further through the book, the threads of Sikhism become more and more intertwined. In exploring the 'ethical dimension' of Sikhism, mention should be made of Ninian Smart's (1998) suggestion that the ethical dimension refers to the law that a religion has as an expression of the doctrines and narratives. Within Sikhism, the ethical dimension is intertwined with the Sikh view of the world and of existence more generally. It has been necessary to outline the beliefs of Sikhism before exploring individual expressions of ethical living. Indeed, in the previous chapters, the teachings have been paired with examples of ethical living; the view of the equality of all people finds expression in the *langar* (see Chapters 3, 5 and 6) which seeks to overcome the poverty that people find themselves in. Similarly, the expression of Guru Hargobind of the necessity of both the 'cauldron' and the 'scimitar' (see Chapter 3) necessitates that a Sikh stand up against any form of injustice. In this chapter, we will explore elements of Sikh ethics; not all of them will link with each other, but they will link with Sikh beliefs. The chapter will begin with a short introduction to the Five Virtues and then move on to individual issues.

## The Five Virtues

As explored in Chapter 2, those striving to live a *gurmukh* life are focused towards Waheguru. In all of their actions they strive to act in worship of Waheguru, and their service is not given in the hope of return or to satisfy their ego. Rather, they act selflessly in order to experience the Divine. Life is a process where people are attempting to train their minds to act with selflessness and in union with Waheguru. One way this can be developed and expressed is through the cultivation of the Five Virtues. In Guru Granth Sahib there is an allusion to the Five Virtues when Guru Arjan was addressing a Muslim about the true five daily prayers:

> First, is the Lord's Praise; second, contentment; Third, humility, and fourth, giving to charities. Fifth is to hold one's desires in restraint. These are the five most sublime daily prayers. (Guru Granth Sahib 1084)

The Five Virtues are:

- Truth (*satya*): Those imbued with truth not only tell the truth but live in a truthful and honest way. This will also involve living in a way that is in harmony with *Satguru*, the Divine. Guru Granth Sahib teaches the importance of this truthful living:

  > He practices Truth, and lovingly focuses on the Truth. (Guru Granth Sahib 841)

  Truth is developed by meditation on the *naam* and through truthful living.
- Contentment (*santosh*): *Maya* leads a person to be discontented with their life as they seek more and more; contentment allows a person to be happy with what they have and not answer the demands of the ego. Contentment is also linked with patience which is needed to travel the path of a gurmukh. It is not arrived at in a day but is a process, and a person should be content with who they are and not constantly striving for the next thing. This also suggests moderation in all things – a person lives in the material world but does not want excess to be the focus of their lives.
- Compassion (*daya*):

  > Through compassion, the naked hermit reflects upon his inner self. He slays his own self, instead of slaying others. (Guru Granth Sahib 356)

  Sometimes this is translated as would 'rather die, than cause another to die', suggesting that compassion can be the ultimate selfless act. A person is more concerned with alleviating the suffering of others than worrying about their own suffering. Compassion as a quality of a Gurmukh is an expression of a person who is receiving of the Guru's grace as with the other virtues. If a person does not have these virtues, they are distant from Waheguru:

  > You have no compassion; the Lord's Light does not shine in you. (Guru Granth Sahib 903)

- Humility (*namrata*) is the suppression of one's ego in the service of the Gurus and others. Guru Granth Sahib uses the imagery of cleansing the dust on the feet of the Gurus to reflect the lack of ego in those who practise humility. With humility, people are able to intuitively connect with the Divine and act accordingly:

  > When this mind is filled with pride, Then it wanders around like a madman and a lunatic. But when it becomes the dust of all, Then it recognizes the Lord in each and every heart. The fruit of humility is intuitive peace and pleasure. (Guru Granth Sahib 235)

- Love (*pyaar*): a person is to seek to develop the love of Waheguru and of others in their mind and in their actions. The love of others essentially reflects the love of Waheguru, as it is showing love to the Divine spark within all; enmity towards others prevents a person from loving Waheguru. Love brings equanimity of mind:

  > Sing, and listen, and let your mind be filled with love. Your pain shall be sent far away, and peace shall come to your home. (Guru Granth Sahib 2)

The Five Virtues, as expressions of characteristics of a gurmukh and way to achieve union with Waheguru, underpin all aspects of Sikh ethics and living.

# Environmental ethics

Possibly the greatest problem in the world today is that of the many threats to the environment. In the Sikh worldview, this threat to the environment is not just physical but also spiritual. In a United Nations publication, the view of Sikhism and the causes of environmental threats were outlined:

> Guru Nanak in his philosophy states that the reality that humans create around themselves is a reflection of their inner state. The current instability of the natural system of the earth – the external environment of human beings – is only a reflection of the instability and pain within humans. The increasing barrenness of the earth's terrain is a reflection of the emptiness within humans. (United Nations Environment Programme and Parliament of the World's Religions, 2020, 57)

This is reflective of the ideal that problems in the material world can be solved if people remember the naam and are motivated to act in selfless ways. The first way that a Sikh will strive to resolve the environmental crisis is through meditation on the naam. This is not, however, the end of their activity. The whole of creation is seen to be imbued with the Divine. In various places within Guru Granth Sahib, the interconnectedness of creation and the Creator is emphasized:

> Air is the Guru, Water is the Father, and Earth is the Great Mother of all. Day and night are the two nurses, in whose lap all the world is at play. (146)

> The Beloved Himself is in all the oceans and lands; whatever God does, comes to pass ... The Beloved Himself enjoys every heart; He is contained within every woman and man ... O Nanak, the Beloved is pervading everywhere, but He is hidden; through the Guru, He is revealed ... The Beloved Himself is contained in all the woods and meadows; as Gurmukh, He reveals Himself. (605)

> The Guru has revealed God to Nanak, in the three worlds, in the water, the earth and the woods. (617)

If a person acts to harm creation, they are acting against Waheguru. If a person seeks to use more of the world's resources than are needed, they are acting out of ego. A Sikh should strive to act in harmony with creation, to solve the ills that face the world. The consequences of such are explained in Guru Granth Sahib:

> Some have cruelty in their hearts – they constantly act in cruelty; as they plant, so are the fruits which they eat. (302)

The need to act in harmony with creation means that a Sikh is acting in harmony with the Creator. The charity EcoSikh is one organization trying to highlight environmental ethics in the *Panth*:

EcoSikh connects Sikh values, beliefs, and institutions to the most important environmental issues facing our world. We draw on the rich tradition of the Sikh Gurus and the Khalsa Panth to shape the behavior and outlook of Sikhs and the world, ensuring that our deep reverence for all creation remains a central part of the Sikh way of life. (EcoSikh, 2021)

# Vegetarianism

Somewhat linked with the issue of environmentalism but also an issue on its own is vegetarianism. Within the Sikh Panth, this is also a contentious issue. There are Sikhs who would argue on both sides of the issue. There are suggestions of the desirability of a meat-free diet; for example, the serving of vegetarian meals within the gurdwara. However, this may reflect the belief that all are welcome and to serve meat would exclude some. A further example is the prohibition against the eating of halal meat. Again, this is only rejecting the eating of meat in certain contexts, reflected by one Sikh complaining about the decision of her local deli to serve halal chicken, which meant she would need to eat elsewhere. The *Rahit Maryada* does not forbid the eating of meat, and Guru Granth Sahib is somewhat ambiguous on the topic of vegetarianism.

On the rejection of meat eating, various *shabad*s in Guru Granth Sahib are cited:

The world eats dead carcasses, living by neglect and greed. Like a goblin, or a beast, they kill and eat the forbidden carcasses of meat. So control your urges, or else you will be seized by the Lord, and thrown into the tortures of hell. (723)

You kill living beings, and call it a righteous action. Tell me, brother, what would you call an unrighteous action? (1103)

You say that the One Lord is in all, so why do you kill chickens? (1350)

Many Sikhs would agree with the approach suggested by one Sikh:

When we realise the power of the ego, we realise that the Divine is present in all. Thus, the eating of flesh only aids the delights of the ego. (Holt, interview)

However, there are also examples of the Gurus in human form eating meat, and shabads in Guru Granth Sahib that suggest that meat eating is a non-issue:

The fools argue about flesh and meat, but they know nothing about meditation and spiritual wisdom. What is called meat, and what is called green vegetables? What leads to sin? ... Those who renounce meat, and hold their noses when sitting near it, devour men at night. They practice hypocrisy, and make a show before other people, but they do not understand anything about meditation or spiritual wisdom. (Guru Granth Sahib 1289)

It would appear from this *Gurbani* that Guru Nanak was more concerned with spiritual aspects of life and the need to meditate and gain spiritual wisdom than arguing about whether people should or should not eat meat. It would appear that Sikh teaching can support vegetarianism or not, as the person decides for themselves. For many, vegetarianism is a way to respect Waheguru; but it also seems as though people who eat meat are not disrespecting Waheguru. There is, therefore, room for both in the Panth. The attitude of one Sikh perhaps sums it up well:

> Ethical eating is part of Sikhi. Vegetarianism *can be* part of ethical eating. (Holt, interview; emphasis added)

# Social justice

Perhaps of all the ethical issues, the need for social justice is the one that lies at the heart of Sikhism. In Chapters 6 and 7, we explored the concepts of *sewa* and *vand chhako*; we also explored aspects of selflessness in the lives of the Gurus in human form (see Chapter 3); and earlier in this chapter, we explored issues of compassion and love. Social justice, and the need to stand up against oppression wherever it is found, is central to Sikhism. The examples of Guru Hargobind and Guru Tegh Bahadur show that the call for social justice is not restricted to speech and action on behalf of other Sikhs; there is no restriction on the use of the 'crucible' or the 'scimitar'.

In addition to the examples and teachings explored throughout this book, we will explore the examples of two Sikhs in the twenty-first century who fought for social justice in different ways.

## Valarie Kaur

Valarie Kaur is an American film-maker and writer who has fought for social justice through film-making, writing, social media and interfaith activities.

Following the killing of Balbir Singh Sodhi post 9/11, Valarie Kaur began to research and document hate crimes that targeted Sikhs and Muslims in the United States. This led to the documentary *Divided We Fall: Americans in the Aftermath*.

She has built on this by making further documentaries and raising awareness on gun violence, racial profiling, immigration and net neutrality. She, and her organization, has produced education materials to work against hate crimes. Her book *See No Stranger: A Memoir and Manifesto of Revolutionary Love* (2020) reflects a project to combat hate, wherever it is found, with love. In the first pages, the example of Guru Nanak is found; on emerging from the Court of Waheguru, Kaur suggests:

> Love made him see with new eyes. Everyone around him was a part of him that he did not yet know. 'I see no stranger,' said Guru Nanak, 'I see no enemy.' (9)

## Deep Sidhu

For some, Deep Sidhu is a controversial figure. He was an actor and lawyer who was arrested for his involvement in the farmers' protests in India in 2021. As an actor it would have been easy for him to remain silent, but in the cause of the farmers he saw a cause for which he needed to stand up. He was a high-profile supporter of the protests of the tens of thousands of farmers who camped for months on the outskirts of the capital Delhi against laws which would ruin their ability to make a living. They were protesting against three laws implemented by Prime Minister Narendra Modi's government that they said could ruin their livelihood.

Many of the farmers were Sikh, and, perhaps, this section should be about them. Many slept on the floor or on wooden cots to peacefully protest against the injustice that was being done to farmers throughout India. Deep Sidhu organized a union to help agitate for the Indian government to repeal the farming laws. In late 2021, Prime Minister Modi repealed the laws. This was not down to Sidhu, but he was part of a larger movement that would not accept the poverty that would result for farmers.

## Same-sex relationships

The Gurus and Guru Granth Sahib were silent on issues of sexuality, and as such some Sikhs reject any type of discrimination or ill-treatment against those in same-sex relationships. This is despite the heteronormative interpretation of the *Rahit Maryada* that makes the family with a mother and father the norm and the ideal. Indeed, in response to the imminent legalization of same-sex relationships in Canada, the Akal Takht issued a *hukumnama* that condemned same-sex marriages and instructed gurdwaras to not allow *anand karaj* for same-sex couples.

Some responses suggest that because Guru Granth Sahib does not comment on issues of sexuality, there is no precedent for rejecting same-sex relationships, and further that the offensive language of the hukumnama in 2005 was reflective of an outdated attitude within society. Many Sikhs, although subject to the authority of Akal Takht (see Chapter 9), would reject this approach and suggest it is a result of certain cultural attitudes within those involved in decision making at Harmandir Sahib. Sukhdeep Singh (2018) articulates the concerns for the homophobic language and approach:

> Apart from (mis)using their position to voice their own homophobia, neither the jathedar nor the SGPC have never gone on to explain the theological reasoning for their edicts and proclamations. Their oft-repeated statement that the 'Sikh religion does not accept same-sex marriage' wouldn't stand a chance if they tried to connect it to the teachings of the Gurus.

The celebration of marriage as an ideal and as a union of two souls is used by people on both sides of the debate. Those who reject same-sex marriage would reject homophobia but reiterate the Akal Takht's view that marriage is assumed in a Sikh context, and in the Guru, to be a union of a man and woman.

This is an emotive issue, but it might be seen that any type of discrimination is rejected, though whether the refusal to accept same-sex marriage is discrimination or not would be answered differently. It is possible, as discussed below in exploring issues of authority in the Panth (Chapter 9), that the issue of same-sex marriage may be more indicative of a generational rather than a Sikh disagreement.

## Thoughts for the classroom

In this chapter, we have only touched on the Five Virtues and four ethical issues. There are many issues in the modern world that have not been explored, such as abortion, euthanasia and divorce. This does not mean that they are not important but that the ones that are included are indicative of the way that Sikhs strive to make ethical decisions. Their approaches to ethics are drawn from the underpinning beliefs that are described in the rest of the book. What is notable, however, is the issue of interpretation. In most of the issues explored there is scope for personal decision making, and this must be based on a person's interpretation of how best to serve others and Waheguru. Perhaps in the issue of environmental ethics, and in the example of Valarie Kaur, there is little to disagree with. However, in discussing the farmers' protests, it is up to the individual as to whether this is an appropriate cause to stand up for. Within vegetarianism and same-sex relationships, we have seen that there are views on both sides; and they raise issues for conceptions of authority and interpretation of Guru Granth Sahib. It is important in exploring many ethical issues to recognize the differing worldviews among Sikhs around the globe. Some 'traditional' Sikhs who like the status quo use interpretive lenses from that cultural perspective, whereas younger, and perhaps more Westernized, Sikhs view Sikhism and their relationship with Waheguru through their own lenses. Maybe within Sikhism there is room for both approaches, but the importance of recognizing the deeply held views of others is paramount in gaining understanding.

# Chapter 9

# Authority in the Sikh Diaspora

Authority is an interesting concept within Sikhism. Throughout the history of Sikhism, even during the time of the Gurus in human form, there were contentions and rivalries for the leadership of the Sikh *Panth*. Outside of the rival claimants such as Sri Chand, Prithi Chand and others, there were isolated incidents where people set themselves up within the Panth, ostensibly to receive some of the following and offerings due to the Guru. It was for this reason that the *masand* system was abolished by Guru Gobind Singh. During his lifetime, as was explored in Chapters 3 and 4, Guru Gobind Singh established the authority within the Panth, in Guru Granth Sahib and also with the Khalsa, to interpret and teach the principles outlined therein.

In this chapter, we will trace threads of authority within Sikhism since the time of Guru Gobind Singh. Following a short exploration of the development of Sikh temporal authority up until the time of the British Empire's control of Punjab, we will explore aspects of authority and diversity within the Sikh Panth today.

## Authority following Guru Gobind Singh

Guru Gobind Singh established or nominated Banda Singh Bahadur as a military commander and gave his charge of some forces just prior to his death. Upon the Guru's death, Banda Singh Bahadur extended elements of the leadership and began to take a role in both spiritual and temporal matters (though not as Guru). He issued coins with the images of Guru Nanak and Guru Gobind Singh and led the army of the Khalsa against the Mughal forces. He saw both success and defeat. Khushwant Singh (1999) suggests that alongside his victories, his attacks lost the Sikhs a lot of support among Muslim and Hindu inhabitants of Punjab and beyond.

Throughout the time of Banda Singh Bahadur and afterwards arose the practice of Sarbat Khalsa, which was essentially a meeting of the Khalsa in the presence of Guru Granth Sahib to establish the path that the Panth would take. From 1721 this was organized under the auspices of Bhai Mani Singh until his death (see below). The meeting which was to take place every two years would establish the collective will of the Khalsa, and all would be subject to the decisions made. The decisions of the Sarbat Khalsa were known as *gurmata*. A number of the decisions made at the biennial meetings surrounded issues of making peace and the carrying on of battles and skirmishes.

Following the execution of Banda Singh Bahadur, the Mughal emperor Zakarya Khan embarked on a terrorizing of Sikhs. They were to be hunted and killed. Easily identifiable by the uncut hair and the symbols of their identity, some members of the Khalsa began to cut their hair to evade capture, while others took refuge in the hills. Sikhs were not idle during this time, and under the leadership of Kapur Singh they sprang surprise attacks against the forces of the empire and caused havoc among them. The emperor, meanwhile, recognized that he could not eradicate the Sikhs completely and so came to an understanding with them: he offered the Sikhs a *jagir* (fief) of one lakh rupees a year, access and residence at Amritsar, and their leader the title of nawab or viceroy. Kapur Singh was chosen by the Sikh community to be nawab.

However, the emperor reneged on the terms of the peace, and it became necessary for the Sikh leaders to organize their forces. Under the direction of Nawab Kapur Singh, the army of the Khalsa was split into two: Buddha Dal (the group of veterans) and Taruna Dal (the army of the young). These were further split into smaller, more manageable forces, with as many as sixty-five bands operating throughout Punjab. At the Sarbat Khalsa of 1748 the forces of the Khalsa were to be unified under the leadership of Sardar Jassa Singh Ahluwalia (though still under the main leadership of Nawab Kapur Singh). As part of this process, the sixty-five groups were organized into eleven *misl*s. Usually described as an army or collection of soldiers, misls became areas of governance within Punjab, with leaders and spheres of influence.

The misls functioned as a Sikh confederacy under the direction of the Sarbat Khalsa. They were largely concerned with the temporal issues of the Panth and had a large influence throughout Punjab, winning many battles and establishing relative peace. There were exceptions: following the slaughter of over twenty-five thousand Sikhs at Wadda Ghalughara in 1762 by the forces of Ahmad Shah, Sikh forces later defeated the armies of the shah at Sirhind and then the shah himself at Amritsar.

As the misls became established, there tended to be incidents of infighting, and the confederacy was not as strong as it was when it was first established; and while the Sarbat Khalsa continued, the involvement in such was restricted to the leaders of the misls or their representatives.

The misls (and Sarbat Khalsa) continued until the time of Maharaja Ranjit Singh, who through prowess in battles and alliances was able to combine all of the Sikh misls under his leadership. He took the title of 'Maharaja' on Baisakhi, 12 April 1801. Commonly known as the Sikh empire (Sarkar-i-Khalsa) (see Atwal, 2020), this time is seen to be a high point of Sikh influence and power in Punjab. Ranjit Singh took control of Amritsar in 1802. He was, however, the temporal or secular leader of the Sikhs who lived in his area of influence. Perhaps as a response to the persecution that Sikhs had faced from the Mughal Empire, Ranjit Singh was not discriminatory in his treatment of those of other religions. Although he formally ended the practice of Sarbat Khalsa, he did not claim religious authority. Indeed, on two occasions he submitted to the punishment of the Akal Takht while Akali Phula Singh served as *jathedar* (leader). His wrongdoings were the marrying of a Muslim woman who did not convert and the offering of a canopy that had been used to the Akal Takht.

Following the death of Ranjit Singh in 1839, the empire slowly crumbled and the areas that it covered gradually came under the influence and control of the British. The increasing influence of the British was exemplified after defeat in the Anglo-Sikh War, when Maharaja Duleep Singh (the son of Ranjit Singh) was deposed and, in time, moved to Britain, becoming a favourite of Queen Victoria and converting to Christianity. He eventually recommitted to Sikhism in 1866.

This brief description of the development of Sikh sovereignty necessarily focused on the temporal and political authority. While it could be seen to go hand in hand with the spiritual authority, they appear to have developed along separate but occasionally intertwined tracks. This was, perhaps, inevitable as spiritual authority had been placed within Guru Granth Sahib, but the main focus of the Panth was survival within the context of numerous invasions and persecutions.

As noted earlier (see the introduction and Chapter 5), the 'spiritual' development of Sikhism during this time seemed to fall into the hands of those Khatri who had traditionally had leadership positions but had held themselves above the expression of Sikhism found in the Khalsa. This period of Sikh belief and expression became known as 'Sanatan Sikhs'. The emphasis was on the teachings of the Gurus but, it is suggested, in light of traditional beliefs that were found in the surrounding areas of Punjab, most noticeably within Hinduism. The suggestion is that there was a great range of diversity within the Panth that enabled people to be Sikh but to continue to make offerings to deities or to follow the life-cycle rites that had always been observed. It was against this background, and the increasing conversions of Sikhs to Christianity, that the Singh Sabha movement developed. Conversions were attributed, by some, to the negative impact of the retention of these cultural practices. Along with the idea of social mobility within the empire, lower-caste Sikhs may have been attracted by the casteless views of Christianity, something many Sikhs felt had fallen out of emphasis in the Panth.

## Singh Sabha

In the nineteenth century many Sikhs observed many issues within the Panth. As already mentioned, there was the concern over Sanatan Sikhism and the increasing appeal of Christianity. There was also the attraction, for some, of the Namdharis (see below) who were found within the Sikh Panth; one of their distinctive teachings was that Guruship in human form had not ended with Guru Gobind Singh. There were also concerns over the management of gurdwaras by *mahant*s (proprietors) who often misappropriated funds or lived immoral lives. They had control of gurdwaras (including Harmandir Sahib) where idols were often displayed alongside Guru Granth Sahib. This issue of mahants would become a major focus in the early twentieth century, but it also shows the diversity within the Panth at this stage, which some saw as a corruption of the message of the Gurus with cultural and religious practices at odds with Sikhism.

The Singh Sabha movement was first established in 1873 in Amritsar. It is interesting to note that it was established by Khatri Sikhs, including descendants of Guru Nanak, who were seeking a return to the teachings of Guru Nanak and had slowly gained control of many gurdwaras. In response to this early incarnation of the Singh Sabha movement, some Khalsa Sikhs established the Lahore Singh Sabha in 1879. The aims of this group in Lahore focused around the articulation and codification of Tat Khalsa (true Khalsa). Over time different groups based on the Amritsar and Lahore organizations developed throughout the Panth; the Lahore model and views found much greater success and eventually became what is meant by Singh Sabha.

As mentioned in both the series introduction and the introduction to this book, we explored the development of the concept of religion. In the nineteenth century the development of the concept of Hinduism made Sikhism just another path in a wider religion. To combat this message Singh Sabha went to great lengths to delineate a separate Sikh identity. There is the suggestion that the focus on *gurpurbs* to celebrate aspects of the lives of Gurus in human form, and events to do with Guru Granth Sahib, can be traced as 'essential' elements of Sikhism in the nineteenth century. Diwali (Bandi Chhor Divas) and Baisakhi were not enough to separate Sikh identity, as they were celebrated at the same time as Hindu festivals. This also included the establishment of definite rituals for life-cycle events (see Chapter 7). Although to suggest that Singh Sabha initiated a process that changed Sikhism would perhaps not be fair, there is evidence of the use of the *Lavan* within weddings since the time of Guru Amar Das; similarly, there are examples of celebrating gurpurbs such as the birthday of Guru Nanak during the time of Ranjit Singh. It may well be that their assertion to be reclaiming the authentic Sikhism that had been lost since the time of Guru Gobind Singh would be seen to be an accurate retelling of the story.

Not all welcomed the activities of the Singh Sabha in establishing the Sikh identity, with the Khalsa as normative. Gurinder Singh (2021) outlines the Akal Takht admonishing members of the Lahore Singh Sabha for trying to have the idols removed from Harmandir Sahib in Amritsar. By this time, the leadership of Akal Takht was in the person of a *sarbah*, or caretaker, appointed by the British. Although the idols predated British involvement, the Akal Takht was seen to be serving the needs of the empire in keeping peace, rather than the needs of the Panth. The authority of the Akal Takht, although enshrined in Sikh history, was seen to be watered down or negated because of the actions of the sarbahs.

Other activities of the Singh Sabha to reinforce the ideal of the Khalsa was through the establishment of schools in villages and the writing and printing of materials that systematized this approach to Sikhism. The relationship between the British Empire and Singh Sabha is complex. On the one hand, it was a reaction against the empire and the Christianization of Punjab and of Sikhs more generally that led to its creation. On the other hand, the structures that they utilized to establish a worldview that could be called Sikhism used the framework of the oppressor in terms of Christianity. Similarly, in emphasizing the martial spirit of the Khalsa, the British Empire reinforced the Sikh ideal that was being suggested as normative – taking *amrit* was required of those Sikh soldiers who wanted to join the British Army.

The two 'wings' of the Singh Sabha movement developed into Chief Khalsa Divan in 1902, and then the anti-British aspect of this movement developed further into a group with the name Akali (this is not to be confused with the precursor to the Nihangs, also named Akali) who were also known as the Gurdwara Reform Movement (in 1920) that agitated for laws and treatment that would further separate Sikhism from Hindu influence. The two major foci of the reform movements in terms of British influence were:

* the establishment of a distinctive Sikh marriage rite; and

* the control of the gurdwaras and the removal of the mahants who enjoyed British patronage.

The first was realized in 1909 with the Anand Marriage Act. The Namdharis, along with the Singh Sabha, had been agitating for the recognition of a distinct Sikh rite, which would mean that they would not have to have a Hindu ritual to be formally married. The Namdharis had been following the practice of replacing the havan (fire) of the Hindu ritual with Guru Granth Sahib, tracing elements of the ceremony to Guru Amar Das. The act read:

1. Short title and extent. (1) This Act may be called the Anand Marriage Act, 1909; and. (2) Its extends to the whole of India [except the State of Jammu and Kashmir].
2. Validity of Anand marriages. All marriages which may be or may have been duly solemnized according to the Sikh marriage ceremony called Anand [commonly known as *Anand Kara*j] shall be, and shall be deemed to have been with effect from the date of the solemnization or each respectively, good and valid in law. (Government of India. Legislative Department, 1909, 2)

The establishment of a ritual distinct from those practised by Hindus led to the development of further outlines for rituals such as death and naming, as well as a formalization of the *amrit sanskar*. It was around this time (1915) that attempts began to be made to codify Sikh beliefs and rituals; this was not accomplished until 1951 with the publication of the *Rahit Maryada* and the establishment of 'official' Sikh rites.

The remaining agitation of the reform movement was to reclaim the gurdwaras from what were seen as corrupting influences. The mahants were generally drawn from Udasis, who were descendants of Guru Nanak and his son Sri Chand. The reformers saw the lack of a distinction from Hinduism as problematic for Sikh identity and felt that gurdwaras should reflect a Sikhism free from Hindu practices.

The Jallianwalla Bagh massacre of 1919 was the impetus for the establishment of the All India Sikh League in 1919, and also the Gurdwara Reform Group in 1920. Agitation against British rule and their interference in Indian laws was spreading throughout the country. One of the leaders of the non-violent resistance was Mohandas Gandhi, and along with others he arranged a general strike. In Punjab the strike took place in Lahore and Amritsar on 6 April. Following the arrest of two of the leaders on 9 April, there was another general strike in Amritsar on 10 April. Groups of people began to congregate, and estimates put the number as at least twenty thousand men, women and children. They were then fired upon by the soldiers, killing between twenty and thirty people and injuring numerous other (numbers differ according to source).

On 13 April, local leaders called for a gathering of Sikhs in the gardens at Jallianwalla to mark the day of Baisakhi. General Dyer 'occupied the only entrance and exit to the garden' and without warning 'opened fire. He killed 379 and wounded over 2,000' having fired for over twenty minutes (K. Singh, 1999, 164). The figures quoted here were the official figures, but other reports place the numbers at over one thousand.

Although not directly linked to the agitation for gurdwaras to come out of British and mahant control, this massacre further motivated Sikhs to take action to remove the Panth from any control of the British, and this was most evident in the gurdwaras.

## Shiromani Gurdwara Parbandhak Committee

On 15 November 1920, the Shiromani Gurdwara Parbandhak Committee (SGPC) was organized at a Sarbat Khalsa with over twelve thousand Sikhs in attendance. This was in response to those in control of Harmandir Sahib refusing the offerings of *karaprasad* from recently initiated dalit Khalsa Sikhs. When the pujaris fled, an ad hoc committee was appointed and the Sarbat Khalsa called to establish a management committee. To try and pre-empt this, the governor of Punjab appointed a management committee of thirty-six Sikhs, two days before the Sarbat Khalsa.

At the Sarbat Khalsa, the Sikhs in attendance rejected this committee of 36 and established a committee of 175 members (including those proposed as the 36). The SGPC was thus organized to oversee gurdwara reform in the Panth, and it held its first meeting on 12 December 1920.

Through a series of non-violent activities, the SGPC were able to take control of a number of gurdwaras, including Gurdwara Panja Sahib at Hasan Abdal and Gurdwara Sacha Sauda at Chuhar Kana. There were many setbacks in the work of the SGPC, including the Nankana tragedy, where at the gurdwara marking the place of Guru Nanak's birth, the mahant opened fire as a group of Sikhs approached and over 130 people were killed. The British eventually agreed to cede control to the SGPC, and the mahant and his associates were arrested. A further obstacle came with the keys' affair where the deputy commissioner of Amritsar took the keys of the Harmandir's treasury away from Sikhs. SGPC officials were arrested for discussing the affair, but through non-violent agitation and a threat to boycott the Prince of Wales's visit to India, the arrested Sikhs were released and the keys given to the SGPC president.

With the governance of Harmandir Sahib in SGPC hands, confidence began to grow, and Khushwant Singh (1999, 207) suggests that 'a decision of the SGPC became like a proclamation of the guru'. Although the SGPC was non-violent, wider elements of the Akali movement were not. This led to the SGPC and the wider Akali movement being declared illegal. As a result of this and attempted government smearing, sympathy grew for those who were imprisoned and the wider cause. This, in turn, led to the passing of the Gurdwaras Act in 1925, after a previous one had been rejected by Sikhs in 1922 as it continued a British role in the control of gurdwaras.

The Gurdwaras Act of 1925 brought the gurdwaras under the auspices of the SGPC, and each gurdwara was to be overseen by an elected committee of Sikhs. Under the control of the SGPC, reform of the gurdwaras could begin in earnest, and the last vestiges of Hinduism and British control could be removed from the Sikh Panth.

This act established the SGPC as an authority within Sikhism, having, as it did and does, control over the major shrines, including the Takhts.

## The role of the Takhts

Alongside this temporal authority were Takhts where matters of the Panth could be discussed. The focus of the greatest amount of authority was the Akal Takht in Amritsar. Since the time of Guru Hargobind, this was seen to be a seat of temporal authority overseen by jathedars who would issue edicts and rulings. During the time of the Gurus, while they were away from Amritsar, the need for the Akal Takht dissipated, as its authority was bound up with the Guru. After Guru Gobind Singh's death, Mata Sundari sent Bhai Mani Singh to become the custodian of Akal Takht, in 1721. There is little information about the timing of the establishment of three of the other four Takhts in existence today, though reference is made to them in literature of the eighteenth century:

- Takht Harmandir or Takht Patna, Patna (Bihar): Patna was the birthplace of Guru Gobind Singh, where he spent the first few years of his childhood.

- Takht Kesgarh, Anandpur (Punjab): This Takht is built on the site of the first initiations into the Khalsa in Anandpur. The Gurdwara began to be built in 1689. The first jathedar was appointed after 1925.

- Takht Hazur/Takht Sachkhand, Nanded (Maharashtra): This is where Guru Gobind Singh set up residence in 1708.

Although not a Takht during this period of history, the fifth Takht in the Panth today is the Takht at Damdama:

- Takht Damdama, Talwandi Sabo (Punjab): It was at Damdama that Guru Gobind Singh recited Guru Granth Sahib to Bhai Mani Singh. It is the final of the five Takhts to have been established as a seat of authority and was named as such on 18 November 1966.

Today, the Takhts are seen to issue edicts that are in their best interests of the *sangat*. The gurmatas and hukamnamas from the Akal Takht are seen by many to be binding for all Sikhs. Each of the Takhts' jathedars is automatically a member of the SGPC.

One example of a decision of the SGPC that was approved by Akal Takht is the *Rahit Maryada*, which was approved in 1945 and published in 1950.

## The *Rahit Maryada*

The *Rahit Maryada* is a statement of Sikh beliefs and practices. It can be seen to follow in the tradition of previous *rehats*:

- The *Tanakhah-nama (Nasihat Nama) Samvat* (1718–19), written ten years after the death of Guru Gobind Singh
- The *Prahilad Rai Rahit-nama*
- The *Sakhi Rahit ki* (1735)
- The *Chaupa Singh Rahit-nama* (1740–65), written by a companion of Guru Gobind Singh
- The *Desa Singh Rahit-nama* from the late eighteenth century
- The *Daya Singh Rahit-nama*

Each of these outlined rules from members of the Sikh Panth. In the *Chaupa Singh Rahit-nama*, for example, there are over eight hundred rules for a Sikh to follow. There are differing interpretations of the authority and authenticity of each of these. The *Rahit Maryada* was written by Sikh scholars under the auspices of the SGPC and approved by the Akal Takht. It can be seen, unsurprisingly, as a product of its context. Those who wrote it were keen to delineate Sikhism as a religion separate from Hinduism and Islam, and as a result some aspects focus on the rules that reject Hinduism rather than on the positive aspects of how Sikhism should be lived. Arising out of the Singh Sabha movement, it also established Khalsa Sikhism as authoritative and normative. Approved by the Akal Takht, the *Rahit Maryada* is seen as binding for the Sikh Panth. However, some would see that the *Rahit Maryada* needs updating to reflect the concerns of the twenty-first century.

## Authority today

The straightforward answer to the question of authority within the Panth is that it lies with Guru Granth Sahib and the Panth. This is understood to have been the will of Guru Gobind Singh. The problem is that *Gurbani* are open to interpretation and, as has been seen, was able to be revered and used as Guru by a wide range of Sikhs, in particular, Sanatan and Khalsa Sikhs, who used the same *bani* to come to different conclusions and ways of worship. The role and authority of Akal Takht, although established by Guru Hargobind, is not without controversy. While recognizing that while Akal Takht is a source of authority, the relationship with such is complicated for many Sikhs. One Sikh has suggested that they see the authority in the Panth as coming from 'Akal Takht but this doesn't work well!' (Holt, interview).

Since 1925 (possibly since 1920), the jathedar of Akal Takht has been appointed by the SGPC. This is outlined in the Gurdwaras Act of 1925 and also would be seen to link with the will of the Panth, because its elected members are representative of such. One concern expressed is that the SGPC is closely linked to the political party of Shiromani Akali Dal (SAD), though both are at pains to point out their separateness.

The issue of the authority of the SGPC as a Panthic organization was challenged in 2015 when a Sarbat Khalsa was called on 10 November. It was held in Chabba on the outskirts of Amritsar, having been denied entrance to Harmandir Sahib and Akal Takht. It was attended by tens of thousands of Sikhs who elected Jagtar Singh Hawara as jathedar of Akal Takht. Jagtar Singh Hawara is in prison on charges of murder, and so Dhian Singh Mand acts in his stead. The SGPC rejected this election and the Sarbat Khalsa as invalid, as the Gurdwaras Act gave only the SGPC the representative authority for the Panth. Interestingly, the 1953 amendment to the Gurdwaras Act excluded Sahajdhari Sikhs from having voting rights to elect people to the SGPC, further reinforcing the Khalsa ideal. The existence of this 'shadow' seat of authority highlights the tensions in the Panth. The SGPC continues to nominate the 'official' jathedar of Akal Takht. It is important to recognize the issue of authority in the Panth and how aspects of it are seen, by some, to be subject to personal and societal influences.

As the diaspora grows, many gurdwaras in places outside of Punjab may seek more consideration of particular issues. One example is of the reaction of some Sikhs to a hukumnama from Akal Takht that condemned same-sex marriages and instructed gurdwaras to not allow *Anand Karaj* for same-sex couples (see Chapter 8), which reflected of an outdated attitude within society.

The virtual sangat has brought to light some of the concerns with the 'traditional' interpreters of authority. No one seems to be agitating for the replacement of structures such as the SGPC, the Akal Takht and the various gurdwara committees. What is being suggested is that there needs to be a way to update the thinking of some of the views and actions that could be considered to be more reflective of older styles of thinking. Examples include some of the more dated language of the *Rahit Maryada*, which addresses issues of gender in a somewhat early-twentieth-century paternalism. Doris Jakobsh (2006a, 35–6) suggests:

> It also sheds light onto the proliferation of what I have called the 'new authorities' among the Sikhs. This is of course not to say that the traditional seats of authority, the aforementioned Akal Takht, SGPC, or gurdwara managements have been replaced. Yet, while they exist, it is my contention that there is a significant shift away from these traditional sites of authority toward the 'new authorities', the intermediaries of cyberspace.

With a greater proliferation of online sites, the knowledge of Sikhism is open to all, and the traditional structures perhaps need to recognize that different sources of authority are being consulted to develop a personal view of Sikhism, which may not be content with the status quo. In recognizing historical developments and diversity in interpretations of the teachings and practices of Sikhism, some may agitate for a move beyond 'traditional' orthodoxy that reflects the concerns of the early twentieth century.

## Thoughts for the classroom

It is evident from the discussion above that issues of authority within Sikhism are complex and perhaps becoming more so. Eleanor Nesbitt (2016, 126) suggests:

> The mechanisms for decision-making and how extensively the resolutions apply, are a subject of increasing discussion, not least among enquiring diaspora Sikhs.

The issue of authority is inextricably linked with the issue of diversity. What is normative Sikhism? Elements of diversity in the Panth, and particularly in the UK, will be explored in the next chapter. It does, however, raise questions for the way that we teach Sikhism. It is not as simple as suggesting that authority lies with the living Guru and with the Panth. How each of these are interpreted leads to differing approaches. Is the concretization of Sikhism a positive thing, where there is orthodoxy and orthopraxy that seek to exclude some practices? But, if there are no boundaries, how is it possible to explain what Sikhism is? Returning to the issue of worldviews, is this something that needs to be applied as a lens to recognize the lived reality of Sikhism in the UK today?

# Chapter 10

# Sikhs and Contemporary Britain

Throughout the previous chapters there have been many examples of how Sikhism is lived in Britain today. This is an important aspect in striving to teach Sikhism in the classroom. Sikhism is a religion that is rich in history, and many aspects of its beliefs and expressions have been influenced or established by events in the lives of the Gurus or through examples of others throughout history. In the previous chapter, we tried to explore the various nuances of authority within the Sikh *Panth*, and as this chapter moves forward, we will try and understand what this means for the lived experience of Sikhs in Britain today. As has already been discussed, the experience of the individual Sikh is dependent on many factors that contribute to their worldview. In this chapter, we will explore various aspects of what could be considered the Sikh experience in Britain today. The values and teachings of Sikhism will form a significant part of this, but it will also be influenced by gender, caste, culture and many other aspects of a person's life experience. Thus, to try and articulate what it is to live as a Sikh today in Britain is perhaps folly, if the individual nature of religious experience is not noted.

## The first Sikhs in Britain

The 'first' Sikh in Britain was Maharaja Duleep Singh, son of Ranjit Singh, in 1854, who was brought across as a favourite of Queen Victoria (see Chapter 9). Following Duleep Singh's migration and the settlement of his family many more Sikhs came across to Britain between the 1850s and the start of the First World War. Two of the most notable Sikhs of this time were Princess Sophia Duleep Singh (youngest daughter of Duleep Singh), who was one of the foremost women involved in the suffragette movement, and Princess Catherine Duleep Singh (another daughter of Duleep Singh), who was also a suffragette, but in the Second World War helped many Jewish families in their escape from Germany. Peter Bance (2012) notes that many Sikhs were here only temporarily, but with the opportunities afforded to them in Britain, many of their stays became more long term and permanent. These first Sikhs faced the issue that would be faced by future generations, whether to adapt 'to the British way of life by relaxing their religious duties and values' or try to 'change and challenge the establishment to become accustomed to [the] Sikh faith' (2).

Peter Bance (2012) outlines four waves of Sikh migration to Britain:

- Between the two world wars where the majority of Sikhs who came to Britain were 'enterprising businessmen, students and pedlars' (viii). Many of these would earn what they could and send money home to care for their families.

- Post Indian independence and Partition (1947) when labour shortages in Britain were met by young people from Punjab, and the arrival of the families of those who had come across between the wars for economic reasons.

- The British Nationality Act of 1948 gave citizenship to every member of the Commonwealth. As such, chain migration of more families, and others taking advantage of this opportunity, continued.

- The expulsion of Sikhs from parts of East Africa in the 1970s meant large numbers settled in Britain.

Particularly significant for migration to Britain were the 'political' acts of Partition in 1947 and Operation Blue Star in 1984 (see Chapter 3). The act of violence towards Sikhs that was Partition was a particular push factor for them to find new opportunities and security. The Partition of India in 1947 essentially cut Punjab into two: West Punjab in Pakistan, and East Punjab in India. It has been described 'as a year when the largest ever migration in human history took place, the magnitude of the massacre was unparalleled, morality had turned into brutality. Punjab experienced the worst of all that happened during this trauma' (Gupta, 1997, 591).

As a result of the identification of Sikhism with Punjab, and the background of many Sikhs having families in Punjab, Punjabi is an integral part of Sikh identity and history. A large number of Sikhs have outlined its importance in describing it as 'our motherland' and the 'land of the Gurus'. One Sikh has suggested the importance of retaining Punjab as part of Sikh identity:

> We need to retain the history and language to follow our faith. If we don't retain the history, someone will re-write it! (Holt, interview)

Perhaps, for this reason, the remaining family ties and the situation of Amritsar and the other sacred sites of Sikhism, Punjab remains an important part of what it is to be Sikh in Britain. A quick look at social media, and appeals in gurdwaras, will highlight some of the important social, political and economic issues that need addressing in Punjab.

There are many Sikhs, however, who see aspects of Punjabi culture as needing reform so that Sikhism can reclaim some of its roots. For example, some Sikhs outlined the machismo and bravado that is present in some aspects of Punjabi culture. Whether this is accurate or not, there are attitudes in the Panth that can be seen to downplay and even subjugate women or reinforce caste (see Chapter 5). This does not mean that these elements need to be replaced by 'British' culture, as elements of that would be similarly discriminatory, and so it is the prioritization of Sikhism over any other influence in the way a person seeks to live their life.

## Assimilation or retrenchment

Within the sociology of religion are the linked concepts of retrenchment and assimilation. On the one hand, there is a 'strain toward greater assimilation and respectability' and on the other, a strain 'towards greater separateness, peculiarity, and militance'. Armand Mauss (1994, 5) further suggests that

> along the continuum between total assimilation and total repression or destruction is a narrow segment on either side of the centre; and it is within this narrower range of socially tolerable variation that movements must maintain themselves, pendulumlike, to survive.

In many ways this is the experience of Sikhism within Britain since the mid-to-late nineteenth century. This can also be related to the experience of many immigrant communities over the past couple of centuries. In terms of the Sikhs in Britain, particularly in the interwar years, there was a general desire to fit into society. This was not common to all Sikhs, but a number felt the need to cut their hair and not display other aspects of Sikh identity, perhaps only feeling the need to wear a turban when attending the gurdwara. This was more than likely not a renunciation of Sikhism but a recognition that any 'difference' had the potential to be used to cause division and discrimination. There was a tenuousness to the position of Sikhs in British society; this tenuousness was also reflected in the gurdwaras which were generally to be found in converted homes.

As time went on, and there began to be an increased confidence in the Sikh community, there was greater push for the 'establishment' to accommodate the needs of Sikhs, rather than Sikhs accommodating to the establishment in the previous phase. This is, perhaps, an indication of the more secure feeling as being a part of British society. It could also be that the next phase of Sikh immigrants were coming into a country where the Sikh presence was more settled, and so did not feel the need to hide any aspects of their identity. Rather than this generation being more religious, it is fairer to say that the groundwork had been laid so that there was an environment that was more conducive to expressing faith as a minority.

Two such examples of this increasing integration of Sikhs were issues surrounding the wearing of the turban and the wearing of the *kirpan*. The issue of the wearing of a turban can be seen to have three distinct phases.

### On buses

In 1959, Sundar Singh Sagar, who was working in the bus garage, applied for the role of bus conductor with Manchester City Council. His initial application was refused because he wore a turban, and this would be against the uniform policy of the council. Sagar worked with the local gurdwara to change the position of the council. It took over seven years, but on 5 October 1966, the council voted to overturn its decision and allow the wearing of turbans. By that point, Sagar was too old for the position, but in 1967, his nephew, Mukhtiar Singh Pardesi, became the first turbaned bus conductor in Manchester.

At the same time as Pardesi taking up his role, Tarsem Singh Sandhu in Wolverhampton was sacked as a bus driver. Previously, he had been clean shaven but had returned to work after a period of ill-health. This led to marches and the division of the local community. Gurhapal Singh and Darshan Singh Tatla (2006, 128) note that one letter to a Wolverhampton newspaper suggested that it was 'time they [the Sikhs] realised this is England, not India'. After a threat of an elderly Sikh to immolate himself, the Indian high commissioner Shanti Sarup Dhawan became involved and made this a transnational issue that would have implications beyond Britain. On 9 April 1969, the Wolverhampton Council reversed its decision.

## Motorbikes

The Road Traffic Act (1972) made it a requirement that people riding a motorbike wear a crash helmet. Due to come into force on 1 June 1973, all efforts to gain an exemption for Sikhs wearing turbans were rebuffed. Baldev Singh Chahal took the government to court claiming, under the Race Relations Act, that in failing to take account of Sikhs, they were contravening human rights. The initial appeal failed, reasoning that no one is being forced to ride a motorbike, and the issue at hand was that if Sikhs wanted to ride a motorbike they were being prevented by the religion and not by law. This led to further discussion around issues of safety and the freedom of religion. The debate led to an amendment to the Road Traffic Act in 1976 that exempted a Sikh, while wearing a turban, from the requirement of wearing a helmet. Some saw this campaign to be symbolic due to the fact that there were few Sikh motorcyclists, but it was an important step in recognizing the rights of Sikhs to practice their religion.

## Racial identity

In 1978 Park Grove School, Birmingham, rejected the application of Gurinder Singh Mandla because a turban did not fit with the school's uniform code. With the support of the Commission for Racial Equality (created as part of the 1976 Race Relations Act), Mandla's family made a legal challenge. The challenge was rejected because the judge ruled that Sikh was not a racial identity but a religious one, and the racial identity of a Punjabi did not necessitate a turban. This led to a sustained campaign and legal appeals. The House of Lords ruled on 23 March 1983 that racial identity was a broader term than the lower courts suggested, and that Sikhs did, indeed, fall under the Race Relations Act because they fit two conditions of an ethnic group: (1) a shared history in the consciousness of the community and (2) possessing shared cultural traditions. This identification led to a debate in the lead up to the 2021 census; some Sikhs wanted Sikh to be identified as an ethnic group where, in the past, most Sikhs had ticked 'Indian' as ethnicity and 'Sikh' as religion. This had supporters and opponents within the community, with supporters arguing that using Sikh as an ethnic identifier would provide access to greater protections and funding opportunities. However, opponents suggest that Sikhism is open to all, and Punjabi and Sikh ethnicity are not synonymous, which seemed to be the argument of proponents, and that protection was already available under the Equality Act (2010) where religion is a protected characteristic.

## Safety helmets

In 1979, the Health and Safety Commission began circulating its intention to establish the wearing of safety helmets as compulsory in the construction industry. The Sikh community again returned to the arguments made in previous cases. The House of Lords issued an amendment to the Employment Act (1989) which exempted turban-wearing Sikhs from this requirement to wear safety helmets in the construction industry. It functioned in the same way as the motorbike helmet exemption. But, interestingly, the exemptions apply only in these particular cases.

## *Kirpan*

The issue of wearing the kirpan did not raise the same issues as early as the wearing of the turban, perhaps because of societal norms or the lack of visibility of many kirpans when worn. In 1979, with the support of the government, it was agreed that British Airways would allow Sikhs to wear kirpans on its flights. In 1982, this was retracted following the hijacking of an Indian Airlines aeroplane by Sikh militants. In 1985, Heathrow airport allowed its workers to wear kirpans of up to three inches, but this did not apply to passengers. The Criminal Justice Act (1988) had an exemption to the ban of carrying of knives for religious reasons, but they were not to be used. This was reiterated in the Offensive Weapons Bill (2018) which contains an exemption for the kirpan.

Despite these exemptions, it is not uncommon for security, and sometimes police, to refuse entry to Khalsa Sikhs wearing a kirpan to sporting or other events. Usually these misunderstandings are resolved quickly when checks are made about the allowance of kirpans, but it also shows a need to further educate those in positions of authority and also the wider public.

The wearing of the kirpan on aeroplanes in a post-9/11 world is much more complex, often depending on the airline, the destination and the originating airport. For some, kirpans are allowed, but for others they are asked to be placed in check-in baggage. The multiplicity of international destinations perhaps makes a unified approach hard to arrive at.

## Gurdwaras

The increasing numbers of purpose-built gurdwaras are also evidence of a more secure British society for Sikhs. Gurdwaras (originally dharmsalas) have served a multiplicity of purposes since the time of the Gurus (see Chapter 3). For example, in addition to a place for *kirtan* and *langar*, Guru Angad had gyms attached for the development of a Sikh's health and skills. Although always being centres of activity in Punjab the gurdwara took on greater significance within the Sikh community in Britain. They are now, more importantly, centres of the community and of Sikh identity. In attending the gurdwara a person is able to meet with others in *satsangat* and solidify who they are as Sikhs. They serve the wider purposes of community and community identity, providing Punjabi and Gurmukhi classes, mother and toddler groups and gathering places for *mela*s and *gurpurb*s.

This continuation of the Sikh and Punjabi way of life is not always seen to be completely positive. In developing the community, and ensuring that all feel part of that inherited identity, some Sikhs suggest that the community in the UK has become too inward facing. One Sikh says:

> Sikhs are insular, inward looking and believe that they can operate in their own silo! We need to adapt and change, grow and make much bigger contribution in all walks of life! Especially in local and national government! We also need take active positions in roles that enable change at Trustee, Director level. (Holt, interview)

This may be a minority view, but the involvement of Sikhs in all areas of life will be explored below. It does, however, highlight an issue for all religious groups. How does a group maintain their distinctive identity when in constant contact with differing values and commitment? Gurdwaras are, on paper, the most welcoming of all religious places of worship, with anyone being able to walk in off the street and receive hospitality. This is true, but often non-Sikhs will be trepidatious about visiting, and the welcoming atmosphere is known only by those who have visited. One interesting initiative, already mentioned, is Guru Nanak FC in Gravesend, which is a football club attached to the gurdwara. Although it initially started with Punjabi players, it now has a multicultural and multifaith feel.

In light of the discussion in the past chapter about authority, it is interesting to note the importance of the different roles of leadership in British gurdwaras. Each gurdwara elects a management committee that is responsible for the day-to-day management of the gurdwara and for the appointment of a *granthi*. Many gurdwaras have the stipulation that to be eligible for the management committee, a person should be an Amritdhari Sikh. Thus, it is possible to suggest that in common with the SGPC the management of gurdwaras may be 'traditional' and reflective of the Khalsa ideal. This is not necessarily negative and ensures people are committed to Sikhism but might restrict the inclusion of certain views and practices.

As mentioned above, each gurdwara committee will choose a granthi (they may also be known as *giani*). Their role is that of a 'reader' of Guru Granth Sahib. In Britain it is extended to include the role of reader at most services, to encourage a regularity and consistency of worship. They may also receive the responsibility to look after the gurdwara in terms of its tidiness and so on. While usually men, the role of a granthi can be fulfilled even by women. One job advert for a granthi in a British gurdwara suggested that the role involves the following responsibilities:

- to install and close Guru Granth Sahib;
- to take part in *akhand*;
- to perform kirtan;
- to conduct services at festivals, weddings, births, baptisms and deaths;
- to say daily *ardas*; and
- to take care of the premises of the gurdwara.

Granthis may have responsibilities in the gurdwara and be called on to offer interpretation of the Guru, but their role is mainly functionary, rather than authoritative. It is often the case that granthis are employed directly from Punjab where there are colleges that train them.

## Education

As has been seen, education in Gurmukhi, Punjabi and wider aspects of Sikhism is an integral part of the role of the gurdwara. It may need gurdwaras to work together, or like-minded Sikhs need to get together. One example of such is a group of Sikhs in the North West of England. Realizing there was no opportunity for Sikh young people to study Sikhism at post the age of fourteen because of their small numbers and the predominance of the Abrahamic religions, they organized a weekly class to be held at a central location so Sikhs could have the opportunity to develop their understanding of Sikhism and gain qualification. This is similar to a weekly Sunday school held in a primary school in Southall to allow Sikhs to learn Gurmukhi and Sikhism from a young age and gain qualifications at the age of six.

Education in the traditions and history of Sikhism is key to keeping the religion alive in people's lives. One further development is the creation of Sikh 'faith' schools that began with what is now the Guru Nanak Sikh Academy in Hayes. One of the largest groups of schools is the Nishkam Academy Trust. These combine the teaching of what could be seen as a 'traditional' curriculum with a Sikh ethos which might also include Sikh studies and Punjabi classes. The Guru Nanak Sikh Academy has a diwan hall attached to the school where assemblies are held in the presence of the Guru. These enable Sikh parents to be confident in the curriculum and experience that their children are receiving and help provide a grounding within Sikhism. These were initially funded by members of the community, and while this continues, the development of the academy's programme has enabled schools to receive funding from the central government. Schools in England with a Sikh ethos or foundation include the Nishkam Academy Trust Schools, the Khalsa Academy Trust and the Guru Nanak Academy Trust.

According to the British Sikh Report (2020) attitudes towards Sikh faith schools are mixed within the Sikh community:

- 54 per cent Sikhs believed there should be a Sikh school in their area (26 per cent did not). However, this figure rose to 71 per cent of Amritdhari Sikhs.

- 42 per cent Sikhs would send their child to a Sikh faith school, while approximately 35 per cent would not. The proportion of those who would send their child to a Sikh school rose to 67 per cent among Amritdhari Sikhs.

- 75 per cent would focus on academic achievement in choosing a school, whereas only 11 per cent thought faith ethos was a factor.

These are interesting figures and perhaps show a greater focus on educational achievement as a factor in the priorities of education for parents. This has, perhaps, been true throughout the Sikh experience in Britain where education is seen as a key factor to success and a way to increase social mobility. This does not mean that development in the faith is not important, maybe that it can be sufficiently accomplished in the home and in the gurdwara. There is, however, an impetus for an increased teaching of Sikhism in the wider education system for the benefit of Sikhs and non-Sikhs:

> Sikhism is the most egalitarian way of life and for the benefit of society (not conversions), it should be taught in a more widespread way in schools.
> Wider community often knows nothing about Sikhs or Sikhi, and assume we're Muslims and our Gurdwara are mosques. Much more cultural awareness is needed. (Holt, interview)

## Prejudice

The last point illustrates one of the issues that many Sikhs face in the community: prejudice. Much of this will be racial prejudice, but perhaps because of more identifiable identity markers, some may be religious. This has been present throughout the Sikh experience in Britain:

> Immigrants looking for housing were subject to undisguised racism: in 1959 in Leamington, thirty residents protested to the town hall when a Sikh was given a council mortgage. (Sanghera, 2021, 165)

Indeed, Enoch Powell's 'Rivers of Blood' speech was given while he was MP for Wolverhampton, home to a large Sikh population. It is, perhaps, impossible for Sikhs not to have drawn links between his speech and Wolverhampton and their own place in the community.

Discrimination is still evident in the twenty-first century; the UK Sikh Survey (2016) highlights the following:

- one in seven Sikhs have experienced discrimination at work;
- one in five Sikhs have experienced discrimination in public;

- one in twelve Sikhs have experience discrimination from public officials; and

- there were over one hundred thousand hate crimes against Sikhs in one year.

These points highlight the fact that the tensions faced with integration into society are still prevalent, and more needs to be done in British society to combat the prejudice and discrimination that Sikhs, and other minorities, face. The responsibility for this falls to wider society, rather than asking Sikhs to be more integrated. Policies, structures and attitudes need to be changed so that Sikhs do not find themselves victims of this prejudice.

# Thoughts for the classroom

Throughout this chapter we have explored the place of Sikhs in Britain and their experiences of retrenchment and assimilation. At times, the focus is on developing Sikh identity so that the beliefs, teachings and practices are not watered down. On the other hand, Sikhs are aware of an increasing awareness of their place within, and from, wider society. As Sikhism has developed, there has been the need for Sikhs to find greater representation of the needs of their communities and the individuals therein. Some of this has happened through the development of representative voices within society, and these are also voices that can be used in the classroom. Groups such as City Sikhs, Sikh Federation and the Sikh Awards (UK) have sought to raise the profile and awareness of Sikhism. Indeed, in academia, the establishment of the Centre for Sikh and Panjabi Studies at the University of Wolverhampton has begun to raise the profile.

Sikhs in the public eye have raised the awareness of wider society towards Sikhism and Sikh principles. Examples include:

- Mandip Gill, an actress who starred in *Doctor Who*;

- Ameet Chana, an actor in *EastEnders*;

- Monty Panesar, an England cricketer;

- Anita Rani, a radio and television presenter;

- Ranvir Singh, a television presenter;

- Preet Gill, MP for Birmingham Edgbaston; and

- Lord Justice Singh, the first Sikh judge of the UK High Court of Appeal.

The most important examples that we use in the classroom are those from our local area. The diversity of the Sikh experience in the UK is significant and should find expression in our classrooms.

Sikhism is a religion that transforms the individual and the world through a remembrance of Waheguru. Sometimes in our writing and teaching we forget that everything in Sikhism has its root in this teaching. Nothing in the Sikh worldview makes sense without an understanding of the Sikh view of Waheguru and existence more widely. It is my hope that as we explore Sikhism as a lived religion, it will become more than a list of observable phenomena and that it will reflect the reality of the spiritual and the temporal, the *nirgun* and *sagun*, and *miri-piri*. It is only then that the richness of Sikhism can be understood by those we teach.

# Glossary

| | |
|---|---|
| 5Ks | The five visible elements worn by Sikhs to symbolize the Khalsa. They include *kesh* (uncut hair), *kara* (steel bangle), *kangha* (comb), *kacheri* (undershorts) and *kirpan* (sword). |
| *Adi Granth* | 'First Volume' – the collection of the writings of the first five Gurus in human form, along with some writings of Hindu and Sufi saints, collected together by Guru Arjan. |
| *Ahankar* | 'Ego/pride', one of the Five Thieves. |
| *Akal Bunga* | The original name of the site of Akal Takht; more precisely, the area where the Akal Takht is housed within the Darbar Sahib. |
| *Akal Purakh* | 'Eternal One' or 'being not subject to death', one of the most common ways of referring to the Divine. |
| *Akal Takht* | 'Throne of the Eternal/Timeless One' – the seat of authority within Sikhism built by Guru Hargobind; more precisely, the throne within Akal Bunga, which is today seen as the most important of the seats of authority in giving guidance to Sikhs. |
| *Amrit* | Used to refer to the water mixture that is used at *amrit sanskar*, the ritual that marks entrance into the Khalsa. It can be translated as 'nectar' and refers to the *naam* – 'the ambrosial Naam' as a name of the Divine. |
| *Amrit sanskar* | The initiation rite where Sikhs become members of the Khalsa. |
| *Amrit vachan* | Refers to the words of the Gurus that are saturated with the grace/energy of Waheguru. |
| *Amritdhari* | Refers to a Sikh who has gone through the *amrit sanskar* and is referred to as a Khalsa Sikh. |
| *Ardas* | A formal prayer of supplication that is used within Sikh life in services in the gurdwara and also by an individual before or after undertaking a task. |
| *Bandi Chhor Divas* | 'The day of liberation' – a festival celebrated to commemorate the release of Guru Hargobind along with fifty-two Hindu princes. It is celebrated at the same time as the Hindu festival of Diwali. |

| | |
|---|---|
| *Baoli* | A well. The baoli at Goindwal was built by Guru Amar Das as a place for Sikhs to visit; seen my many as a place of pilgrimage. |
| *Beadbi* | Sacrilege – such acts are usually performed against Guru Granth Sahib. |
| *Braham-giani* | God-conscious being whose characteristics may be reflective of someone in the stage of *karam khand*. |
| *Darbar* | 'Throne' – often refers to the seat of the Guru. |
| *Darbar Sahib* | Often used to refer to the complex in Amritsar that houses the Harmandir Sahib and Akal Takht. |
| *Dasam Granth* | 'Book of the tenth' – a contraction of *Dasven Padshah Ka Granth* or 'Book of the Tenth Emperor'. It contains the writings of Guru Gobind Singh. |
| *Dasvandh* | Literally, 'one-tenth'. A Sikh is expected to give one-tenth of their income to social or charitable purposes; introduced during the Guruship of Guru Arjan. |
| *Daya* | 'Compassion', one of the Five Virtues. |
| *Degh* | 'Cauldron' – the idea within Sikhism that people will be protected from 'want' through *sewa*. |
| *Dharam* | Also transliterated as 'dharma', meaning 'duty'. |
| *Dharam Khand* | One of the five realms/stages of consciousness. In this realm, a person acts and reaps the consequences of their actions. |
| *Dharam Yudh* | 'War of justice' – a war fought to protect the rights of people, for self-defence, when other solutions have failed, and should be fought honourably. |
| Dharamsala | 'Abode of dharma' – refers to a Sikh place of worship before it was gradually replaced by gurdwara during the time of Guru Hargobind. |
| *Diwan* | The hall in the gurdwara where Guru Granth Sahib is placed on a *takht*. |
| Five Thieves | These are inclinations drawing people away from the truth and making them subject to *maya*. They are *kam* (lust), *krodh* (rage or uncontrolled anger), *lobh* (greed), *moh* (attachment or emotional attachment) and *ahankar* (ego/pride). |
| Five Virtues | Virtues found in a person seeking to live a *gurmukh* life. They are *sat* (truth), *santokh* (contentment), *daya* (compassion), *nimrata* (humility) and *pyare* (love). |

| | |
|---|---|
| *Gian Khand* | One of the five realms/stages of consciousness. In this realm of wisdom, a person is engaged more in the development of wisdom or mental satisfaction. |
| *Granthi* | 'Relator' or 'narrator' – someone who reads Guru Granth Sahib in worship. |
| *Gurbani* | Teachings/writings of the Guru. |
| *Gurmat* | Teachings of the Guru. |
| *Gurmukh* | 'Guru focused'. Such a person has recognized the truth of reality and is aware of the *naam* within everything. They have seen through the clouds of *maya* and understood the truth of their relationship with the Divine. |
| *Gurmukhi* | 'From the mouth of the Guru' – a language established to preserve the words of Guru Nanak. Guru Angad drew on existing languages to develop a unique composite language. |
| *Gurpurb* | 'Festival/celebration of the Guru' – the name given to a festival in Sikhism that celebrates an aspect of a Guru's life. |
| Guru | A person possibly best described as a teacher who brings another from darkness to light. The darkness of *maya* is shattered by the teachings of the Gurus as a person comes to know the truth of the *naam* within themselves. Within Sikhism, there are ten Gurus in human form and Guru Granth Sahib. |
| Guru Granth Sahib | The Living Guru, Guru Granth Sahib was installed as the Guru of the Sikhs by Guru Gobind Singh. The Guru contains writings of some of the Gurus in human form as well as Sufi and Hindu sants. |
| Guru Nanak Nishkam Sewak Jatha | A Sikh organization founded by Baba Puran Singh in Kenya in the 1950s. Its headquarters are in England, and there are slight differences in elements of practice with those recorded in the *Rahit Maryada*. |
| *Guruprasaad* | Guru's grace or by Guru's grace – part of the *Mool Mantar*. |
| Harmandir Sahib | 'Abode of Akal Purakh/Waheguru'. 'Har' is a name of the Divine. Harmandir Sahib is known as the Golden Temple, originally built by Guru Arjan. It is perhaps the holiest place of Sikhism, where Guru Granth Sahib is housed. |
| *Haumai* | 'Self centredness/ego'. By the focus on the *haumai* a person deludes themselves that life is all about them and the seeking of worldly pleasures to satisfy the ego. As part of *maya*, it provides the illusion that there is a duality in the world and that Waheguru and creation are separate. |

| | |
|---|---|
| *Hukam* | 'Command' – refers to the will or command of Waheguru. |
| *Hukamnama* | A command in the name of the Guru. |
| *Ikonkaar* | The first word of the *Mool Mantar* is *Ik*, meaning 'One and it is represented in the numeral, rather than the word, 1'. This suggests the indivisible and concrete unity of the Divine. *Onkaar* can be variously translated as 'One God', but it refers to the nature of the Divine as one. |
| *Janamsakhis* | Narratives of the events of the life of Guru Nanak. Initially, some of these were pictures that illustrated events from Guru Nanak's life. They soon became written narratives. The main *Janamsakhis* are: *Bhai Bala Janamsakhi*, *Vilayat Vali Janamsakhi*, *Hafizabad Vali Janamsakhi* (these two are often combined as the *Puratan Janamsakhi*), *Bhai Mani Singh's Janamsakhi* and *Miharban Janamsakhi*. |
| *Japji* | 'To recite/chant' and 'ji' is an honorific. Composed by Guru Nanak, the *Japji* is the first teaching/hymn in Guru Granth Sahib covering Angs 1–8. The *Japji* is recited by Sikhs each morning. |
| Jat | A caste of peasant farmers from which some early Sikhs had already been drawn, but the time of Guru Arjan marked a much larger number joining the *Panth*. Many Sikhs come from a Jat Sikh background. |
| *Jathedar* | 'Leader'; originally appended to Bhai Gurdas as the leader of Akal Takht, it refers to the person who makes the decisions about justice and issues related to Sikhism. Today, there are five jathedars who sit in each of the seats of authority. They are appointed by the Shiromani Gurdwara Parbandhak Committee (SGPC). The Akal Takht is the most important of the five Takhts. |
| *Kam* | 'Lust', one of the Five Thieves. |
| *Karam* (karma) | In Sikhism, *karam* has three main interpretations – the law of cause and effect, the grace of the Guru and actions. |
| *Karam Khand* | One of the five realms/stages of consciousness. This realm is the stage of spiritual progression where the grace of Waheguru breaks through and enables people to experience bliss. |
| *Karaprasad* | A mixture of flour, clarified butter and sugar – it is food shared in the gurdwara suggesting that all are equal; sometimes seen to be 'sacred' or 'blessed'. |
| *Karta Purakh* | *Karta* means 'Doer' or 'Creator' and *Purakh* refers to an individual being. Therefore, Waheguru is the being who is the creator. |

| | |
|---|---|
| Keshdhari | Sikhs who may keep/wear aspects of the 5Ks, such as uncut hair, but have not undergone the *amrit sanskar*. |
| Khalsa | 'Pure' – the name given to Sikhs who have undergone the *amrit sanskar*. This was given by Guru Gobind Singh who 'founded' the Khalsa. |
| Khatri | Sikhs also known as Sanatan Sikhs who were rooted in the ruling elite of India. They generally had leadership of gurdwaras and placed themselves outside of the Khalsa ideal. |
| *Kirat karo* | One of the three pillars of Sikhism – to earn an honest living. |
| *Kirtan* | The act of worship in Sikhism, where *Gurbani* is sung. |
| *Krodh* | 'Rage' or uncontrolled anger, one of the Five Thieves. |
| *Lavan* | A hymn composed by Ram Das, used/recited at weddings in Sikhism. |
| *Lobh* | 'Greed', one of the Five Thieves. |
| *Manji* | Either the system or the people appointed within the system (sometimes called *masand*s) established by Guru Amar Das. Twenty-two Sikhs (men and women) were appointed to teach *Gurbani*, provide guidance and form a link between the Guru and the wider *sangat*; also responsible for the collection of offerings and later *dasvandh*. |
| *Manmukh* | Self-willed or self-focused. Under the influence of *haumai* and of the Five Thieves, a person can be seen to become *manmukh*. Such a person is focused on the ego or the self and is shrouded in the cloud of *maya*. |
| *Masand* | Sikhs (men and women) who were appointed to teach *Gurbani*, provide guidance and form a link between the Guru and the wider *sangat*; also responsible for the collection of offerings and later *dasvandh*. |
| *Maya* | Materialism or the illusion of reality that leads people away from the Truth. |
| *Mina* | 'Charlatan' – an appellation given to Prithi Chand, the eldest son of Guru Amar Das, who tried to claim the Guruship. His followers became known as 'Mina' and grew for a time, but eventually died out. |
| *Miri-piri* | The two swords of spiritual and temporal authority with which Guru Hargobind was installed. Building on the existing belief of *tegh* and *degh*, it has become shorthand for the concept of saint-soldier |

| | |
|---|---|
| | in Sikhism – the principle that a Sikh should protect others from injustice and inequality by the use of the bowl and the sword. |
| *Misl* | The system established to appoint *masand*s/*manji* to teach *Gurbani*, provide guidance and form a link between the Guru and the wider *sangat*; also responsible for the collection of offerings and later *dasvandh*. |
| *Moh* | 'Attachment' or emotional attachment, one of the Five Thieves. |
| *Mool Mantar* | The opening of Guru Granth Sahib – a description of the Divine. 'One Universal Creator God, The Name Is Truth Creative Being Personified No Fear No Hatred Image Of The Undying, Beyond Birth, Self-Existent. By Guru's Grace' (Ang 1). |
| *Mukti* | 'Freedom' or 'liberation' – usually from the cycle of rebirth and the world of ego. The realization of the true nature of reality and union with the Divine is seen to be *jivan mukti*; often used synonymously with *sach khand*. |
| *Naam* | Literally means 'name' and appears over two and a half thousand times in Guru Granth Sahib. Within Sikhism naam can be seen to have three different, but related, meanings: Waheguru – the all-pervading spirit/power that is throughout the universe and lies latent in every person and is actualized or realized by engagement with the Guru; it can refer to *Gurbani* – the words of the Gurus; it refers to the praise and glorification of Waheguru. |
| *Naam Simran (Naam Japo)* | 'Meditation on the *naam*' – it is an act that is central to Sikh worship and life and enables the Sikh to meditate on the qualities of Waheguru. |
| Namdharis | A group that considers itself as Sikh; many in the wider Sikh community reject this. They were founded in the late nineteenth century by Balak Singh. One key belief is that the line of Gurus did not end with Guru Gobind Singh but that he went into seclusion. |
| Nihangs | They have historically been known as 'Akalis' (a servant of the Timeless One) and trace their existence back to Guru Gobind Singh. They are known to be fearless and are a fairly militaristic group within Sikhism, known for their wearing of blue and weapons, including the *kirpan* and *chakar*s. |
| *Nimrata* | 'Humility', one of the Five Virtues. |
| *Nirbhau* | *Nir* means without or no, and *bhau* means fear. According to this description, Waheguru is literally without fear or fearless. |

| | |
|---|---|
| *Nirguna* | Beyond all attributes, and 'transcendent'. Waheguru is both *nirguna* and *sagun*. |
| *Nirvair* | *Nir* meaning without, and *vair* meaning hatred or enmity. Therefore, Waheguru is without hatred to enmity and is free from rancour towards anything or anyone. |
| *Nitnem* | 'Daily routine' – collection of *Gurbani* to be read a minimum of three times. |
| *Paintis Akhari* | An acrostic poem of Guru Nanak's that utilizes all thirty-five letters of the Gurmukhi alphabet at the beginning of each line to describe the qualities of *Ikonkaar*. |
| *Panj pyare* | The five pure ones who volunteered to sacrifice themselves at the birth of the Khalsa. The first five initiated Sikhs. Also refers to the five witnesses/participants at the initiation into the Khalsa. |
| *Panth* | 'Path' or 'way'; usually used today to refer to the Sikh community and sometimes known as the Guru's nation. |
| *Puris* | As part of the *manji* system, Guru Amar Das created fifty-two puris, which were smaller centres of governance. The number fifty-two mirrored the number of bodyguards held by the emperor. |
| *Pyare* | 'Love', one of the Five Virtues. |
| Rag | Different musical modes/measures (rags) – the hymns of Guru Granth Sahib are set to rags. |
| *Rahit Maryada* | A code of conduct for Sikh belief and practice, adopted in its final version by Shiromani Gurdwara Parbandhak Committee (SGPC) in 1945. |
| *Ramalla* | A cloth that is placed as a cover on Guru Granth Sahib. |
| Ramsar | A spot on the outskirts of Amritsar where Guru Arjan dug a pool which he named Ramsar after his father and also where Guru Arjan and Bhai Gurdas worked on the compilation of the Adi Granth. It is also at this spot that Guru Arjan composed the prayer *Sukhmani* (psalm/jewel of peace), which can be found in Angs 262–96 of Guru Granth Sahib. |
| Ravidasis | Followers of the sant Ravidas who lived prior to Guru Nanak, and some of whose compositions are in Guru Granth Sahib. They have traditionally been part of the Sikh *Panth* but have become a separate group in recent years because of the souring of relations with Sikhs. |
| *Sach Khand* | One of the five realms/stages of consciousness. *Sach* means 'truth', and as such the final realm is the 'realm of truth'; it is the dwelling |

|  | place of *Nirankar* (the Formless One). In this realm, no more karma is attached to a person and the karmic process has ended because of the intervention and grace of Waheguru. |
|---|---|
| *Sagun* | Refers to Waheguru possessing all attributes, or being immanent; Waheguru is both *sagun* and *nirguna*. |
| Sahajdhari | 'Slow adopter' – used by some to describe some Sikhs who live most, if not all, aspects of a Sikh life but do not take *amrit*. |
| *Sangat* | 'Company' or 'fellowship'; more broadly, this refers to the community of Sikhs or a gathering of Sikhs. The Gurus taught living in community, which raised people's understanding of who they are and the nature of reality. A related concept is *satsangat* or 'true *sangat*', to denote a group of people who meet to edify each other in seeking a *gurmukh* life. |
| *Santokh* | Contentment, including an overcoming of attachment, one of the Five Virtues. |
| Sants | Loosely translates as 'saint' but does not really connote the meaning of the word. Guru Arjan describes sants as 'those who do not forget the Lord with each breath and morsel of food whose minds are filled with the Mantra of the Lord's Name – they alone are blessed; O Nanak, they are the perfect Saints' (Guru Granth Sahib 319); may refer to someone who has realized the true nature of existence. |
| *Saram Khand* | One of the five realms/stages of consciousness. It is variously translated but it can mean the 'realm of effort' but also modesty and humility. In this realm it is suggested that the person becomes more humble as their knowledge of the Divine increases. |
| *Sat* | 'True' or 'Truth', a quality of Waheguru. Commonly attached to *Naam* (Satnaam) to emphasize that the Divine is the 'True Name'; or Guru (Satguru), again, to suggest the 'True Guru'. Also used to describe the community of Sikhs as *satsangat*. |
| *Satguru* | 'True Guru' – a name for Waheguru. |
| *Satnaam* | 'True Name', 'Name is Truth', suggesting a name of characteristic of the Divine. |
| *Sewa* | Shortened from *karasewa* meaning 'selfless service'. |
| *Sewadars* | People who engage in *sewa*. |
| *Shahid* | 'Martyr', a word to denote martyrs within the Sikh tradition. |

| Shiromani Gurdwara Parbandhak Committee (SGPC) | An organization responsible for the management of gurdwaras in India. They nominate the *jathedar* of the Akal Takht. |
| Sikh | 'Disciple', a follower of the Gurus/Sikhism. |
| Sikh Dharma of the Western Hemisphere | Also known as 3HO, it is an American Sikh organization founded in 1970. |
| Sikhi | A verb – a way to describe the active learning from the Guru and the search for the reality of the nature of humanity and existence. It has begun to be the preferred term, which is a better descriptor of the Sikh way of life. |
| Sikhism | The name of the religion that Sikhs follow – a contested term. |
| Singh Sabha | A movement in the late nineteenth and early twentieth centuries that sought to systematize Sikhism. |
| *Sukhmani* | The Psalm/Jewel of Peace, a prayer of Guru Arjan, which can be found in Angs 262–96 of Guru Granth Sahib. |
| *Takht* | 'Throne' or seat of authority. |
| *Tat Khalsa* | Literally, 'true Khalsa'. |
| *Tegh* | 'The sword', a symbol to denote that all will be protected from persecution and violence. Often used by the Gurus alongside *degh* as a symbol of the two purposes of the Guru and the *sangat*. |
| Thara Sahib | 'Pillar of patience' – the place where Guru Tegh Bahadur waited patiently for entry into the Harmandir Sahib. |
| *Tirath* | A place of pilgrimage. |
| Udasi | An ascetic group which follows the teachings of Sri Chand, a son of Guru Nanak. |
| Valmikis | A form of Sikhism based on the teachings of Valmiki; mainly followed by dalits. |
| *Vand Chhako* | One of the three pillars of Sikhism – the responsibility to share one's wealth. |
| *Waheguru* | Supreme Lord; a name that is used commonly to refer to Akal Purakh or the Divine. |
| *Zafarnama* | 'Epistle of victory', written by Guru Gobind Singh to Emperor Aurangzeb; so named to reflect the spiritual victory of the Guru and the moral failures of the emperor. It is found today in the Dasam Granth. |

# References

Ammerman, N. T. (2021). *Studying Lived Religion: Contexts and Practices*. New York: New York University Press.

Atwal, P. (2020). *Royals and Rebels: The Rise of the Sikh Empire*. London: Hurst.

Bance, P. (2012). *The Sikhs in Britain: 150 Years of Photographs*. London: Coronet House.

Bindra, P. S. (2005). *Bhai Swaroop Singh Kaushish's* Guru Kian Saakhian: *Tales of the Sikh Gurus* (English adaptation). Amritsar: Singh.

Bowie, R. A., Panjwani, F. and Clemmey, K. (2020). *Texts and Teachers: Opening the Door to Hermeneutical RE*. Canterbury: National Institute of Christian Education.

British Sikh Report (2020). *British Sikh Report 2020: An Insight into the British Sikh Community*.

Cole, W. O. (2010). *Sikhism – an Introduction: Teach Yourself*. London: Hodder.

Cole, W. O., and Sambhi, P. S. (2006). *The Sikhs: Their Religious Beliefs and Practices*, 2nd edn. Brighton: Sussex Academic.

Commission on RE (2018). *Religion and Worldviews – the Way Forward: A National Plan for RE*. London: Commission on RE.

Cooling, T. (2002). 'Commitment and Indoctrination: A Dilemma for Religious Education?' In L. Broadbent and A. Brown (eds), *Issues in Religious Education* (pp. 42–53). New York: Routledge.

Cooling, T., Bowie, B., and Panjwani, F. (2020). *Worldviews in Religious Education*. London: Theos.

Crenshaw, K. (1989). 'Demarginalizing the Intersection of Race and Sex: A Black Feminist Critique of Antidiscrimination Doctrine, Feminist Theory and Antiracist Politics'. University of Chicago Legal Forum. University of Chicago Law School, 139–68.

Cunningham, J. D. (1915). *A History of the Sikhs: From the Origin of the Nation to the Battles of the Sutlej*. Delhi: Low Price.

Dogra, R. C., and Gobind Singh, M. (1995) *Encyclopaedia of Sikh Religion and Culture*. Delhi: Vikas.

EcoSikh (2021). 'EcoSikh'. Retrieved from About EcoSikh: https://ecosikh.org/about/#ourMission.

Fenech, L. E. (2000). *Martyrdom in the Sikh Tradition: Playing the 'Game of Love'*. New Delhi: Oxford University Press.

Fenech, L. E. (2014). 'The Evolution of the Sikh Community'. In P. Singh and L. Fenech (eds), *The Oxford Handbook of Sikh Studies* (pp. 35–48). Oxford: Oxford University Press.

Fenech, L. E., and McLeod, W. H. (2014). *Historical Dictionary of Sikhism (Historical Dictionaries of Religions, Philosophies, and Movements Series)*, 3rd edn. Lanham: Rowan and Littlefield.

Government of India, Legislative Department (1909). 'Anand Marriage Act, 1909'. Retrieved from Government of India, Legislative Department: https://legislative.gov.in/sites/default/files/A1909-07.pdf.

Goyal, A., and Singhania, A. (2019). *Voices from Punjab: The Strength and Resilience of 15 Punjabi Women Living in the UK*. Kibworth Beauchamp: Matador.

Grewal, J. (2010). 'W.H. McLeod and Sikh Studies'. *Journal of Punjab Studies*, 17: 115–44.

Grewal, J. S. (1998). *Contesting Interpretations of the Sikh Tradition*. New Delhi: Manohar.

Gupta, H. R. (1994). *History of the Sikhs Vol. I: The Sikh Gurus 1469–1708*. New Delhi: Munshiram Manoharlal.

Gupta, S. K. (1997). 'Sikhs and the Partition of the Punjab'. *Proceedings of the Indian History Congress*, 58: 591–8.

Hans, S. (1988). *A Reconstruction of Sikh History from Sikh Literature*. Jalandhar: ABS.

Holt, J. D. (2019). *Beyond the Big Six Religions: Expanding the Boundaries in the Teaching of Religions and Worldviews*. Chester: University of Chester Press.

Holt, J. D. (2022). *Religious Education in the Secondary School: An Introduction to Teaching, Learning and the World Religions*. Abingdon: Routledge.

hooks, b. (1994). *Teaching to Transgress: Education as the Practice of Freedom*. London: Routledge.

Jackson, R. (1997). *Religious Education: An Interpretive Approach*. London: Hodder.

Jain, K. (2021, 2 November). 'Modi's Diwali Extravaganza Shows Why We Need to Tell the Many Stories of Rama'. Retrieved from Religion News Service: https://religionnews.com/2021/11/02/modis-diwali-extravaganza-shows-why-we-need-to-tell-the-many-stories-of-rama/.

Jakobsh, D. R. (2006a). 'Authority in the Virtual Sangat: Sikhism, Ritual and Identity in the Twenty-First Century'. *Heidelberg Journal of Religions on the Internet*, 02.1: 24–40.

Jakobsh, D. R. (2006b). 'Sikhism, Interfaith Dialogue, and Women: Transformation and Identity'. *Journal of Contemporary Religion*, 21.2: 183–99.

Josephson, J. A. (2012). *The Invention of Religion in Japan*. Chicago: University of Chicago Press.

Juergensmeyer, M. (1979). 'The Forgotten Tradition: Sikhism in the Study of World Religions'. In M. Juergensmeyer (ed.), *Sikh Studies: Comparative Perspectives on a Changing Tradition* (pp. 13–23). Berkeley: Graduate Theological Union.

Kaur, V. (2020). *See No Stranger: A Memoir and Manifesto of Revolutionary Love*. New York: One World.

Kaur Singh, N.-G. (1993). *The Feminine Principle in the Sikh Vision of the Transcendent*. Cambridge: Cambridge University Press.

Kaur Singh, N.-G. (2000). 'Why Did I Not Light the Fire? The Refeminization of Ritual in Sikhism'. *Journal of Feminist Studies in Religion*, 16.1: 63–85.

Kaur Singh, N.-G. (2005). *The Birth of the Khalsa: A Feminist Re-memory of Sikh Identity*. New York: State University of New York Press.

Kaur Singh, N.-G. (2011). *Sikhism*. London: I.B. Tauris.

Kaur Singh, N.-G. (2019). *The First Sikh: The Life and Legacy of Guru Nanak*. Haryana, India: Penguin/Random House.

Kaur Takhar, O. (2016). *Sikh Identity: An Exploration of Groups among Sikhs*. Abingdon: Routledge.

Lopez, D. (1995). *Curators of the Buddha: The Study of Buddhism under Colonialism*. Chicago: University of Chicago Press.

Macauliffe, M. A. (1909a). *The Sikh Religion: Its Gurus, Sacred Writings and Authors Volume I*. Oxford: Clarendon.

Macauliffe, M. A. (1909b). *The Sikh Religion: Its Gurus, Sacred Writings and Authors Volume IV*. Oxford: Clarendon.

Macauliffe, M. A. (1985). *The Sikh Religion, Volume III*, third reprint. New Delhi: S. Chand.

Mair, M. (1989). *Between Psychology and Psychotherapy: A Poetics of Experience*. New York: Routledge.

Malcolm, J. (1812). *Sketch of the Sikhs: A Singular Nation, Who Inhabit the Provinces of the Punjab, Situated between the Rivers Jumna and Indus*. London: John Murray.

Masuzawa, T. (2005). *The Invention of World Religions*. London: University of Chicago Press.

Mauss, A. (1994). *The Angel and the Beehive: The Mormon Struggle with Assimilation*. Illinois: University of Illinois.

McGuire, M. (2008). *Lived Religion: Faith and Practice in Everyday Life*. Oxford: Oxford University Press.

McLeod, W. H. (1968). *Guru Nanak and the Sikh Religion*. Oxford: Clarendon.

McLeod, W. H. (1976). *The Evolution of the Sikh Community: Five Essays*. Oxford: Clarendon.

McLeod, W. H. (1980). *Early Sikh Tradition: A Study of the Janamsakhis*. Oxford: Clarendon.

McLeod, W. H. (2007). 'Sikhs and Caste'. In T. Ballantyne (ed.), *Textures of the Sikh Past* (pp. 104–31) Delhi: Oxford University Press.

Mello, R. (2001). 'The Power of Storytelling: How Oral Narrative Influences Children's Relationships in Classrooms'. *International Journal of Education & the Arts*, 2.1: 1–6.

Mobad (2001). 'Sikhism and the Sikhs, 1645–46 from "Mobad", Dabistan-i Magahib', translated by Irfan Habib. In J. S. Grewal and I. Habib (eds), *Sikh History from Persian Sources: Translations of Major Texts* (pp. 59–84). Delhi: Tulika.

Nesbitt, E. (2016). *Sikhism: A Very Short Introduction*. Oxford: Oxford University Press.

Oberoi, H. (1994). *The Construction of Religious Boundaries: Culture, Identity and Diversity in the Sikh Tradition*. Chicago: University of Chicago Press.

Ofsted (2021, 21 May). 'Research Review Series: Religious Education'. Retrieved from: https://www.gov.uk/government/publications/research-review-series-religious-education/research-review-series-religious-education.

Oldenburg, R. (1999). *The Great Good Place*. New York: Marlowe.

Ondaatje, M. (1992). *The English Patient*. New York: Vintage.

Prothero, S. (2010). *God Is Not One: The Eight Rival Religions That Run the World and Why Their Differences Matter*. New York: HarperOne.

Pruthi, R. (ed.) (2004). *Sikhism and Indian Civilisation*. New Delhi: Discovery.

Puri, S. (1993). *Advent of Sikh Religion: A Socio-political Perspective*. New Delhi: Munshiram Manoharlal.

Rogers, A., and Beveridge, H. (1909). *Tuzuk-i-Jahangiri or Memoirs of Jahangir*. London: Royal Asiatic Society.

Sanghera, S. (2012). *The Boy with the Topknot: A Memoir of Love, Secrets and Lies*. London: Penguin.

Sanghera, S. (2021). *Empireland*. London: Penguin.

Sanghera, S. (2022). *Marriage Material*. London: Penguin.

Schimmel, A. (2004). *The Empire of the Great Mughals: History, Art and Culture*. London: Reaktion.

Shani, G. (2008). *Sikh Nationalism and Identity in a Global Age*. Abingdon: Routledge.

The Sikh Network (2016). 'UK Sikh Survey 2016 Findings'. Retrieved from the Sikh
    Network: https://www.thesikhnetwork.com/wp-content/uploads/2016/11/UK-Sikh-Survey-2016-
    Findings-FINAL.pdf.

Sikhnet (n.d.). 'Guru Har Rai and Bani'. Retrieved from Sikhnet: https://www.sikhnet.com/stories/
    audio/guru-har-rai-and-pot.

Singh, D. P. (1999). 'The Literary Genius of Guru Gobind Singh'. *Sikh Review*, 47.4: 35–9.

Singh, G. (trans.) (1960). *Sri Guru Granth Sahib*, vol. 1. New Delhi: Allied.

Singh, G. (2021). 'The Institution of the Akal Takht: The Transformation of Authority in Sikh History'.
    *Religions*, 12: 390–402.

Singh, G., and Brar, K. S. (2021, 5 November). 'One Month Later: A Nihang Sikh and a Journalist
    Discuss the Lynching at Singhu Border'. Retrieved from Outlook: https://www.outlookindia.
    com/website/story/india-news-explainer-why-the-alleged-desecration-of-holy/399815.

Singh, G., and Singh, T. (1950). *A Short History of the Sikhs: 1496–1765*. Calcutta: Orient Longman.

Singh, G., and Singh Tatla, D. (2010). *Sikhs in Britain: The Making of a Community*. London: Zed.

Singh, H. (1983a). *Berkeley Lectures on Sikhism*. Delhi: Guru Nanak Foundation.

Singh, H. (1983b). *The Heritage of the Sikhs*. New Delhi: Manohar.

Singh, J. (1996). 'Caste System and Sikhs'. In G. Singh (ed.), *Perspectives on the Sikh Tradition*,
    2nd edn (pp. 273–366). Patalia: Academy of Sikh Religion & Culture.

Singh, K. (1993). *Sikhism: An Oecumenical Religion*. Chandigarh: Institute of Sikh Studies.

Singh, K. (1999). *A History of the Sikhs: Volume I: 1469–1839*, 2nd ed. New Delhi: Oxford
    University Press.

Singh, K. (2004a). *Janamsakhi Tradition: An Analytical Study*. Amritsar: Singh.

Singh, K. (2004b). *Sri Gur Sobha: Sainapati*. Chandigarh: Institute of Sikh Studies.

Singh, K. (2009). *A History of the Sikhs. Volume II: 1839–2004*, 2nd ed. New Delhi: Oxford
    University Press.

Singh, P. (1926). *The Book of the Ten Masters*. London: Selwyn & Blount.

Singh, P. (2014a). 'Gurmat'. In P. Singh and L. E. Fenech (eds), *The Oxford Handbook of Sikh
    Studies* (pp. 225–9). Oxford: Oxford University Press.

Singh, P. (2014b). 'The Guru Granth Sahib'. In P. Singh and L. E. Fenech (eds), *The Oxford
    Handbook of Sikh Studies* (pp. 125–35). Oxford: Oxford University Press.

Singh, P. P. (2006). *The History of Sikh Gurus*. New Delhi: Lotus.

Singh, R. (2021). *Patshahi Mehima: Revisiting Sikh Sovereignty*. UK: Khalis.

Singh, S. (2003). *Philosophy of Sikhism*. Amritsar: Shiromani Gurdwara Parbandhak Committee.

Singh, S. (2018, 13 February). 'Homophobia Has No Place in Sikhism'. Retrieved from
    Sikhnet: https://www.sikhnet.com/news/homophobia-has-no-place-sikhism.

Singh, T. (1981). *Life of Guru Hari Krishan: A Biography and History Hardcover*. Delhi: Delhi Sikh
    Gurdwara Management Committee.

Singh, T., and Singh, G. (2006). *A Short History of the Sikhs, Vol. 1 (1469–1765)*. Patiala: Publication
    Bureau Punjabi University.

Singh, W. (1969). *Aspects of Guru Nanak's Philosophy*. Lahore: Lahore Book Shop.

Singh Mandair, A.-P. (2005). 'The Emergence of Modern "Sikh Theology": Reassessing the
    Passage of Ideas from Trumpp to Bhāī Vīr Singh'. *Bulletin of the School of Oriental and African
    Studies, University of London*, 68.2: 253–75.

Singh Mandair, A.-P. (2009). *Religion and the Spectre of the West: Sikhism, India, Postcoloniality, and the Politics of Translation*. New York: Columbia University Press.

Singh Mandair, A.-P. (2013). *Sikhism: A Guide for the Perplexed*. London: Bloomsbury.

Singh Mann, G. (2001). *The Making of Sikh Scripture*. Oxford: Oxford University Press.

Singh Mann, G., and Singh, K. (2011). *Sri Dasam Granth Sahib: Questions and Answers*. London: Archimedes.

Smart, N. (1998). *The World's Religions*, 2nd ed. Cambridge: Cambridge University Press.

Smith, J. Z. (2004). *Relating Religion: Essays in the Study of Religion*. Chicago: University of Chicago Press.

Streets, H. (2004). *Martial Races: The Military, Race and Masculinity in British Imperial Culture, 1857–1914*. Manchester: University of Manchester Press.

Tatla, D. S. (2008). 'Sikhism and Development: A Review'. Working Paper 21. Birmingham: International Development Department, University of Birmingham.

Theos Think Tank (2021). 'Nobody Stands Nowhere'. Retrieved from: https://www.youtube.com/watch?v=AFRxKF-Jdos (accessed 30 July 2022).

Trumpp, E. (1877). *Adi Granth or the Holy Scriptures of the Sikhs*, trans. from the original Gurmukhi. London: William H. Allen.

Uberoi, J. (1996). *Religion, Civil Society and the State: A Study of Sikhism*. New Delhi: Oxford University Press.

United Nations Environment Programme and Parliament of the World's Religions (2020). *Faith for Earth: A Call for Action*. Nairobi: UNEP.

Wittgenstein, L. (1968). *Philosophical Investigations*. Trans. G. E. Anscombe. New York: MacMillan.

Wood, B. (2020). 'Teaching Worldviews at GCSE'. In M. Chater (ed.), *Reforming RE: Power and Knowledge in a Worldviews Curriculum* (pp. 165–8). Woodbridge: John Catt Educational.

# Index